Ramadhan *is the word we use collectively as Muslims to describe the name of the Holy Month. However, countries and regions have their own languages and with these languages come their unique changes to the word Ramadhan, including the way it's said or spelt. We grew up calling it* **Rooza**, *which essentially translates as 'fasting', and to me, Rooza it shall aways be.*

Rooza

A journey through Islamic cuisine inspired by Ramadhan and Eid

Nadiya Hussain

Photography by Chris Terry

To all the mothers: the mothers that do everything that everyone else does and then some more. The table would not be what it is without you.

Contents

Introduction **6–11**

Turkey
12–17

Iraq
18–25

Afghanistan
26–31

Tunisia
32–35

Aleppo, Syria
36–39

Malaysia
40–43

Algeria
44–49

Somalia
50–53

Egypt
54–59

Maldives
60–63

Libya
64–67

Bangladesh
68–71

Lebanon
72–77

Thailand
78–81

Mauritius
82–87

Iran
88–91

North Africa
92–95

India
96–99

Middle East
100–103

Nepal
104–107

Cambodia
108–113

Sri Lanka
114–117

Indonesia
118–121

Syria
122–125

Bengal
126–129

West & South Africa
130–133

South Asia
134–139

Pakistan
140–143

Yemen
144–149

Singapore
150–155

Eid-ul-Fitr
156–183

Thanks **186**
Index **188–190**

Introduction

As the month of Ramadhan fast approaches, you begin to hear the word 'Ramadhan' and 'fasting' being murmured, whispered and announced everywhere. Maybe that's just me or maybe it's not. Adults and children are speaking about it in schools, in friendship groups, with colleagues and at places of work, waiting at bus stops, quite literally, anywhere and everywhere. I find myself talking about Ramadhan to anyone who will listen. As we lead up to the holiest month in the Islamic calendar, there is an eagerness and anticipation in the air for those intending to observe, and often a powerful curiosity for those who are not.

Things are so different now to when I grew up observing Ramadhan. Ramadhan was then contained inside our homes and within our small communities. Though the change isn't huge, these days we are starting to see shop windows wishing observers Ramadhan Mubarak ('have a blessed Ramadhan') or Ramadhan Kareem ('have a generous Ramadhan'), which is something I never imagined, but when I see it, it fills my heart with hope. We have even started to see supermarkets prepare for the month by having aisles dedicated to Ramadhan, the shelves filled with rice, flours, lentils, oils, butter, dried fruit, nuts and so much more. Seeing everything under a bright banner elevates the excitement to a whole other level.

Whenever I get asked about Ramadhan, I try to describe this beautiful month in the way that I feel it in my heart and through my lived experience. The only way I can describe Ramadhan is as an old friend, a distant friend. The kind that you don't see for months and months, but you know that no matter how far away they are or how infrequent the interactions, you can pick up right where you left off. Like a good friend, Ramadhan visits every year, like clockwork, exactly when you need them the most.

The anticipation for this holy month is nothing short of magnificent, even though we know what it entails. Fasting requires hard work, determination and faith. No eating or drinking (yes, not even water) from the moment the sun comes up to the time it sets. It is the most exciting time in our house and with our wider families. We channel our excitement by decorating the house with banners, balloons and sparkly lights, all in preparation for this month of fasting and worship.

When the month of Ramadhan finally arrives, we all work as normal, but for just one month of the year our day-to-day lives revolve around Ramadhan, and not the other way around. We spend time perfecting our prayers. We nap when the exhaustion sets in. We gather our energy so we can spend time reading the Quran. Giving charity

Introduction

Introduction

Introduction

Introduction

makes up a huge part of our worship and even the smallest of things, the way we speak to each other, is softer, kinder and more measured. This is the month that we are the best versions of ourselves in every way.

For me as a mum and as the head of the kitchen, what we eat is so important. After having not eaten from sunrise, what I lay on the table at sunset really matters to me. It is the one meal we sit down and eat together after having fasted all day. It has to be nutritious, filling and, most of all, it has to be delicious. So, I pride myself on making delicious meals every night. I dedicate a few hours, outside of work, household chores and worship, to make sure I know exactly what we are eating. From small, nibbly bits to one-pot meals, staples like rice and pasta and, of course, dessert. Not to mention fresh fruit, dates and ice-cold water.

What I cook can be inspired by traditional foods, my travels, something I may have watched on TV or read in a book, or even by an entire cuisine that I know nothing about. Whichever way, I know that whatever I cook will be received well by my hungry brood, who are always complimentary and ever grateful for the work that goes into preparing this feast, all while fasting myself.

Introduction

This book is filled with thirty meals inspired by countries that have worshippers who observe Ramadhan. These recipes are motivated by each of these countries and are foods that are enjoyed by them all year round and during this holy month. As easy as it would be for me to make familiar foods, I really enjoy trying new foods from new countries with distinctive cuisines during this month. These recipes will keep you feeling excited about each meal you lay on the table. There is also a whole section dedicated to Eid-ul-Fitr – the celebration at the end of the month where we can eat 'as normal' again – filled with celebration-worthy dishes and sweet treats for the whole family.

As the mother of an ever-growing family, Ramadhan is the only time of year that I know I will see my children for thirty days on the trot for dinner at our table, without a second's delay, and I won't have to call them twice. Whilst I know that will change as they get older, as they move on and out of our family home, it is this month that binds us as a family, intertwines us and holds us together through faith, worship, dedication and the meal we share at the end of another day. Whilst small for some, it is huge for us. It is this dedication to our faith and the delicious food that we are blessed with that will bring them back to the very same table, year after year.

Turkey

CHICKEN SHISH TAOUK
Chicken Kebabs with a Yoghurt Flatbread, Cucumber Dip and Pickled Radishes

Turkish food is something that has blown up in the last few years and where I live, there is a Turkish restaurant around every corner. With one of our very close friends being Turkish, we have also had the pleasure of being able to enjoy Turkish food at its finest at home. So, this take on a Turkish shish with delicious sides and yoghurt flatbread is an homage to our friend Emir.

Let's start by making the chicken shish. Put the plain yoghurt in a large bowl. In a small pan, heat your oil to a high heat, add the cumin seeds and as soon as they start to pop and spit, take off the heat. Pour and scrape all the contents on to the yoghurt.

Now mix in the ground cumin, thyme, paprika, salt, the juice and zest of the lemon and the garlic paste. Add in your diced chicken thighs and mix till everything is evenly coated.

Cover and leave to marinate. If you can make this ahead, then 6 hours is great (ideally overnight for the best flavour), but if you have no time, just pop it into the fridge for 1 hour. And if you absolutely have to make it now, make it now!

Preheat the oven to 200°C. Lightly grease a baking tray that will fit all six skewers. Drizzle a little extra oil on top.

After marinating, skewer the chicken on to six metal or wooden skewers and bake in the oven for 25–30 minutes till cooked all the way through.

Meanwhile, let's make the flatbread by putting the flour in a large bowl, adding the salt and oil and rubbing the oil in with your fingers so you don't have any clumps of oil. Spoon the plain yoghurt in and, using a palette knife, start to mix, then get your hands in and bring the dough together, kneading just enough till you have a smooth, shiny dough.

Leave to rest, covered under a tea towel, for 10 minutes.

Serves: 6

For the chicken shish taouk
500g plain yoghurt
3 tablespoons oil, plus extra for drizzling
1 tablespoon cumin seeds
2 tablespoons ground cumin
2 tablespoons dried thyme
1 tablespoon paprika
1½ tablespoons salt
1 lemon, zest and juice
3 tablespoons garlic paste
1.5kg chicken thighs, diced into equal pieces

For the yoghurt flatbread
500g strong bread flour
1 tablespoon salt
3 tablespoons oil
500g plain yoghurt
melted butter, for brushing

For the cucumber dip
1 large cucumber
2 cloves of garlic, minced
3 spring onions, thinly sliced
6 tablespoons full-fat mayonnaise
whole milk, to loosen
sumac, for sprinkling

➡

Now make the cucumber dip by grating the cucumber, using your hands to drain out any excess liquid. Pop the grated cucumber into a bowl. Get your minced garlic and spring onions in, along with the mayonnaise, and mix through. Pour in just enough milk to loosen the dip so it doesn't clump, but also it shouldn't be runny. Sprinkle over the sumac and set aside.

Make the pickled radishes by pouring the apple cider vinegar into a small pan and adding the caster sugar. Bring to the boil and as soon as the sugar has dissolved, add the radishes and bring to the boil again. Turn the heat off and leave the radishes to sit in the juice.

Make the flatbreads by dividing the dough into six equal pieces. Roll each piece out to a round that is about 3mm thin.

Pop a griddle pan on the hob and bring to a medium heat, then place a piece of dough on the griddle and cook for 3-4 minutes on each side. Take off the heat and brush with butter. Repeat with all the dough pieces.

Drain the radishes, reserving the liquid (this can be used for dressings or pickling other things). Take the kebabs out of the oven. To serve, add the kebab meat to the flatbread, removing carefully from the skewer, then drizzle over the cucumber dip, sprinkle over some pickled radishes and it is ready to enjoy.

For the pickled radishes
200ml apple cider vinegar
3 tablespoons caster sugar
300g radishes, thinly sliced

6 metal or wooden skewers

Turkey

BAKLAVA

Baklava is a dessert of layers of buttery filo with a buttery centre, all baked and doused in a sweet, sticky syrup. It is one of the most sophisticated and elegant desserts, but it is pretty straightforward to cook and I love making it. I always thought it was Middle Eastern, but baklava has spread its sweet love across many other countries, including Turkey. I like to serve it with clotted cream just like I had in Istanbul many years ago, and a swirl of raspberry jam for tang.

Makes: 24 baklava

Start by browning the butter. Pop the butter into a small pan and start to melt it, then bring it to the boil, lower to a medium heat and allow the milk solids to toast. When you swirl the pan and are able to see flecks of brown and it starts to smell very toasted, take off the heat and set aside.

Preheat the oven to 180°C. Take a 40cm x 25cm baking tray and measure to make sure your filo sheets will fit comfortably without creasing. If not, cut to size using the tray as a guide. Grease and line this tray with two sheets of baking paper, one on top of the other, allowing a bit of overhang.

Brush the inside of the tray with the browned butter and put one filo sheet in, then add another sheet and butter again. Do this till you have added seven sheets to the base.

Put the walnuts, pistachios, orange zest and cinnamon in a food processor and blend to a fine mixture. Pour on to the filo, spreading to an even layer.

Now butter and add each layer of the leftover filo, placing them on top of the nut mixture till you have done all seven layers.

Press down firmly and use a sharp knife to cut into equal squares, making sure you get right to the base and through each and every layer. Any leftover butter can be poured right on top.

Bake in the oven for 35 minutes, till golden brown.

Make the syrup by putting the caster sugar in a pan with the orange juice, lemon zest and juice, honey and cardamom. Bring the syrup to a boil and leave to simmer for 10 minutes till golden and a little thicker.

For the baklava

200g salted butter

2 x 270g packs of filo pastry, ready-rolled (14 sheets in total)

200g walnuts

100g pistachios

1 orange, zest only (reserving the juice for later)

2 teaspoons ground cinnamon

For the syrup

300g caster sugar

juice of an orange (see above)

1 lemon, zest and juice

100g honey

4 cardamom pods, husks removed and seeds crushed

To serve

400g clotted cream

150g raspberry jam

Take the baklava out of the oven and while it is still hot, pour the syrup all over the baklava. Set aside to cool completely.

To serve, I like to decant my clotted cream and ripple in the raspberry jam. Take a few squares of the baklava and serve with a dollop of the raspberry clotted cream.

BEEF KIBBEH
with Lamb Murag and Rice

These kibbeh are a total labour of love but are worth every second. If you like meat, then there is meat in the bulgur wheat coating and also a gently spiced meat filling on the inside. Hearty and wholesome, they go so well with the lamb murag and rice.

Start by making the stuffing for the kibbeh. Pour a splash of oil into a frying pan. When the oil is hot, add the beef mince, break it up and cook till browned. Now add the onions, walnuts and salt and keep cooking till the onions are soft. Take off the heat, add the parsley and mix through, then set aside and leave to cool completely.

While that cools, make the dough. Start by putting the fine semolina in a bowl with the boiling water, mix and set aside.

Pop a large pan on the hob with a litre of salted water. As soon as the water is boiling, add in the bulgur wheat and boil for 8 minutes, then drain and set aside.

Pour a splash of oil into a frying pan and as soon as the oil is hot, add the beef mince and cook till broken up and golden brown. Now add your cumin, black pepper, salt and tomato purée, mix and cook through for 5 minutes.

Take off the heat, add the soaked semolina and bulgur wheat, mix well and set aside to cool completely. Once cool, put the mixture in a food processor and blitz to a smooth paste. Now add the plain flour and blend one more time till you have a mixture that can hold its shape.

Using wet hands, divide the mixture into 24 balls. Take each ball and, again with wet hands, create a hole in the centre, slowly working your way in to create a large hole with thinner walls. Fill with 1 tablespoon of the filling. Seal shut and you can keep them as a ball or make a traditional point on each side – this will give you a lovely crispness on either end of the kibbeh.

Set aside in the fridge till they are ready to fry. Freeze any leftover mixture for next time.

➜

Serves: 6

For the kibbeh stuffing

oil, for frying
500g beef mince
3 onions, diced
100g walnuts, finely chopped
salt
large handful of fresh parsley, finely chopped

For the dough

40g fine semolina
150ml boiling water, plus 1 litre for the bulgur wheat
350g bulgur wheat
oil, for frying
200g beef mince
1 teaspoon ground cumin
1 teaspoon black pepper
1 teaspoon salt
1 tablespoon tomato purée
125g plain flour

For the murag

1kg diced lamb
6 tablespoons oil, plus extra for the onions
3 onions, diced
1 tablespoon salt
3 tomatoes, diced
1 teaspoon sugar
6 tablespoons baharat spice
2 tablespoons tomato purée
500ml hot water
225g green beans, topped, tailed and halved

For the rice

600g basmati rice
900ml cold water

Now for the murag. Make sure your lamb is patted dry and any moisture removed from it. To a large pan, add the oil and heat over a medium heat. Add all the lamb and cook till golden brown.

Take the meat out, pour in a little extra oil and cook the onions with the salt till lovely and golden and very soft. Now add your diced tomatoes, along with the sugar and the baharat spice, then add in the tomato purée. Cook the spices into the mix for about 5 minutes, then add back in all your lamb, mix through and pour in the water. Cook with the lid on, over a medium heat, for 45 minutes.

Meanwhile, make the rice. Wash the rice thoroughly with cold water till the water runs completely clear. Drain the rice and put into a medium pan with 900ml cold water from the tap. Boil the rice, making sure to stir occasionally so the rice doesn't stick to the base. Keep boiling till the water has almost completely evaporated. Lower the heat, pop the lid on and leave to steam for 15 minutes.

After 45 minutes take the murag off the heat and add the green beans. Cook with the lid off for another 15 minutes till the green beans are just tender.

Now let's fry the kibbeh. Take a large pan and pour oil into it about two-thirds of the way up. I like to use a large frying pan with high sides. Heat the oil to about 180°C. Gently drop the kibbeh into the hot oil, cooking a few at a time and making sure not to overcrowd the pan. Cook for about 8 minutes till crisp on the outside. Drain on kitchen paper, then fry up all the rest.

Everything should be ready at once to serve and enjoy.

KLEICHA
Date Swirled Cookies

Dates are a huge part of Ramadhan and not just to break your fast with. They are a great ingredient to bake and cook with too. This date and nut paste makes for a sweet and aromatic filling in these swirly biscuits, perfect with a cup of tea for a light treat after breaking your fast.

Makes: 24 kleicha

Let's start by making the dough. Put the plain flour in a bowl with the cubed butter. Rub the butter into the flour till there are no large lumps of butter and the flour looks less fine.

Add the ground cinnamon and icing sugar and mix through. Make a well in the centre and add the egg in. Bring the dough together gently, being sure not to knead it – just bring it together so you don't have any floury bits left.

Shape into a square, wrap in cling film and leave in the fridge for at least 30 minutes.

Meanwhile, make the filling by putting the pitted dates in a bowl with the hazelnuts. Pour boiling water on top till they are submerged and leave to soak for 10 minutes. After 10 minutes, drain completely, reserving any water, and blend to a smooth paste. Add a few tablespoons of the reserved water if necessary.

Preheat the oven to 180°C and line a baking tray with some baking paper.

Dust the worktop with some icing sugar, unwrap the dough and roll the dough out to a 24cm square. Brush the date paste all over in an even layer. Roll up and freeze for 30 minutes.

After freezing, slice into 1cm swirly biscuits. Lay them out on the prepared baking tray and bake for 15-20 minutes, till they are golden brown.

Take them out, brush generously with the golden syrup and then wait for them to be just cool enough to eat, but still lovely and warm.

For the dough
225g plain flour
120g salted butter, chilled and cubed
1 teaspoon ground cinnamon
2 tablespoons icing sugar
1 egg, lightly beaten
icing sugar, for dusting

For the filling
150g pitted dates
100g hazelnuts
boiling water, to cover

To finish
3 tablespoons golden syrup, warmed

KABULI PULAO
with Qorma-e-Sabzi
Lamb Pulao with Greens

Serves: 6

I had this very dish at a tiny restaurant that serves authentic Afghani food. When I go to a restaurant that I have never eaten at before and where the cuisine is new to me, I always ask the waiting staff what they recommend, and this was it. I love rice in all its forms and this recipe perfectly captures the essence of the Kabuli pulao from what I can remember. Lightly scented rice served with spinach and a sweet and savoury carrot topping. Joy in every single mouthful.

Start by making the pulao. To a large pan add all the ghee and, over a high heat, allow the ghee to melt. Add the cloves, bay leaves and stick of cinnamon and let the whole spices sizzle in the melting ghee.

Add the sliced onions and cook till they are really soft and golden. Now add your garlic paste and salt and cook through for a few minutes. Get the lamb cubes in with the garam masala and cook till the meat is brown. Pour in the 100ml hot water and bring to the boil. Reduce the heat slightly and cook till there is no more liquid left and there is a golden-brown mixture coating the meat.

Wash the basmati rice till the water runs clear. This will take a few washes, but it's important to remove as much starch as possible. Drain the rice and add to the meat. On a high heat, mix the rice with the meat and onions, mixing and scraping the base for about 5 minutes to remove any rice that may be sticking.

Pour in the boiling water and, over a high heat, mix and allow the whole thing to come to a boil till almost all the liquid has dried off and you can see every grain of rice. As soon as you get to that point, lower the heat completely and put the lid on. Leave to steam for about 30 minutes.

While the pulao cooks, let's make the qorma-e-sabzi. Pour the oil into a medium non-stick pan and bring to a high heat. Add the sliced spring onions with the salt and cook for a few minutes.

→

For the pulao
150g ghee
4 cloves
3 bay leaves
1 large cinnamon stick
2 onions, thinly sliced
2 tablespoons garlic paste
2 tablespoons salt
500g diced boneless lamb
3 tablespoons garam masala
100ml hot water
500g basmati rice
650ml boiling water

For the qorma-e-sabzi
3 tablespoons oil
1 bunch of spring onions, thinly sliced
1 teaspoon salt
1 lemon, juice only
1kg frozen spinach
2 teaspoons ground coriander
1 teaspoon ground black pepper
small handful of fresh coriander
small handful of fresh dill

For the carrot topping
2 carrots, grated
50g raisins
40g almonds, toasted
3 tablespoons vinegar
2 teaspoons honey

As soon as the spring onions are soft, add the lemon juice and the frozen spinach. Water should release from the frozen spinach - keep cooking till most of the liquid has evaporated. Add the ground coriander and black pepper and cook till completely dry and there is no excess liquid in the base when you are stirring. Take it off the heat as soon as it is ready and stir in the fresh coriander and dill.

Make the quick carrot topping by putting the grated carrots in a bowl with the raisins and toasted almonds. Mix well. Put the vinegar and honey in a bowl and mix. Drizzle all over the carrots and stir through.

Take the rice off the heat and serve on a platter or in the pan with the carrot mixture sprinkled over and the qorma-e-sabzi alongside.

SHEER PIRA
Milk Fudge

This fudge is sweet, milky and everything you want if you are after a sweet fix. Made with whole milk powder and a really easy sugar syrup, it is ready to enjoy as soon as it is set or is even better packed up and gifted to neighbours. I like to top mine with nuts and dried red cranberries for colour and a slight tart hit.

Makes: 10 bars

Line and lightly grease a 900g loaf tin with baking paper and set aside.

Start by pouring in the water and adding the sugar to a shallow non-stick frying pan, along with the crushed cardamom seeds and rose extract.

Bring to the boil and as soon as the water is hot and the sugar has completely dissolved, boil to 120°C.

Now put the milk powder in a bowl, pour in the hot sugar water and mix till it all comes together. Work quickly to press the mixture into the prepared tin.

Press in the cranberries and pistachios, being sure to press in firmly, then carefully add the gold leaf.

Leave to set completely, then break into pieces and serve.

250ml water
200g caster sugar
3 cardamom pods, husks removed and seeds crushed
½ teaspoon rose extract
150g full-fat milk powder, sifted
25g dried cranberries, finely chopped
25g pistachios, toasted and chopped
gold leaf, to decorate

Tunisia

LABLEBI
Chickpea Stew

I love chickpeas, especially after a whole day of fasting. They really are wholesome and filling and this is such a delicious way to enjoy them. The lablebi is sweetly spiced with caraway and thyme and served with a poached egg and crunchy baguette – a perfect one-bowl meal.

Serves: 6

Get a large pan and pour the oil straight into the pan. Pop over a medium heat and as soon as the oil is hot, add the sprig of thyme in there and leave to one side. Add the dried red chillies and allow the chillies to toast and blacken very slightly. As soon as that happens, take the pan off the heat and carefully remove the chillies. Sprinkle with salt to keep them crisp and set them aside.

Now go in with the bay leaves, cinnamon stick and caraway seeds and toast them gently with the pan back on a low to medium heat. Add the minced garlic and toast till very golden brown. As soon as it is a golden brown, get the onions in with the salt and cook the onions till they are tender and golden.

Add the first three tins of drained chickpeas to the pan and mix through. Take the fourth tin, crush the chickpeas completely, add to the pan with the water and bring to a boil. As soon as it comes to the boil, leave to simmer over a medium heat. You will know it is ready when the whole chickpeas are surrounded by a thick chickpea sauce and not a watery one.

While that cooks away, it's great to get all the toppings ready to serve with the lablebi.

Dish out the hot lablebi once it is off the stove. Remove the bay leaves and the cinnamon stick. Now serve with a poached egg, the tuna, a spoonful of harissa, a lemon wedge, black olives and a sprinkling of parsley. Warm up those crusty baguettes and serve alongside.

For the lablebi

100ml oil

large sprig of fresh thyme

6 dried red chillies

pinch of salt

2 bay leaves

1 large cinnamon stick

2 teaspoons caraway seeds

1 bulb of garlic, cloves peeled and minced

1 onion, finely diced

1 tablespoon salt

4 x 400g tins of chickpeas, drained

1 litre water

To serve

6 poached eggs

3 x 145g tins of tuna in brine, drained

180g jar of harissa

6 lemon wedges

354g jar of pitted black olives, drained

large handful of fresh parsley, chopped

6 small crusty baguettes, warmed

SAMSAS

Samsa is a traditional dish often made during Ramadhan. They are not like the samosas you frequently find, filled with spiced savoury meat. These are stuffed with a mixture of ground down nuts, sweet potato, orange and cinnamon. Doused in sweet syrup, they are then coated again with nuts. I like to serve mine with a simple strawberry coulis.

Pierce the sweet potatoes all over with a fork, place directly on to a microwave plate and cook for 10 minutes till very soft. You can also do this in the oven.

Take out and leave to cool enough so they can be handled and then scoop out all the flesh and pop into a bowl. Mash to a smooth paste with the cinnamon, orange zest and walnuts. Set aside.

For the pastry, pop the butter into a pan and melt till brown. As soon as it starts to bubble and brown flecks appear, you have browned the butter. Take off the heat.

Preheat the oven to 190°C and have a baking tray at the ready.

Cut the filo sheets down the length and create 14 strips of filo, leaving the sheets you're not working with under a damp tea towel. Butter two sheets together. Take a dollop of the filling and place at the bottom of the end of the strip. Fold a corner over to create a visible triangle, encasing the filling. Now take the filled triangle and fold over again and keep going till you have a fully encased triangle. Make the other six and butter them all over with any leftover butter.

Pop on to the tray and bake for 20 minutes.

Make the syrup by pouring the orange juice into a pan with the water and caster sugar. Bring to the boil and leave to simmer till the syrup is thick and golden.

Take the triangles out of the oven and dip straight into the syrup till completely coated, then coat with pistachios and set aside.

For the strawberry coulis, put the fresh strawberries, icing sugar and lemon juice in a food processor and blend. Serve alongside the samsas as a dip or a drizzle.

Makes: 7 samsas

For the filling
2 medium sweet potatoes
1 teaspoon ground cinnamon
1 orange, zest only (reserving the juice for later)
100g walnuts, finely chopped

For the pastry
150g butter
270g pack of filo pastry, ready-rolled (7 sheets)
100g pistachios, finely chopped

For the syrup
juice of an orange (see above)
100ml water
150g caster sugar

For the strawberry coulis
227g punnet of strawberries
100g icing sugar
squeeze of lemon juice

Aleppo, Syria

BULGAR POT
with Sliced Lamb

This durum wheat salad is hearty and wholesome and perfect for sharing. Simply spiced with cumin and cinnamon, I love it topped with sumac-spiced lamb to give it a tang. Drizzled with a fresh coriander and parsley dressing, this is exactly the kind of recipe that gets me up and about, enthused to cook iftar. Iftar is the Arabic word for the meal that we eat to break our hours-long fast. There are so many versions of this word that span languages and regions. This is a word that is much anticipated and met with excitement.

Serves: 6

Start by making the bulgur. Put the butter in a large pan over a high heat and melt and brown it till it smells very toasted and you can see the toasted milk solids.

Add the diced onions and cook till the onions are starting to soften and break under the pressure of the spoon. Now add the ground cinnamon, ground cumin and salt and cook through on a low heat.

Rinse the bulgur wheat under cold water till the water runs clear. Drain and add the bulgur to the onion mix, stir in the pan over a medium heat and toast for 5 minutes. Increase the heat to high, pour in the hot vegetable stock or water and bring the whole thing to a boil until the water has evaporated completely. Pop a lid on and leave to steam for 20 minutes on the lowest heat.

For the lamb, put your thinly sliced pieces of lamb into a bowl with the salt, oil and sumac. Mix through till you have everything really well combined.

Put a griddle pan on to a high heat and griddle the pieces of lamb into a few pieces at a time, till you have done all the lamb, then set aside to rest.

Make the dressing by putting the lemon zest and juice into a food processor, along with the honey, garlic, fresh parsley, coriander, toasted pine nuts, oil and a pinch of salt and blend to a rough paste.

Spoon the bulgur out on to a large platter, lay the lamb slices on top and drizzle generously with the dressing. Sprinkle over the pomegranate seeds and serve in the middle of the table.

For the bulgur

200g butter
2 onions, diced
¼ teaspoon ground cinnamon
1 teaspoon ground cumin
1 tablespoon salt
500g bulgur wheat
500ml hot vegetable stock or water

For the lamb

1kg boneless lamb, thinly sliced
2 teaspoons salt
3 tablespoons oil
75g sumac

For the dressing

2 lemons, zest and juice
3 tablespoons honey
6 cloves of garlic, peeled
small handful of fresh parsley
small handful of fresh coriander
100g toasted pine nuts
100ml olive oil
large pinch of salt
pomegranate seeds, for sprinkling

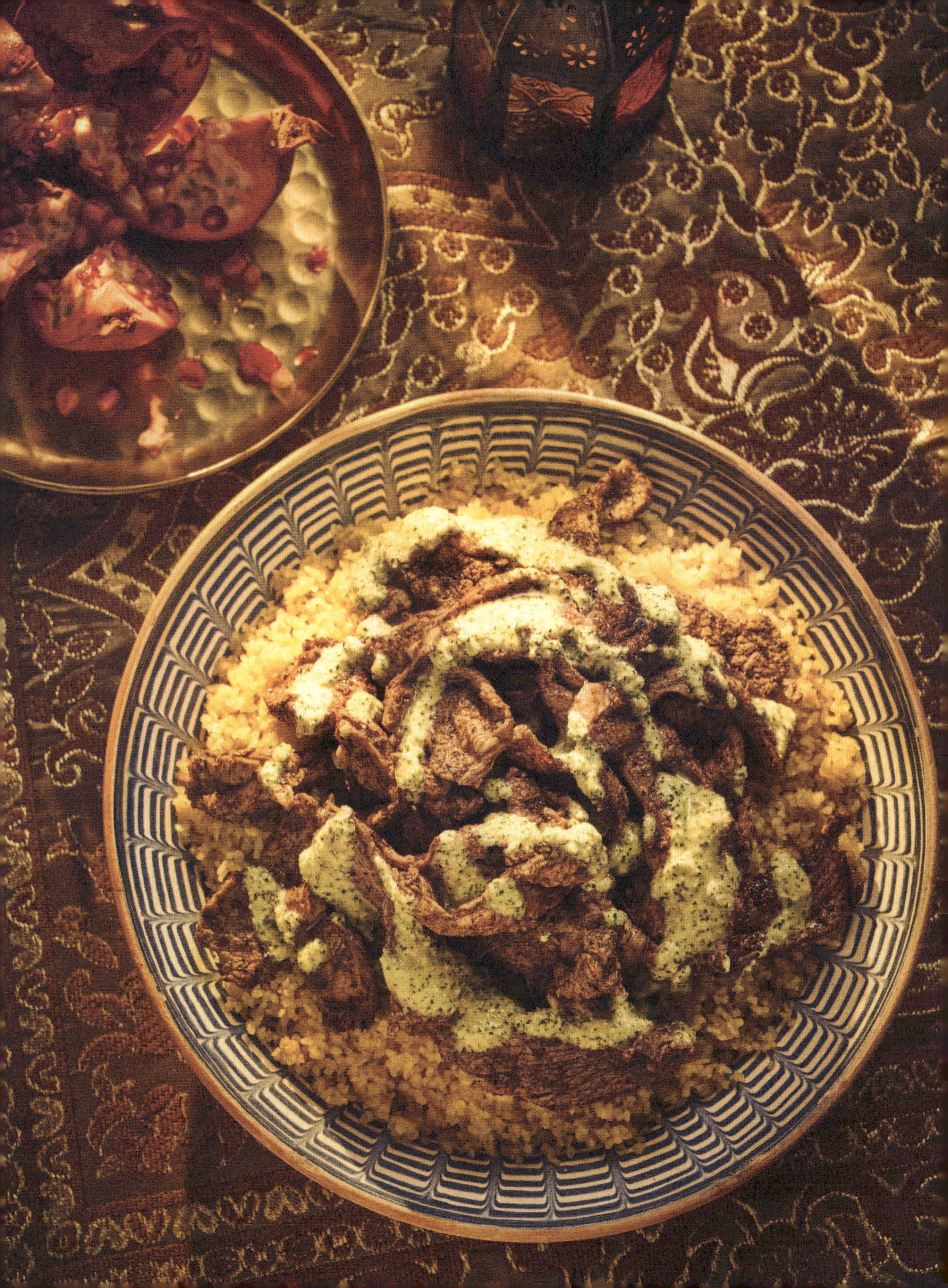

Aleppo, Syria

MUSHABBAK
Semolina Churros

If you like a deep-fried dessert that is sweet and crunchy, then this is for you. The semolina gives this yeasted dough the perfect crunch. Served with a pistachio cream, it is a sight for sore eyes.

Makes: 50–60 Mushabbak

For the dough, start by putting the fine semolina in a bowl with the plain flour, caster sugar, yeast, baking powder and salt. Whisk so everything is well combined.

Make a well in the centre, pour in the oil with the lukewarm milk and whisk till you have a smooth batter. Cover with a tea towel and leave to sit for 15 minutes.

Meanwhile, make the syrup by putting the caster sugar in a pan with the water, lemon juice, rose extract and salt. Bring the whole thing to the boil and simmer for just 5 minutes and then take off the heat.

Now it is time to deep fry the batter. Pour the oil into a large pan, adding enough to go two-thirds of the way up. Bring the oil to 180°C.

Spoon the batter into a piping bag with a star tip attached. Squeeze the batter into the oil in 2-3cm pieces and cut, then keep doing this till you have a few in the pan without overcrowding. Fry till golden, making sure to turn as and when you need to.

Use a slotted spoon to remove from the pan and add straight into the syrup to soak for 10 seconds, then take out and leave on a plate. Do this till you have finished all the batter.

For the cream, put the pistachios into a food processor with the icing sugar, oil, salt and milk and blend to a smooth paste. You can use this cream as a dip or you could also put it in a piping bag and pipe all over the fried delights before serving.

For the dough
450g fine semolina
70g plain flour
50g caster sugar
15g fast-action yeast
½ teaspoon baking powder
½ teaspoon salt
3 tablespoons oil
300ml lukewarm milk
oil, for frying

For the syrup
400g caster sugar
420ml water
1 lemon, juice only
1 teaspoon rose extract
pinch of salt

For the cream
200g pistachios, toasted
100g icing sugar
50ml olive oil
½ teaspoon salt
8 tablespoons milk

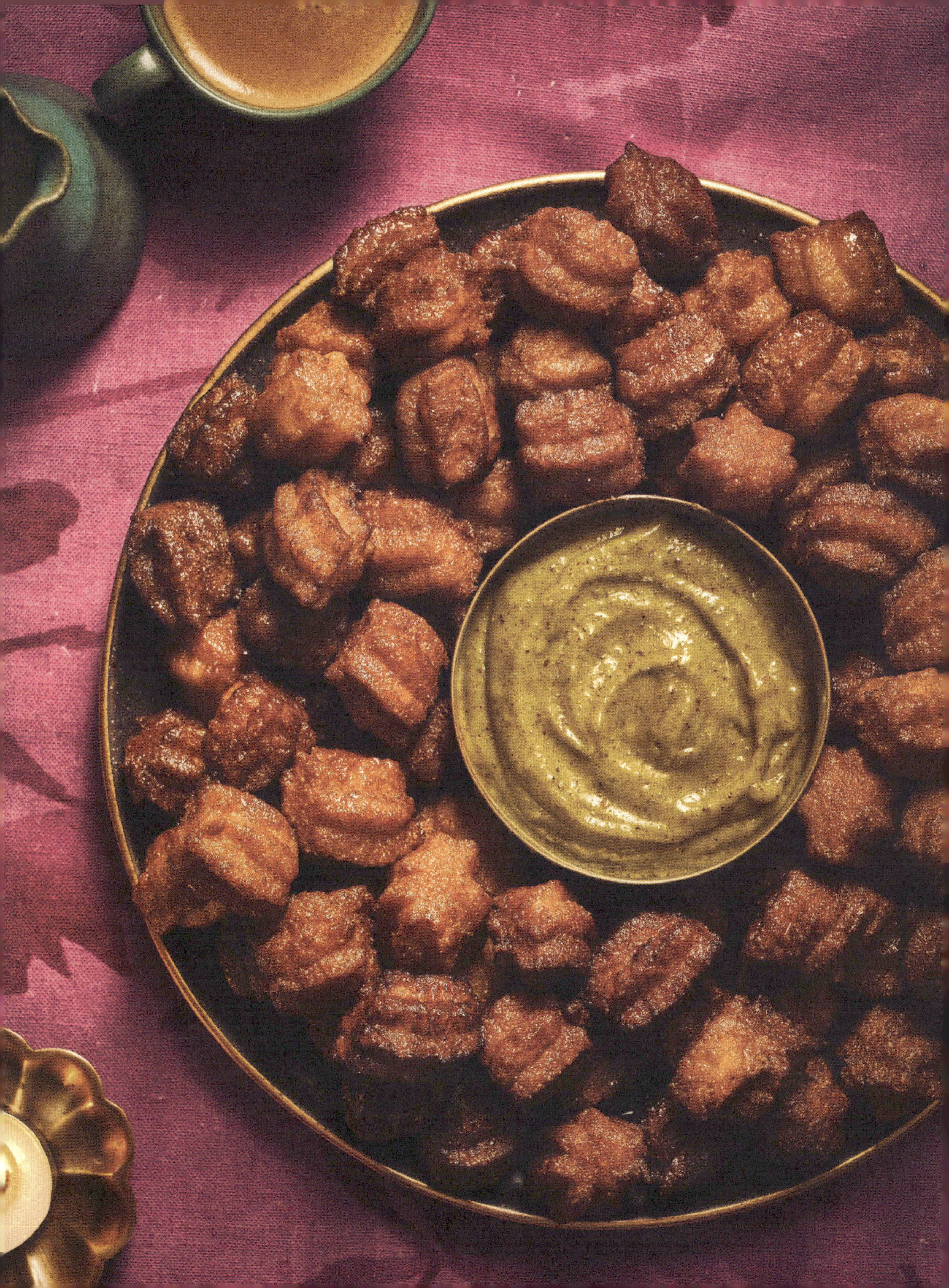

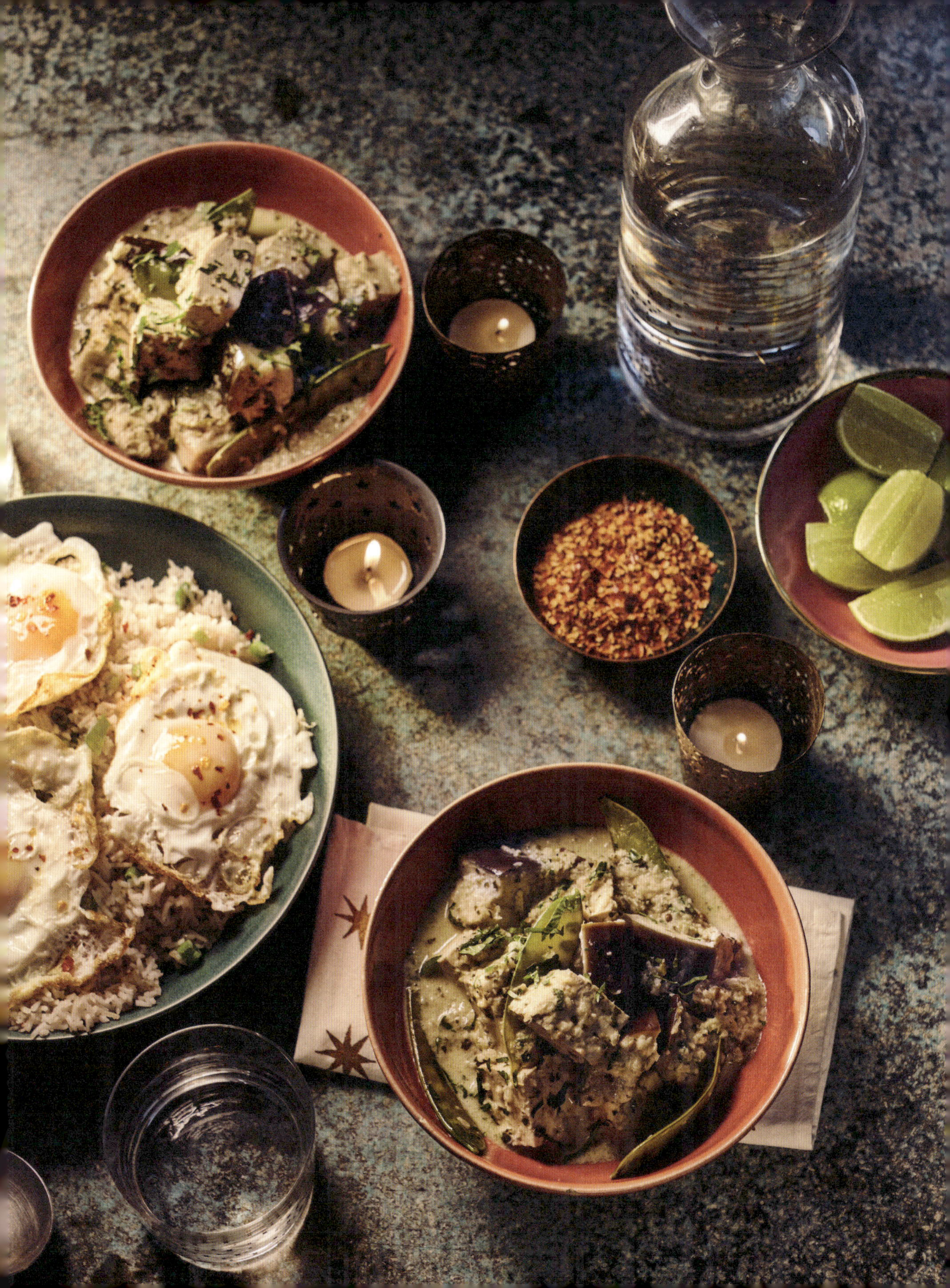

VEGETABLE TOFU CURRY
with Nasi Goreng Ikan Billis

I love food from different parts of the world, but sometimes meeting someone who is from a part of the world that I have never travelled to can spark my curiosity. I love the flavours of Singaporean cooking and the blend of spices and coconut milk, and I love this curry made with tofu and served with anchovy rice. So much happening, and all in a good way!

Let's start by making the paste. Put the onion, garlic, ginger, lemon-grass stalks, lime leaves, zest and juice of the limes, coriander with the stalks, coriander seeds, peppercorns, fish sauce and oil in a blender or food processor. Blend the ingredients for a few minutes. Now pour in the water and blend to a smooth paste.

Take a large pan and pop over a medium heat. Put the paste mixture in the pan and start to cook the paste – this will really enhance these great flavours further. Cook till the paste starts to come away from the sides and is much darker in colour.

Now add the tofu and aubergine and cook in the paste for just a few minutes. Pour in the coconut milk and leave to simmer till the sauce is as thick as the consistency of double cream. Cook gently for 30 minutes. Stir in the mangetout and cook for just another 10 minutes.

For the rice, put the anchovies and oil into a hot wok, then break the fillets down to a paste. Add the rice and stir through, then add the spring onions, stir again and set aside.

Fry the eggs in hot oil in a frying pan till you have an egg that is frilly around the edges with a runny, warm yolk. Sprinkle chilli flakes over the eggs.

Serve the eggs with the rice and the curry, sprinkling over a generous amount of fresh coriander and serving with lime wedges.

Serves: 6

For the paste
1 onion, roughly chopped
1 bulb of garlic, cloves peeled
8cm piece of peeled ginger, roughly chopped
2 lemongrass stalks, roughly chopped
8 fresh/dry lime leaves
2 limes, zest and juice
small handful of fresh coriander with the stalks
2 tablespoons coriander seeds, toasted
1 teaspoon whole black peppercorns
4 tablespoons fish sauce
100ml oil
100ml water

For the tofu
2 x 280g packs of firm tofu, diced into 2cm cubes
1 large aubergine, diced into 2cm cubes
2 x 400ml tins of coconut milk
260g mangetout

For the rice
100g anchovy fillets with the oil
3 x 250g packets of microwave rice or 750g leftover cold rice
1 bunch of spring onions, thinly sliced

For the eggs
6 eggs
oil, for frying
chilli flakes

To serve
handful or fresh coriander, chopped
lime wedges

Malaysia

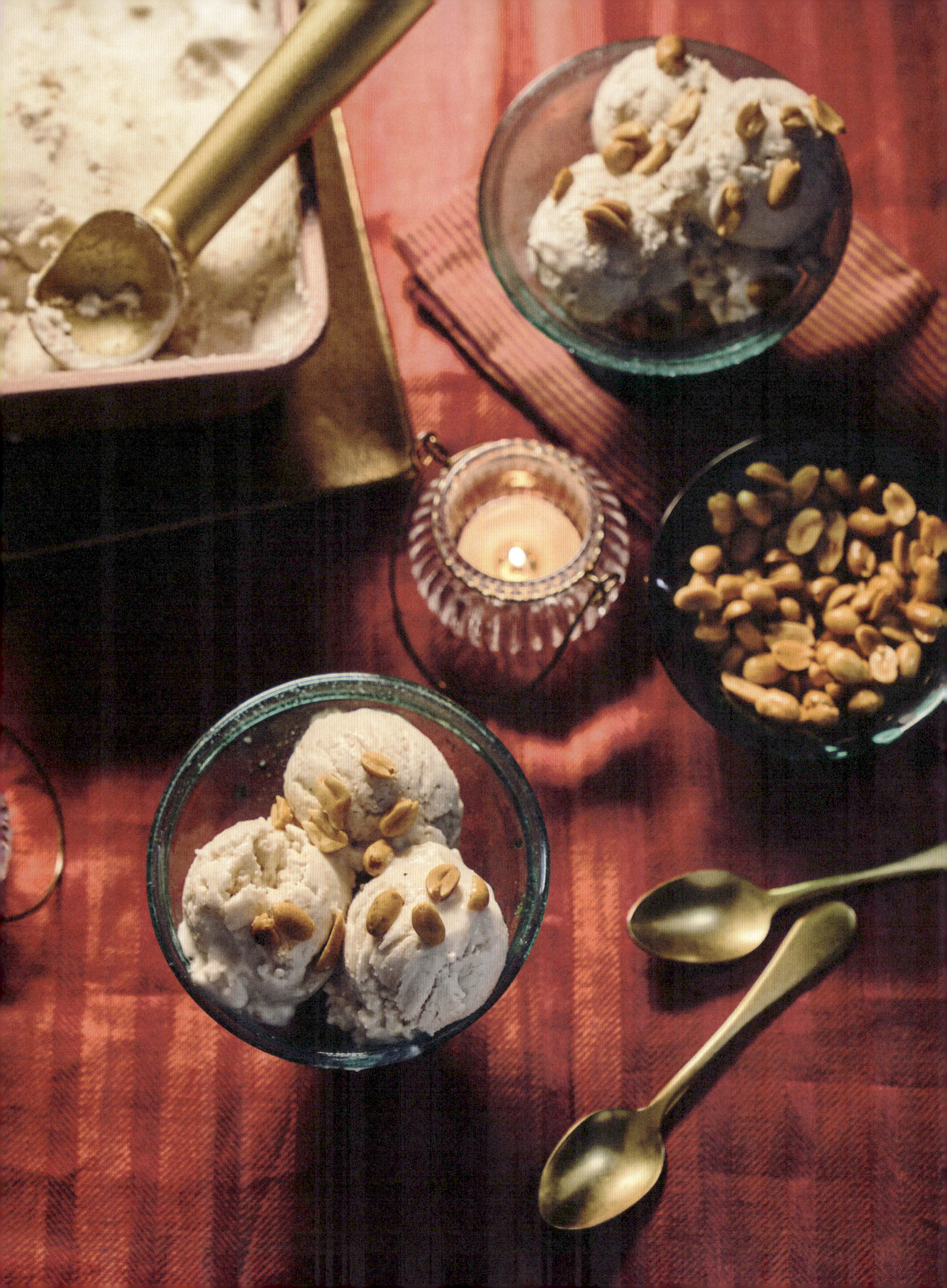

COCONUT ICE CREAM

Ice cream is a great way to explore the many intense flavour combinations in Malaysian cuisine. I love this coconut ice cream recipe, it's so simple to make and you get the creamy coconut with the hint of salty peanut. Perfect for a light dessert after dinner.

Serves: 6

Start by putting the coconut in a small non-stick pan and toasting till the coconut is very golden. Set aside to cool completely, which won't take long.

Put the coconut cream in a bowl with the condensed milk and vanilla extract and whisk till thick and fluffy. Add the toasted coconut and mix through.

Transfer the mixture to a freezer-safe Tupperware, pop the lid on and leave to freeze overnight.

Make the topping by melting the butter till it is golden and brown. Add the peanuts, mix through and cook in the butter till the nuts are dark brown. Take off the heat and sprinkle in the salt.

Take the ice cream out 15 minutes before serving. Scoop into dishes, sprinkle over the peanuts and serve.

For the ice cream

50g desiccated coconut

3 x 400ml tins of coconut cream, chilled

397g tin of condensed milk

1 tablespoon vanilla extract

To serve

3 tablespoons unsalted butter

200g peanuts, roughly chopped

large pinch of salt

Algeria

TAGINE DE POULET
Chicken Tagine served with Beid Hamine and Rice

Serves: 6

Algerian food is something my mind never even ventured to until a few years ago when I realized there were so many Algerian Muslim pop stars in the charts, which twigged my curiosity, though less for the music and totally for the food. Algerian food has been heavily influenced by Arab countries, Berbers, Turks and Europeans. This chicken is so light, yet hearty and warming. Served with rice and some onion and coffee-infused eggs, you will love this.

Start with enough oil in a large pan to lightly cover the base. When the oil is hot, add the garlic and fry till very golden brown. Now add your onions with the salt and cook till the onions are really soft.

Add your chicken thighs, potatoes and carrots, then add all your spices and mix through to make sure everything is combined. Add the preserved lemons, green olives and stock. Mix and bring everything to the boil, then leave to simmer for 30 minutes with the lid on.

Now let's get on to the beid hamine. Put the eggs in a pan with the onion skins, coffee grounds and salt. Pour in as much cold water as you need to cover the eggs and bring to the boil, then leave to simmer for 10 minutes till you have hard-boiled eggs. Take the eggs out, crack the shells all over, put back into the hot liquid and leave to sit.

Take the rice and wash it till the water is completely clear. Drain and put into a pan with the cold water and stick of cinnamon. Bring the rice to the boil, stirring to stop it from sticking to the base, and boil till you can see every grain of rice and the water has evaporated. Pop the lid on and leave to steam on the lowest heat.

To finish the chicken off, take off the lid, mix the cornflour with the water and add to the pan. Mix and allow to thicken for 10 minutes.

Drain the eggs and peel them. Sprinkle the fresh parsley and coriander over the chicken and everything is ready to serve.

oil, for frying
1 bulb of garlic, cloves peeled and thinly sliced
2 onions, thinly sliced (reserving the skins for the beid hamine)
1 tablespoon salt
6 chicken thighs, bones still in, skin still on
3 medium potatoes, peeled and quartered
6 carrots, peeled and cut into 2-3cm pieces
2 teaspoons ground cinnamon
2 teaspoons ground turmeric
4 teaspoons ground cumin
3 teaspoons paprika
3 preserved lemons, quartered
200g whole green olives
700ml chicken stock or water
4 tablespoons cornflour
4 tablespoons cold water

For the beid hamine
6 eggs
skins of 2 onions (see above)
1 tablespoon coffee grounds
1 tablespoon salt
cold water, to cover

For the rice
600g basmati rice
750ml cold water
1 large cinnamon stick
2 teaspoons salt

To serve
fresh parsley
fresh coriander

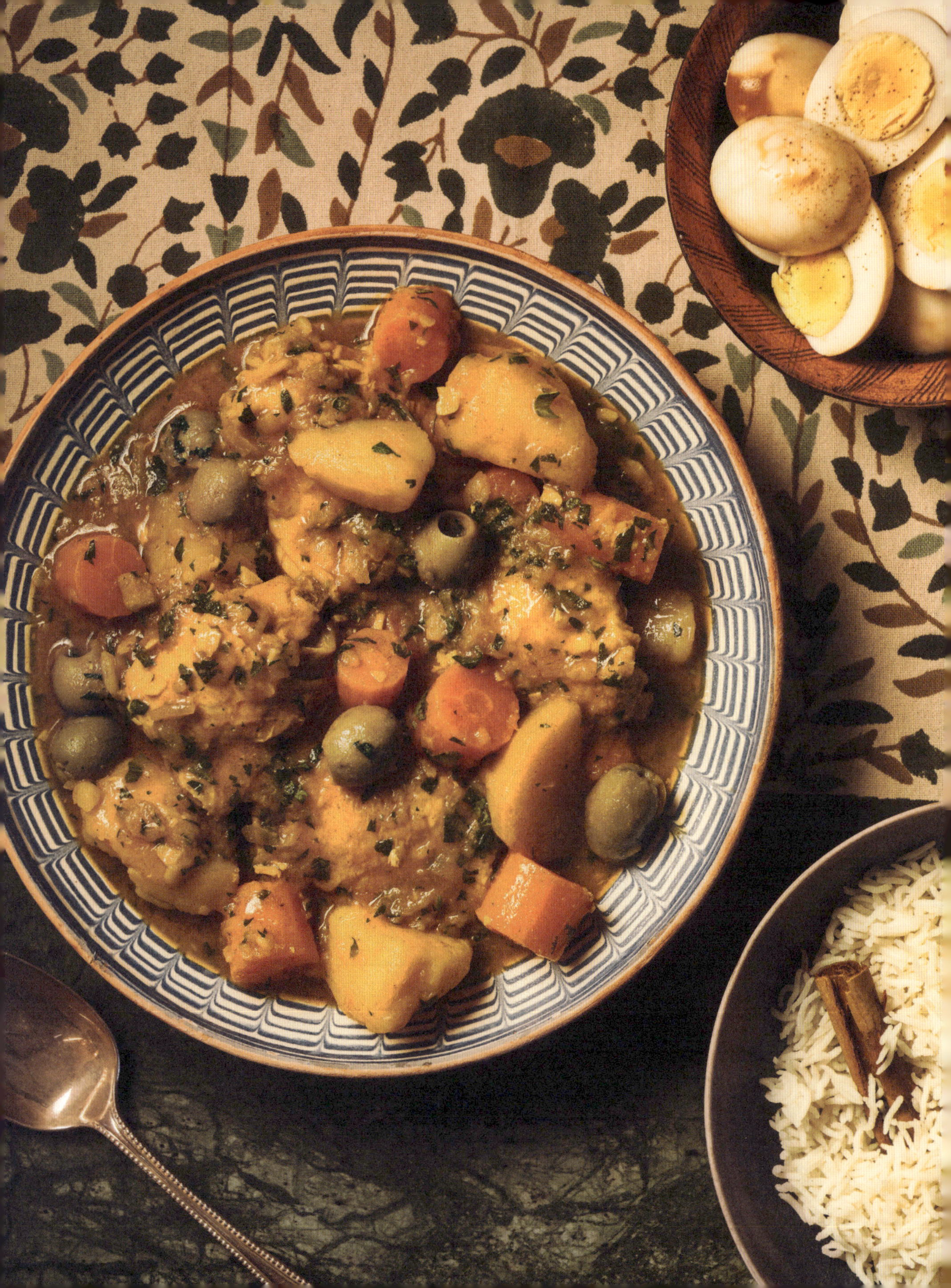

46

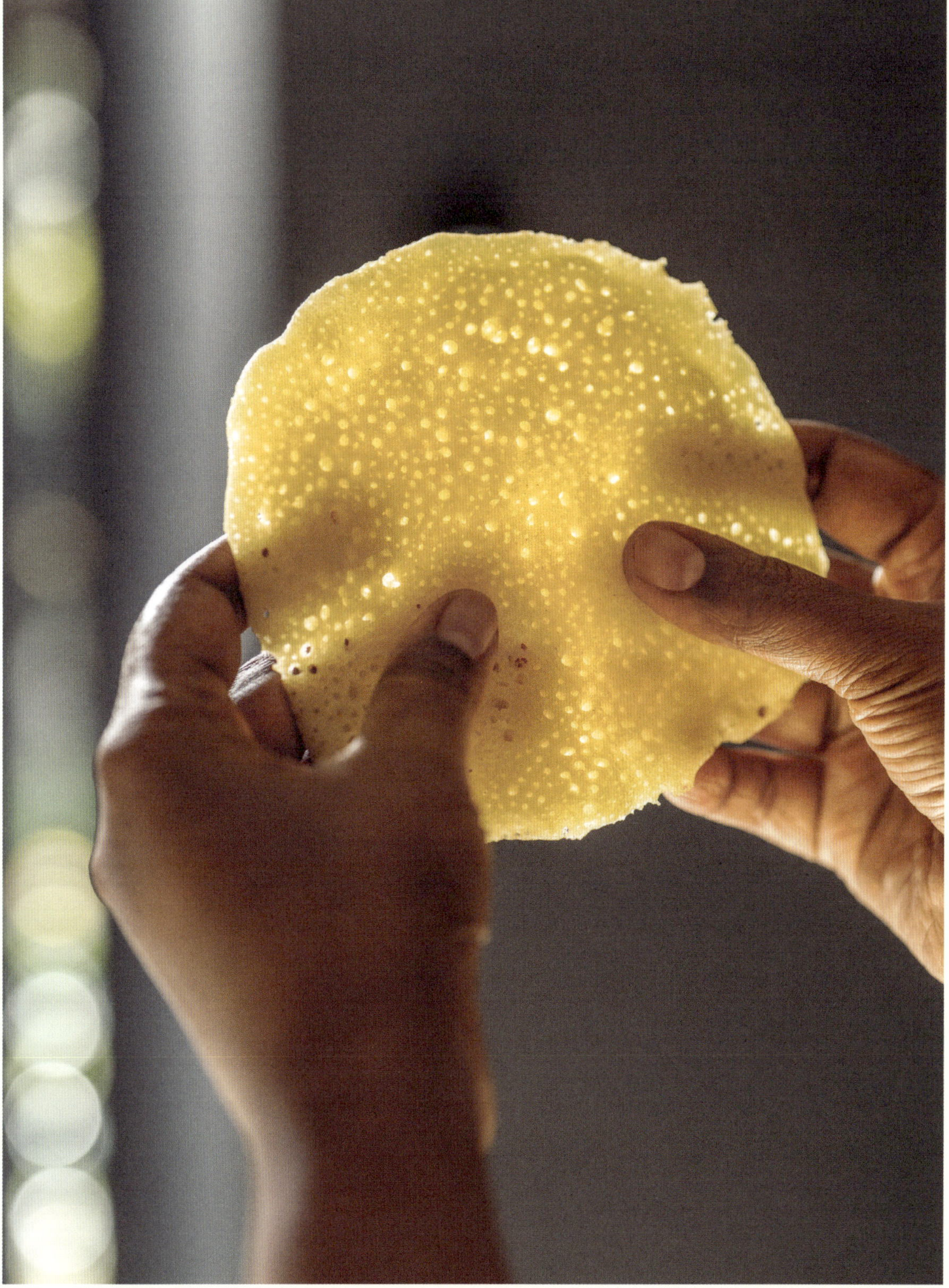

BAGHRIR
Yeasted Semolina Pancakes

If you love pancakes, then you will love these. Baghrir are made with yeast, so they have that delicious deep flavour of yeast and yet are just so soft and versatile. I love to serve these with honey mixed with lavender for something a little bit different.

Serves: 6

Start by making the batter for the pancakes. Put the semolina, plain flour, yeast, baking powder, sugar, salt and water in a blender. Blend to a smooth batter, transfer to a bowl, cover and set aside for 15 minutes.

Heat a non-stick pan on a medium to low heat, give the batter a good stir and spoon in 2 tablespoons, encouraging a round shape, and cook for 3-4 minutes till dry and lots of holes are created on the surface. Don't be tempted to flip it over or we will lose the holes. Once cooked, set aside on a serving dish and continue till you have made them all.

For the lavender honey, put the runny honey, butter and just 1 small sprig of lavender in a blender (or use a stick blender) and blend till you have an even mixture. Pour into a serving dish and serve alongside the hot pancakes.

For the pancakes
290g fine semolina
90g plain flour
14g fast-action yeast
2 teaspoons baking powder
1 teaspoon sugar
1 teaspoon salt
710ml lukewarm water

For the lavender honey
227g jar of runny honey
100g butter, melted
Fresh lavender

Algeria

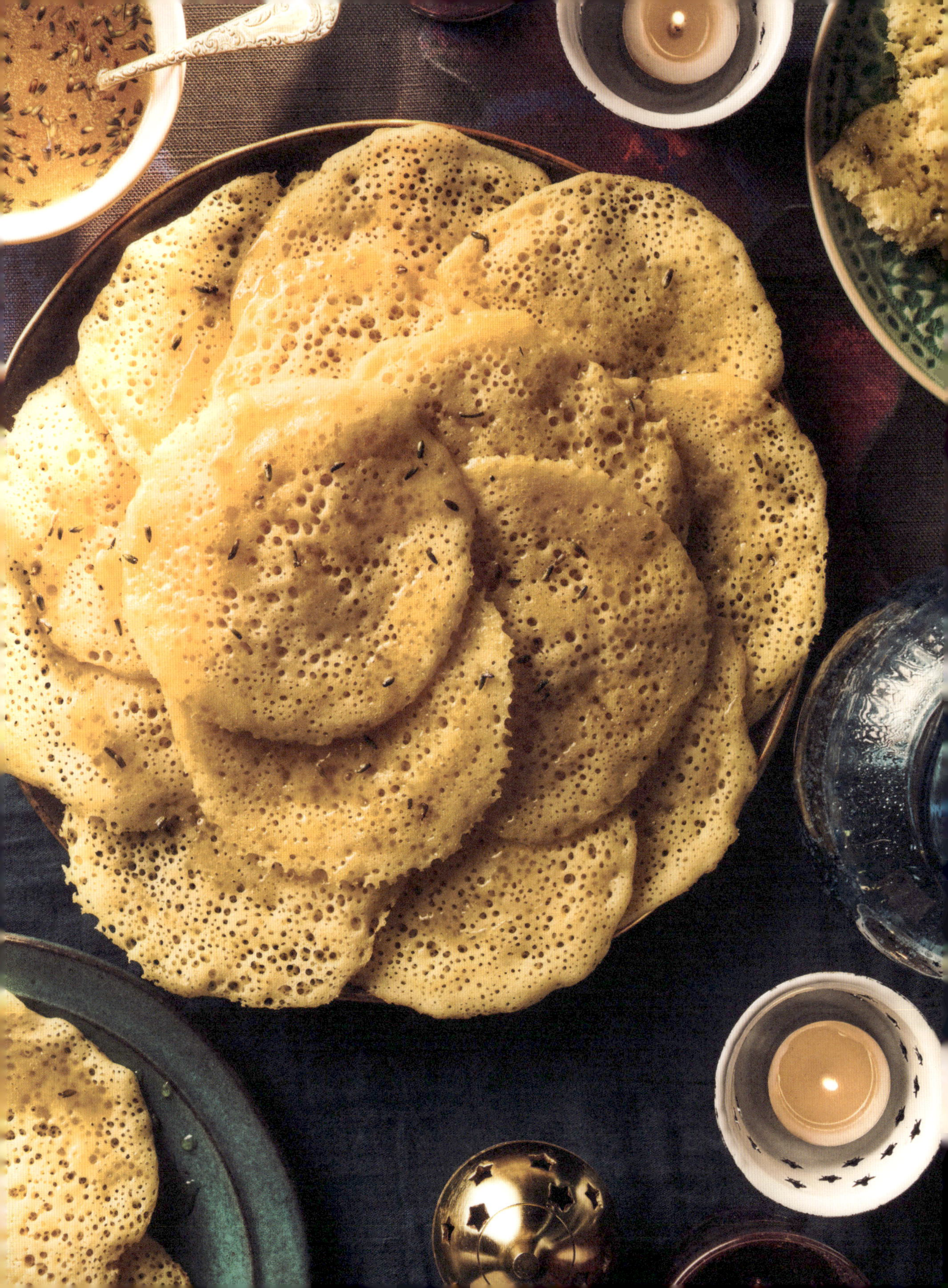

Somalia

LAMB SUQAAR
with Injera (Pancakes)

Somali food is right up there as one of my favourite cuisines. The flavours are always rich and deep, as they are in this lamb suqaar, where it is the intensity of the toasted coriander seeds that takes it to another level of deliciousness. I also love making my version of injera – fermented pancakes. They are traditionally made with teff flour, something that I don't find easy to source, but after a little trial and error I realized we can get close-ish to the real thing using wholemeal flour.

Serves: 6

Start by making the batter for the injera. Put the wholemeal and plain flours in a bowl along with the yeast, salt and baking powder. Whisk the dry ingredients so they are mixed well. Make a well in the centre, add the warm water and vinegar and whisk till everything is combined and there are no dry spots of flour. Cover and leave the batter to rest for an hour.

Meanwhile, let's make the lamb suqaar. Pour the oil into a large pan and warm the oil on a high heat. Add your onions in along with the salt and cook the onions till they are deep dark brown, which can take about 12 minutes, making sure to stir occasionally.

Now add your diced peppers and garam masala and cook till the peppers are soft. Add the toasted coriander seeds and tamarind and mix through for a minute. Get your lamb in and cook through on a high heat till the meat begins to brown.

Meanwhile, make the tomato paste by putting the tomatoes, garlic and coriander in a blender and blending to a smooth paste. Pour this straight on to the lamb and cook on a medium to high heat till all the moisture has evaporated and you have a thick sauce that coats the meat. This can take 30-40 minutes.

While that cooks away, make the injera. Take a medium non-stick pancake pan and place it on a medium heat. Brush very lightly with a small amount of oil.

Pour a ladleful of batter into the pan, spread around the edges to form a circle and then carefully swirl the pan to fill the centre, adding more batter if you need to. Leave to cook for about

For the injera
250g wholemeal flour
125g plain flour
14g fast-action yeast
1 teaspoon salt
½ teaspoon baking powder
680ml lukewarm water
2 tablespoons apple cider vinegar
oil, for greasing

For the lamb suqaar
100ml oil
2 onions, finely diced
1 tablespoon salt
2 peppers, diced
3 tablespoons garam masala
4 tablespoons coriander seeds, toasted till dark in colour, lightly crushed
3 tablespoons tamarind paste
1kg diced boneless lamb

For the tomato paste
3 tomatoes
8 cloves of garlic, peeled
small handful of fresh coriander

➜

3 minutes till dry on top, then flip over for 10 seconds and slip on to a plate and cover with a tea towel while you make the rest.

To serve, place an injera on a plate, add the lamb in the centre, sprinkle over the coriander and enjoy with lemon wedges on the side.

To serve

handful of fresh coriander, finely chopped

lemon wedges

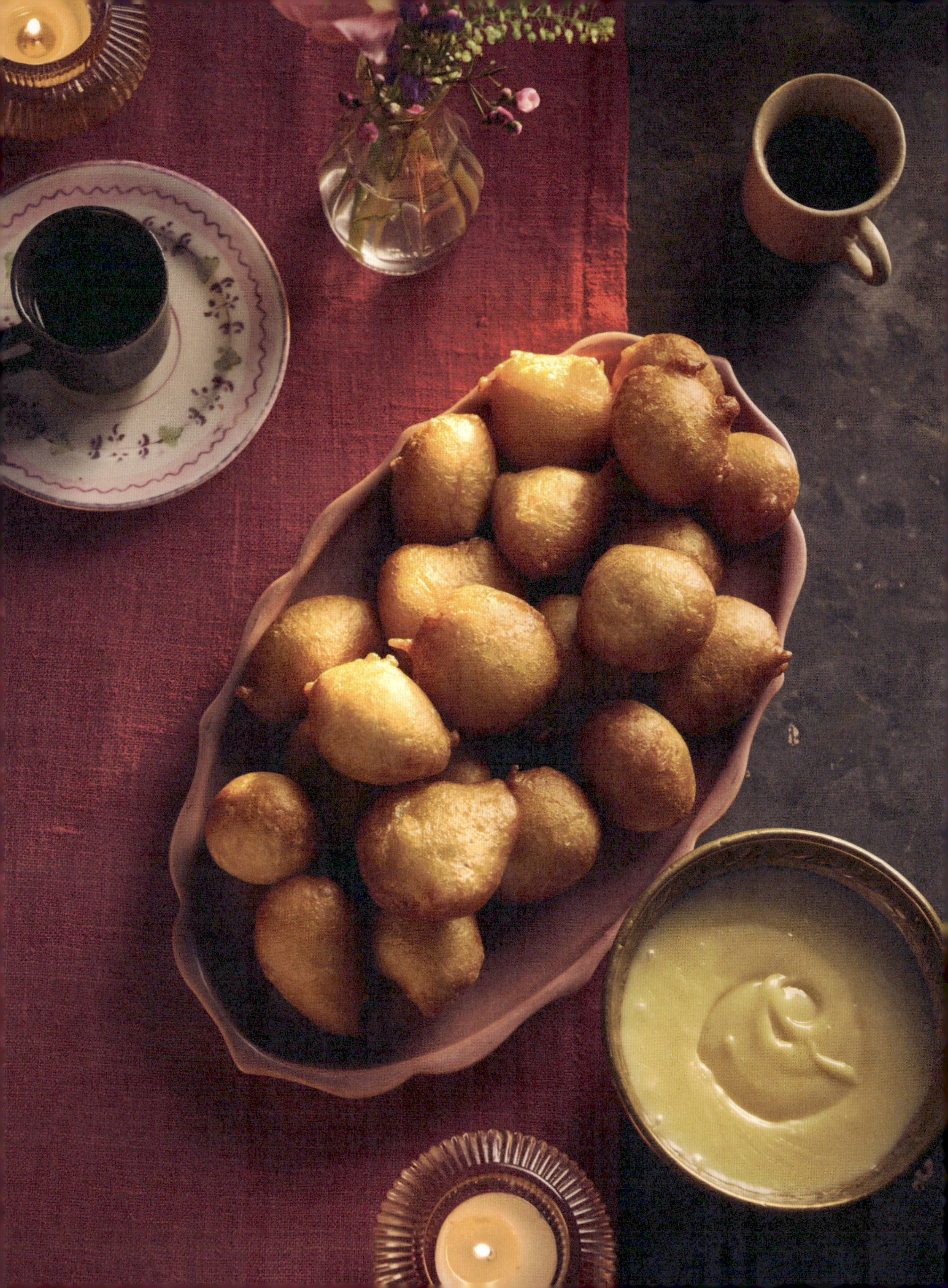

Somalia

PUFF PUFFS

If you like doughnuts, you will love these. A yeasted dough that is dropped into hot oil to create these yummy, moreish, too-good-to-stop puff puffs.

Makes: 25–30 puff puffs

Start by making the batter. Put the plain flour in a bowl with the yeast, caster sugar and salt and mix really well. Pour in the lukewarm water and mix till you have a smooth batter and no spots of flour. Cover and set aside.

While that sits, let's make the chocolate sauce by breaking up the chocolate into a jug. Put the double cream into a small pan and bring to the boil. As soon as it comes up to the boil, remove and pour straight on to the broken chocolate, leaving it to sit for 3 minutes.

Add the butter and cardamom powder and use a stick blender to make a smooth chocolate sauce. Set aside and let's start to fry the puff puff.

Take a large pan and fill with oil about two-thirds of the way up. Heat the oil to 180°C. Have a tray lined with kitchen paper to absorb any excess oil and a slotted spoon at the ready.

The batter for the puff is really sticky and gloopy, so grease an ice cream scoop, pick up a scoop and drop it into the oil, greasing your scoop if and when it needs oiling. Keep doing this till you have fried them all.

Pop the puff puffs on to a serving platter and serve with the white chocolate sauce in the centre or drizzle all over.

For the batter
600g plain flour
10g fast-action yeast
150g caster sugar
½ teaspoon salt
550ml lukewarm water
oil, for frying and greasing

For the chocolate sauce
300g white chocolate
200ml double cream
1 tablespoon butter
4 cardamom pods, husks removed and seeds crushed to a fine powder

Egypt

KHOSHARI
with Buftek

Serves: 6

We stopped off at the airport in Egypt on a trip abroad and amongst all the fast-food chains there was a place that served up khoshari, all made up in bowls, ready to eat. It literally had everything we needed to fill ourselves up before the flight. If you enjoy lots of textures and flavours, you will love everything about this.

We should begin by prepping the beef steaks. Use a meat hammer to bash each steak till it is thin, about 25mm. Put the steaks on a large tray.

Put the blended onions in a bowl with the salt and pepper and mix through well. Now smother the mixture all over the beef steaks, cover and leave to marinate for 4 hours.

After 4 hours, take each steak and dip into the beaten egg, then coat generously with the breadcrumbs. Set aside on a tray.

Now on to the khoshari. This is all about the different layers and textures. So, let's start with the rice.

Wash the rice till the rice water runs completely clear. Put the rice in a pan with the cold water and the cinnamon stick. Cook the rice by bringing to the boil and stirring occasionally to stop the grains from sticking to the base. Once all the water has evaporated, lower the heat completely, put the lid on and leave to steam.

Now on to the tomato sauce. Pour the oil into a pan, enough to cover the base in a thin, even layer. Get the oil nice and hot. As soon as it's hot, add the thinly sliced onions, making sure to separate them with your hands as you drop them in.

Fry the onions till they are crisp and very golden brown. You may need to do this in two batches dependent on your pan size. Remove the onions with a slotted spoon on to a plate lined with kitchen paper to drain. Sprinkle salt over generously to keep the onions crisp.

To the same pan, add the minced garlic, making sure the oil is still hot and adding a little more oil if you need to. Fry till golden.

➜

For the buftek

6 beef rump steaks
2 onions, blended to a purée
2 teaspoons salt
4 teaspoons ground black pepper
2 medium eggs, lightly beaten
250g dried white breadcrumbs
oil, for frying

For the khoshari

300g basmati rice
450ml cold water
1 large cinnamon stick
oil, for frying
3 onions, thinly sliced
8 cloves of garlic, minced
2 teaspoons salt
400g carton of passata
2 teaspoons chilli flakes
2 teaspoons apple cider vinegar
100g salted butter
3 teaspoons ground cumin
200g macaroni
400g tin of brown lentils, drained and rinsed
400g tin of chickpeas, drained and rinsed
fresh chives, for sprinkling
lime wedges, to serve
salt

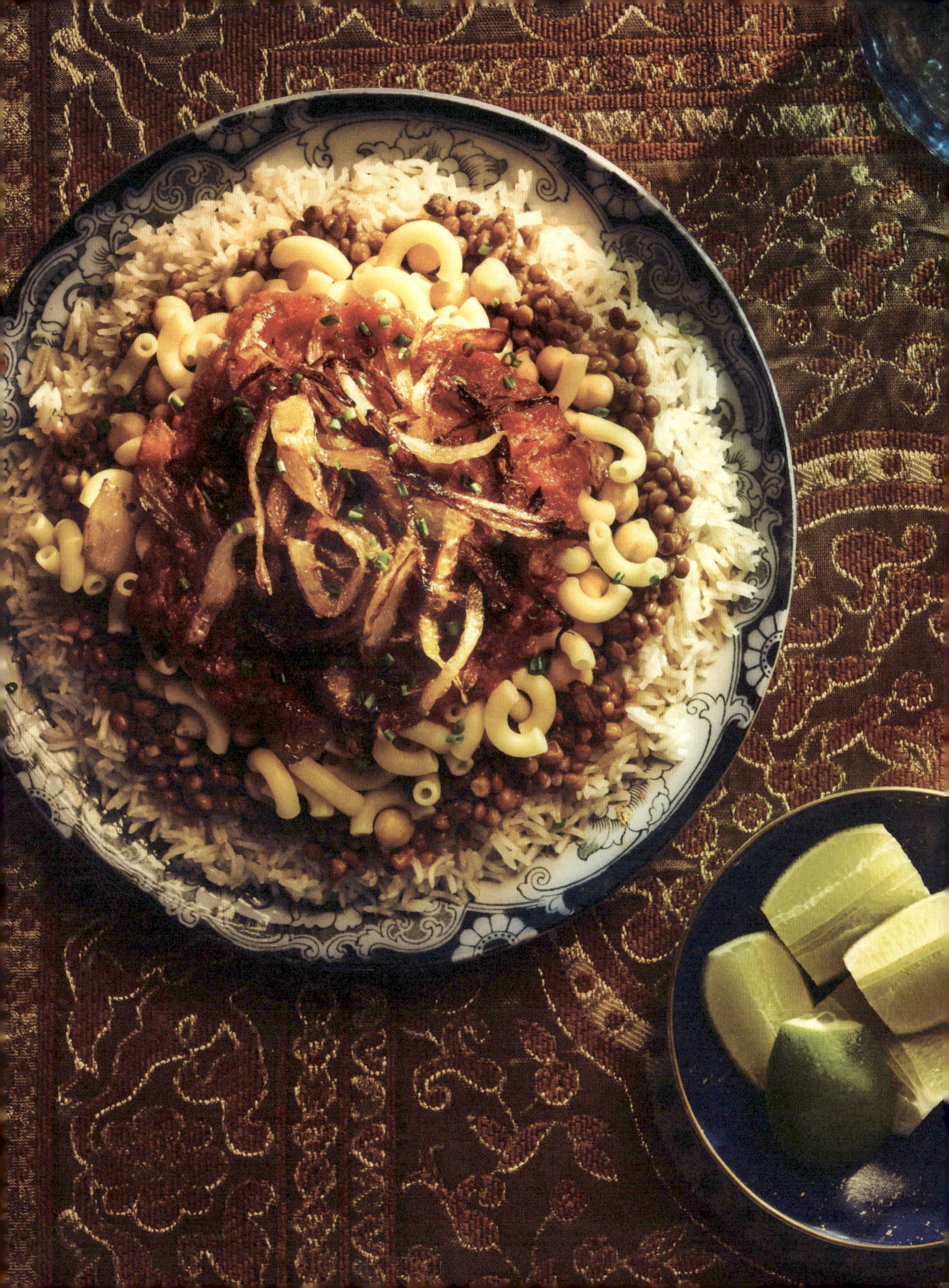

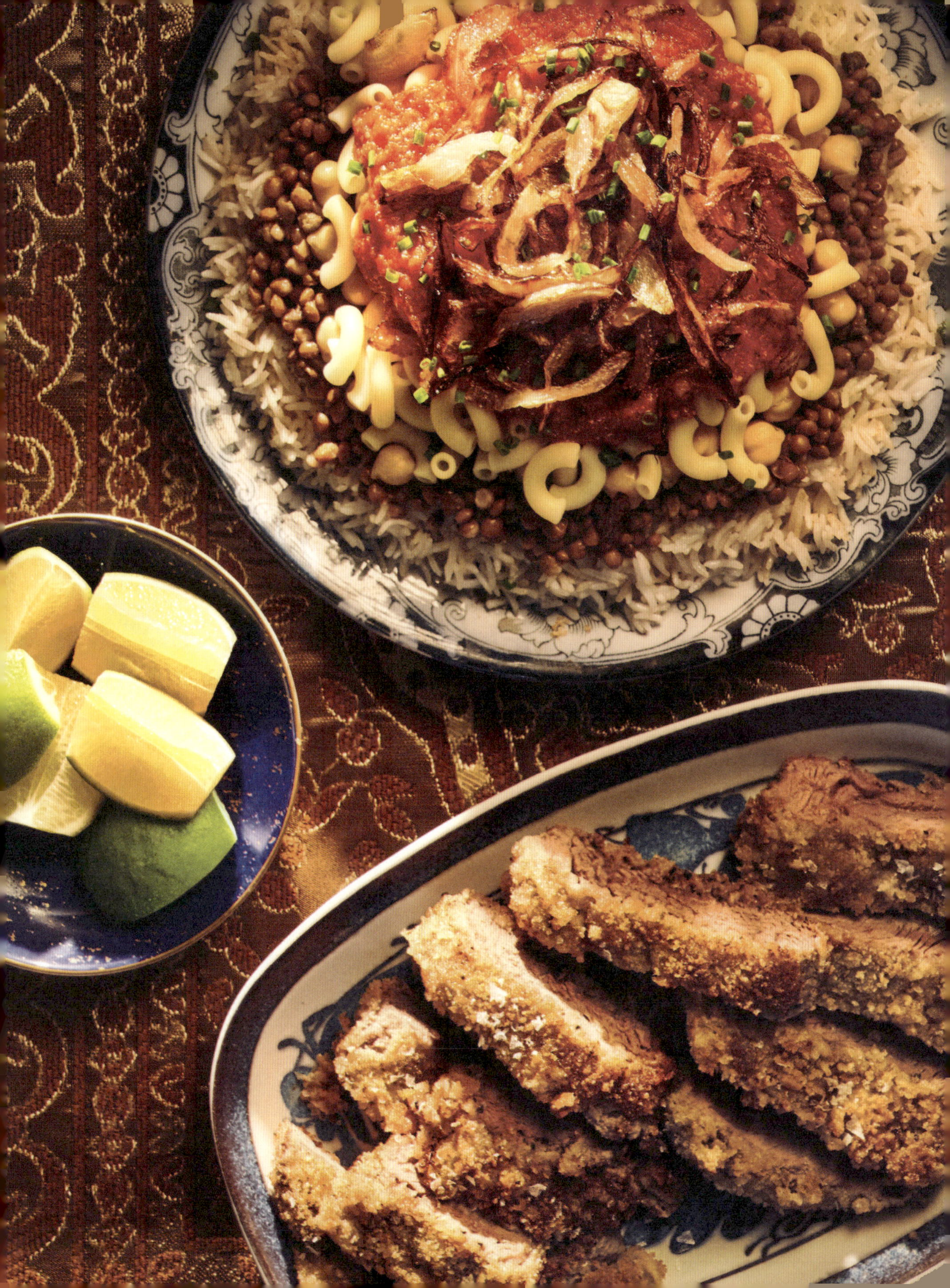

Add the salt and the passata, along with the chilli flakes and apple cider vinegar and cook over a medium heat for 10-15 minutes till thickened. Set aside.

Take the rice off the heat. In a small pan, warm the butter till melted and browned slightly. Add the ground cumin, mix through, and drizzle all over the rice. Fluff up the rice and set aside with the lid on.

Now boil the macaroni till tender and not too soft or as per the instructions on the packet. Make sure to season the water really well.

While the pasta is boiling, pour some oil into a large frying pan, enough to cover the entire base, and fry the beef in batches (you may need to do these two at a time). Fry for 5 minutes on each side, till golden brown and cooked through. Repeat for the rest of the steaks.

Drain the pasta and we are ready to begin layering the khoshari. Take a large platter and layer the rice on first in one even layer, removing the cinnamon stick. Add the layer of lentils and season with salt, then the chickpeas and season again. Add the macaroni, top with the tomato sauce and then the crispy onions.

Sprinkle over the chives and it is ready to eat. Plate up with lemon wedges and enjoy.

UMM ALI

This is very similar to the traditional bread-and-butter pudding but made with croissants. You can use any stale bread, but I love the buttery nature of the croissant. Simply spiced, bursting with raisins, this dessert is perfect for making in advance and enjoying in the middle of the table with family.

Serves: 6

Start by greasing a 31cm x 20cm roasting dish with some soft butter. Set that aside.

Pour the whole milk, along with the half tin of condensed milk, into a jug. Sprinkle in the ground cardamom, ground cinnamon and vanilla extract. Whisk it all together and set aside.

Take the large croissants, rip into pieces and get them into the buttered roasting dish. Pour in the milk mixture and leave the whole thing to soak for 30 minutes.

Preheat the oven to 170°C.

Before baking, sprinkle over the raisins, desiccated coconut and almond flakes. Bake for 25 minutes, till the top is golden brown. Take out and leave to cool for 15 minutes before eating.

Make the rose honey by putting the dried rose buds in a mortar and pestle with the salt and crush the petals to a fine powder. Add the honey and the rose to a small bowl and mix well.

Serve a portion of the pudding drizzled all over in the honey, pour on some double cream and enjoy.

butter, for greasing
950ml whole milk
½ x 397g tin of condensed milk
1 teaspoon ground cardamom
1 teaspoon ground cinnamon
2 teaspoons vanilla extract
6 large croissants
100g raisins
3 tablespoons desiccated coconut
25g almond flakes
double cream, to serve

For the rose honey
4 dried rose buds
¼ teaspoon salt
200g honey

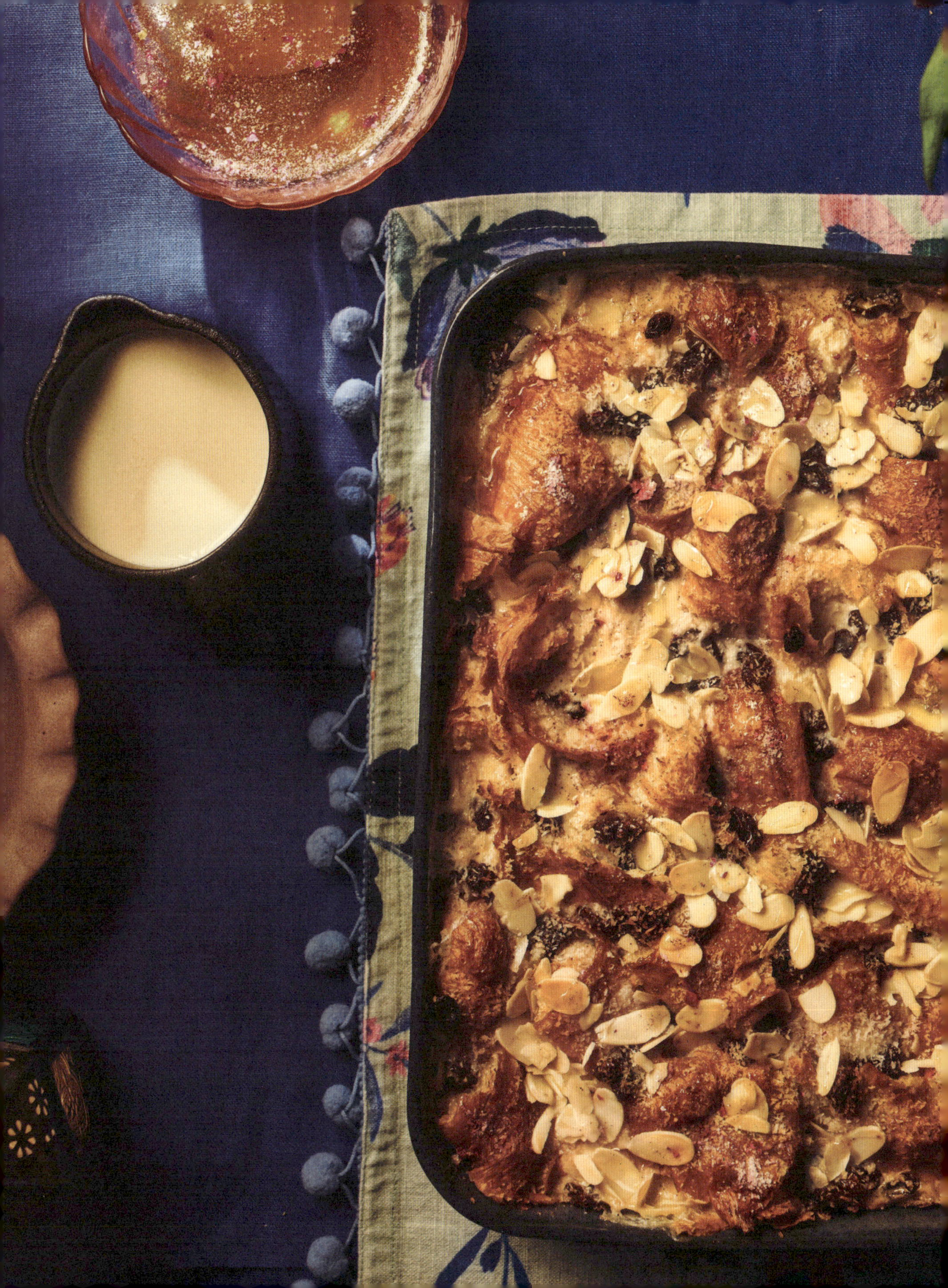

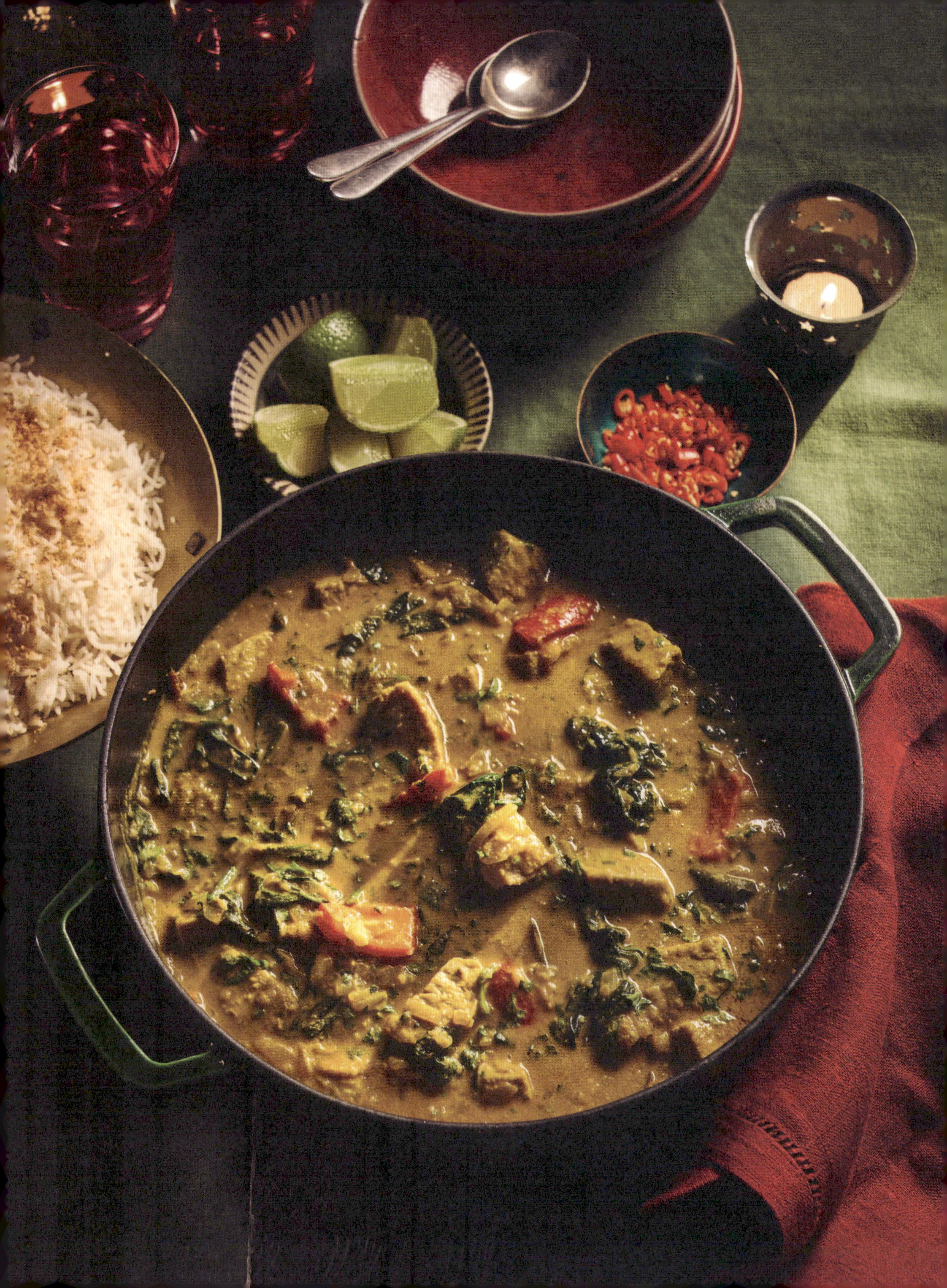

Maldives

KANDU KUKULHU
Maldivian Tuna Curry with Rice

Serves: 6

My husband has relatives who live and work in the Maldives and that got me thinking about all the delicious things that they could be eating on those sunshine islands. Tuna curry is a whole thing out there and I love making this delicious curry that cooks tuna in a way that doesn't dry it out at all. Aromatic with cardamom and creamy with coconut.

Start by making the curry. Get a large pan and put it over a medium heat. Pour in the coconut oil and let the oil warm up. As soon as the oil is warm, add the curry leaves and cardamom seeds. As soon as the seeds start popping, add the minced garlic and ginger and gently begin cooking through.

Add the onions and the salt and cook over a medium heat till the onions are a golden brown and very tender – soft enough so that if the onions are pushed with a spoon they disintegrate. Now add the ground fennel, cumin, turmeric and chilli powder.

Cook the spices for a few minutes and then pour in the coconut milk along with the red pepper chunks and cook till the sauce is lovely and thick. Add the fresh spinach and cook with the lid on for 20 minutes. Five minutes before the end of the cooking time, add in the fresh tuna chunks. Stir to coat in the sauce, put the lid back on and cook until the fish is just cooked through.

For the rice, wash the basmati till the water runs completely clear. Pop the rice back into a pan with the cold water and salt and bring to a boil, making sure you stir occasionally. As soon as every grain is visible and the water has evaporated, reduce the heat and leave the lid on to allow it to steam for 10 minutes. Once the rice has cooked, take off the heat.

Melt the butter in a small pan and toast the coconut in the butter till golden. Add the coconut to the rice and fluff through.

Take the curry off the stove and serve with sprinklings of fresh coriander and chilli and the lime wedges alongside the rice.

For the curry
3 tablespoons coconut oil
10 fresh/dry curry leaves
2 cardamom pods, husks removed and seeds only
4 cloves of garlic, minced
5cm piece of peeled ginger, minced
2 onions, finely diced
2 teaspoons salt
2 teaspoons ground fennel
2 teaspoons ground cumin
2 teaspoons ground turmeric
2 teaspoons chilli powder
2 x 400ml tins of coconut milk
1 large red pepper, cut into chunks
100g fresh spinach
600g tuna chunks

For the rice
600g basmati rice
900ml cold water
1 teaspoon salt
75g butter
25g desiccated coconut

To serve
handful of fresh coriander
sliced red chillies
lime wedges

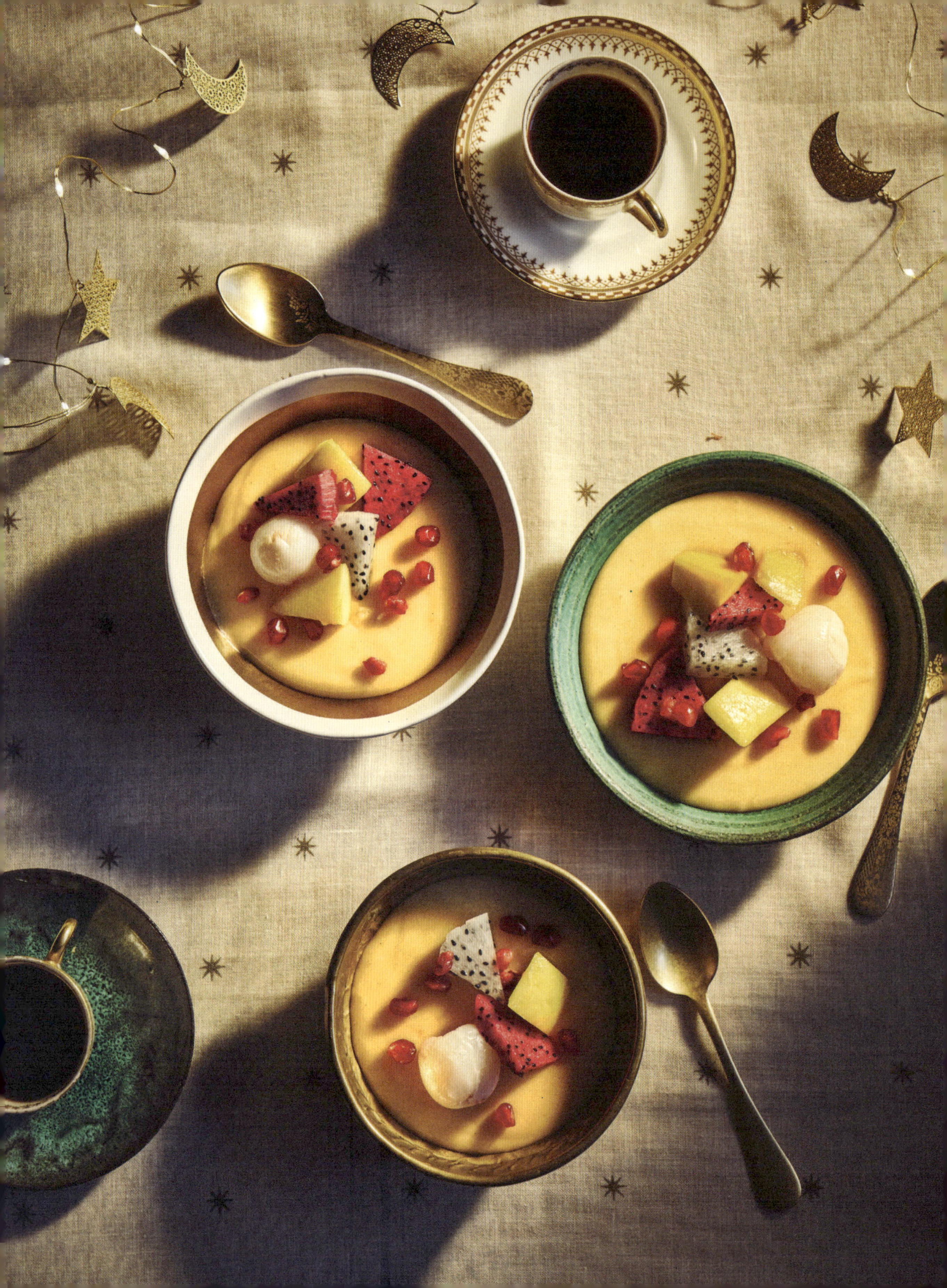

Maldives

BIS HALVA POTS
Maldivian Custard with a Tropical Fruit Salad

Usually served as custard slices, I like to make these in pots just to make life a little easier and let them set in there. Best served with lots of colourful tropical fruit.

Serves: 4

Start by making the custard. Put the 12 eggs in a large heatproof bowl along with the condensed milk. Whisk well, place the bowl on top of a pan of simmering water and cook the eggs till they are hot and thicker. This can take about 20 minutes.

Pop a non-stick pan on to a low heat. Add the clarified butter and melt. Pour in the egg mixture and cook till the mixture starts to pull away from the sides. This can take about 40-45 minutes. As soon as you get it to this stage, pour the mixture into four pots.

Set in the fridge overnight.

Before taking out to serve, make the fruit salad by putting the mango, lychees, dragon fruit and pomegranate seeds in a bowl and mixing them all up.

Serve the custard pots with the fruit on top.

For the custard

12 medium eggs

397g tin of condensed milk

120g clarified butter, plus extra for greasing

For the tropical fruit salad

1 large mango, cut into chunks

567g tin of lychees in syrup, drained

1 dragon fruit, cubed

1 pomegranate, seeds removed

KUFTA BIN BATINIAL

If you love aubergines, you will love this recipe. Grilled aubergine slices, filled with delicious mince and baked to perfection.

Start by preparing the aubergines by cutting them into ½ cm slices across their length, so they are paddle shapes rather than rounds.

Preheat the oven to 200°C. Have a roasting dish at the ready to assemble the dish.

Lay the aubergine slices on a flat sheet, drizzle over some oil and sprinkle over some salt. Bake for 20 minutes or until they are soft enough to roll. Take out and leave to cool.

Make the sauce by putting the oil in a pan with the garlic and cooking until the garlic is golden. Add the red pepper and chilli, along with the salt, and cook till the pepper is tender. Pour in the tinned chopped tomatoes and cook till the mixture just starts to thicken and is less watery. Take off the heat.

For the kofta mix, put the mince into a bowl with the minced garlic, onion, salt, ground cumin, nutmeg, black pepper and cinnamon. Get your hands in and make sure all the dry spices have combined into the mince. Now add the eggs, parsley and breadcrumbs and give everything a thorough mix.

Take your cooled aubergine flats, add the mince to the thickest part and roll to envelop the mince. Repeat with all the aubergine slices and lay them into the roasting dish. Once they are all packed in, spread over the tomato sauce and bake in the oven for 40 minutes.

Take out and leave to cool for 10 minutes before eating. Sprinkle over some parsley to serve.

Serves: 6

For the aubergines
3 large aubergines
oil, for drizzling
salt

For the sauce
oil, for frying
4 cloves of garlic, thinly sliced
1 red pepper, finely diced
4 teaspoons chilli flakes
1 teaspoon salt
2 x 400g tins of chopped tomatoes

For the kofta
1kg beef mince
3 cloves of garlic minced
1 onion, finely diced
1 teaspoon salt
1 teaspoon ground cumin
1 teaspoon ground nutmeg
1 teaspoon ground black pepper
1 teaspoon ground cinnamon
2 eggs, lightly beaten
large handful of fresh parsley, chopped
80g dried white breadcrumbs

To serve
small handful of fresh parsley, chopped

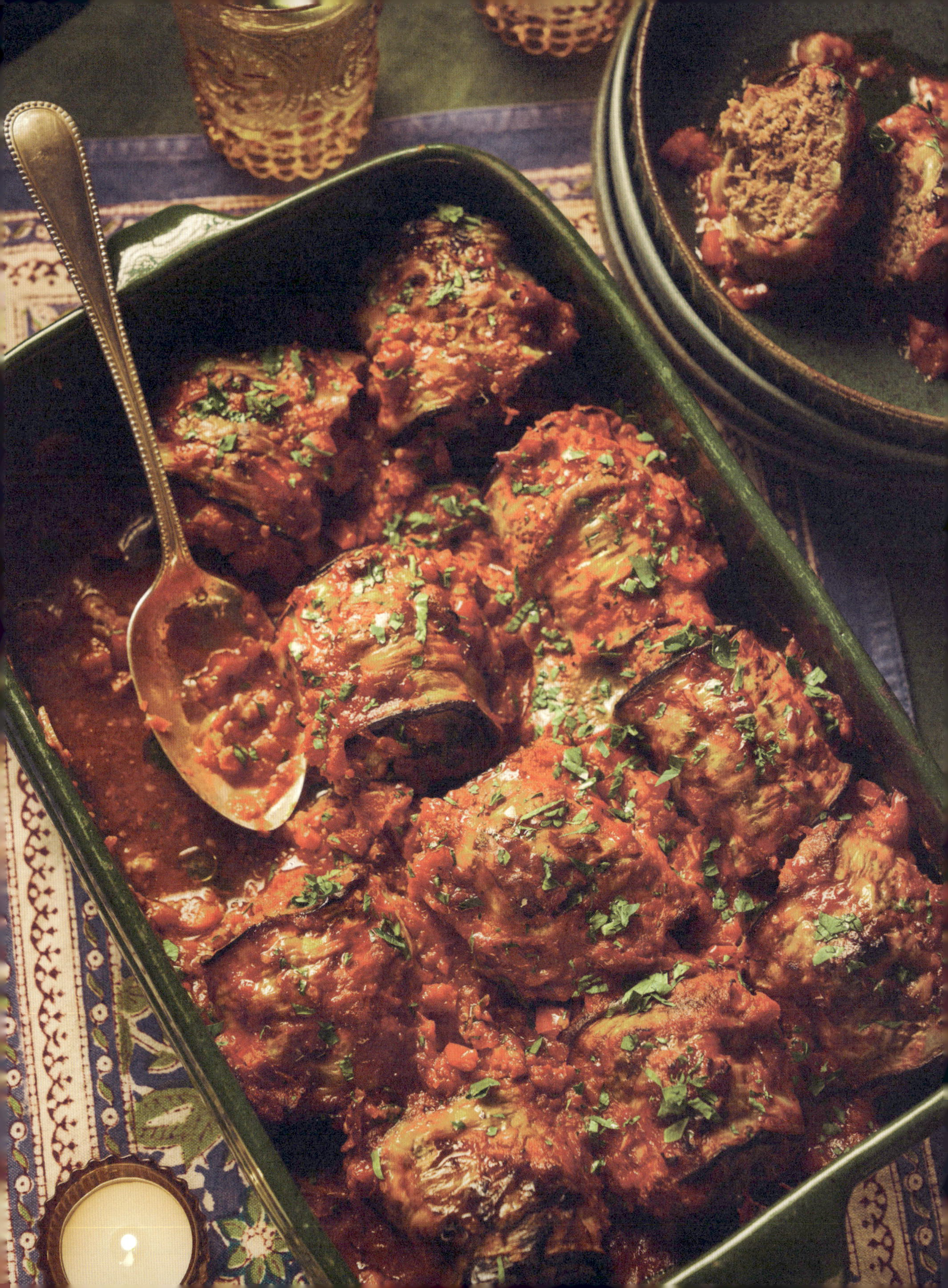

DIBLAH

These diblah are not just fun to make, they are also delicious to eat. The crisp pastry is fried in swirls till crisp and then dipped into a sugary sweet syrup.

Makes: 15 diblah

For the pastry, put the flour in a large bowl with the baking powder. Drizzle in the melted butter and use your fingers to incorporate it into the flour.

Make a well in the centre, add the eggs, vanilla, water and orange blossom water and bring the dough together, using a knife to begin with and then getting your hands in and making sure there are no floury parts. Knead the dough till it is just smooth and shiny.

Cover with a damp tea towel and leave to rest for 30 minutes.

Make the syrup by putting the caster sugar, water, honey and orange blossom water in a small pan. Bring to the boil and allow the sugar to dissolve. Simmer for 10 minutes over a low heat and then take off the heat.

Now on to making the spirals. Take the dough and roll out on a lightly floured surface until the pastry forms a 30cm square. Cut that rectangle into 15 strips lengthways, that are 2cm wide.

Pour the oil into a small frying pan with sides until about two-thirds of the way up. Heat until the oil is about 180°C.

Take one pastry strip and weave one end into the spike of a dinner fork. Holding on to the other end, dunk the fork and pastry slowly into the oil and spin your fork to create the spiral as the pastry lands in the oil. Leave the fork in while spiralling all the time, then gently remove the fork as soon as the spiral starts to hold its shape. While that cooks, do another.

When each spiral is ready, take out using a slotted spoon to remove any excess oil and then dunk it straight into the syrup. Take out with another spoon and place on to a rack for any excess syrup to drip off.

When they are all done, sprinkle with toasted sesame seeds, if you like.

For the pastry

375g plain flour

1½ teaspoons baking powder

3 tablespoons melted unsalted butter

3 medium eggs, lightly beaten

2 teaspoons vanilla extract

6 tablespoons cold water

6 teaspoons orange blossom water

oil, for frying

For the syrup

600g caster sugar

300ml water

6 tablespoons honey

4 tablespoons orange blossom water

To serve

toasted sesame seeds (black and white), optional

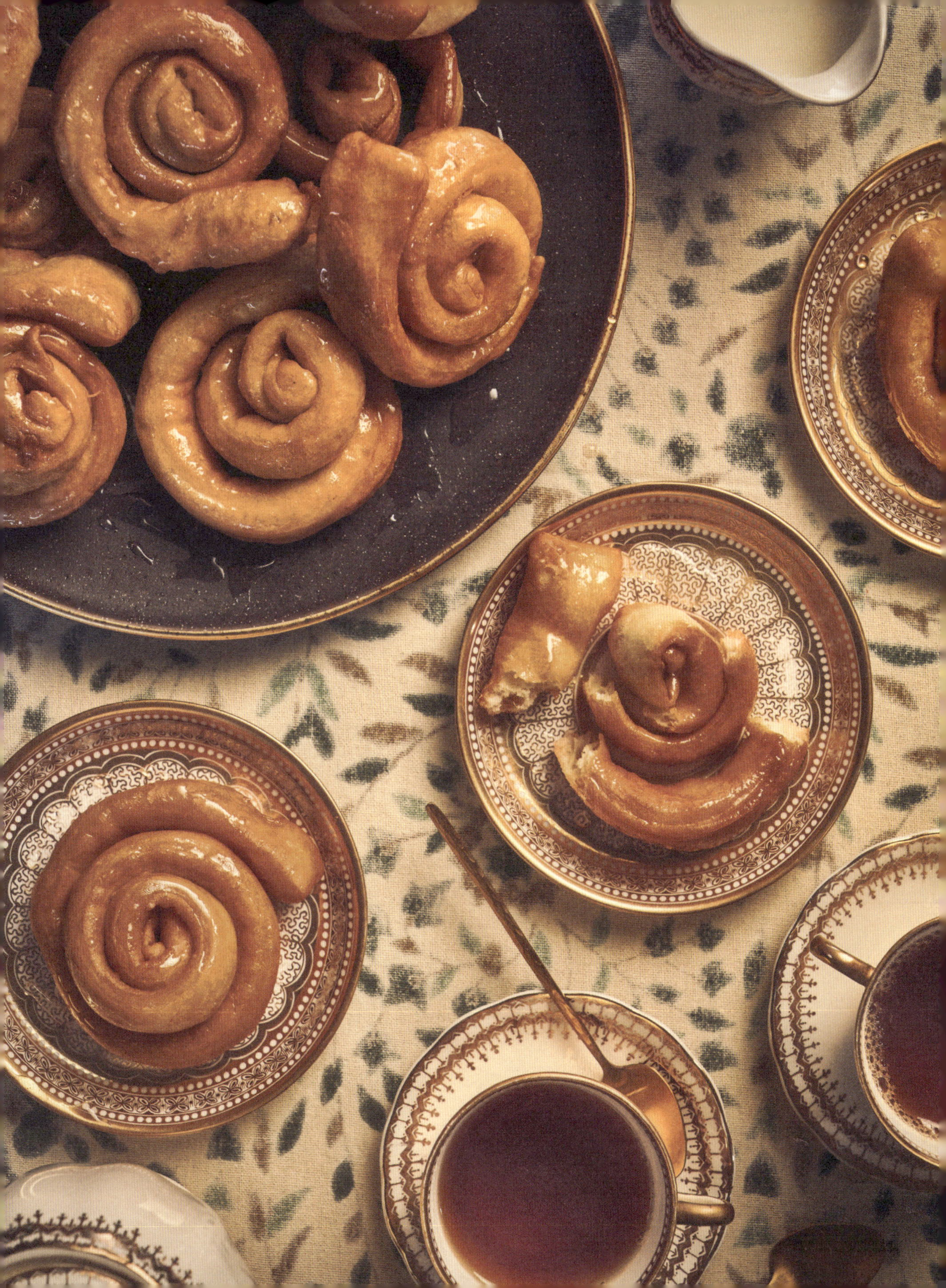

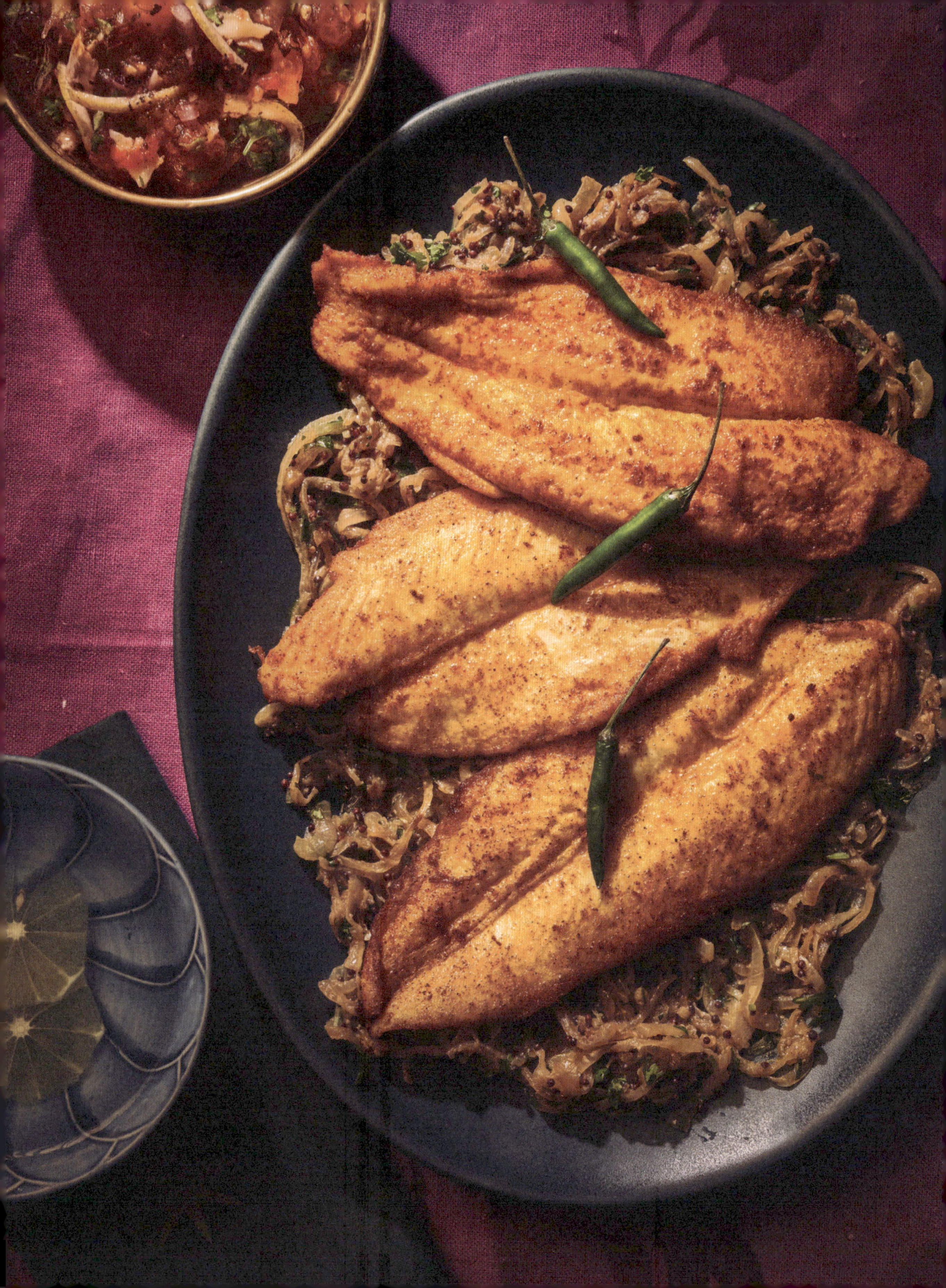

Bangladesh

MAAS BIRAN
with Baath and Tomato Sathni

This is the kind of thing that I make often. During Ramadhan as I experiment with other cuisines, this fried fish is a go-to for whenever we want a little taste of home. Simply fried, the sweet onions are what make this dish! Served with rice and charred tomato chutney, it is everything and more.

Let's start by marinating the fish. Put the oil in a jug along with the turmeric, salt and chilli powder and give it all a good mix. Put the fish on a tray and then pour the spiced oil all over the fish. Get your hands in and make sure it is all completely covered.

Take a large frying pan and fry the fish off a few fillets at a time over a high heat. This should take about 4 minutes on each side. Once you have fried them all, pop on to a plate and set aside.

Pour the oil for the onion into the same pan. As soon as the oil is hot, add the garlic and mustard seeds and cook until golden and the mustard seeds start popping. Now add all the onions with the salt and cook on a medium to high heat till the onions are caramelized. Add the coriander, fish and all the juices on top of the onions and leave to warm through with the lid off.

For the sathni, take a blowtorch and blacken the tomatoes and the garlic completely. You can also do this under a grill, and remove as soon as they are completely black. Set aside to cool for a moment.

Put the red onion in a bowl with the salt, coriander, lemon juice and rind. Use your hands to macerate it all together. Chop the tomatoes and garlic, making sure to keep the skin of the tomatoes and the garlic. Add them in and mix altogether, using your hands.

For the rice, wash the basmati till the water runs completely clear. As soon as the water is clear, put in a pan with the black cardamom pod and cold water. Bring to the boil, stirring occasionally and making sure the rice doesn't stick to the base. As soon as the rice grains are visible and the water evaporated, reduce the heat, put the lid on and leave to steam for 15 minutes.

As soon as the rice is ready, serve with the fish and sweet onions with the sathni on the side.

Serves: 6

For the fish
100ml oil
1 teaspoon ground turmeric
1 teaspoon salt
2 teaspoons chilli powder
6 large tilapia fillets

For the onion
100ml oil
4 cloves of garlic, minced
2 teaspoons mustard seeds
4 onions, thinly sliced
1 teaspoon salt
small handful of fresh coriander, thinly sliced

For the sathni
6 tomatoes, pierced
4 cloves of garlic, unpeeled
1 red onion, finely diced
½ teaspoon salt
small handful of fresh coriander
¼ lemon, juice and rind thinly sliced

For the rice
600g basmati rice
1 black cardamom pod
900ml cold water

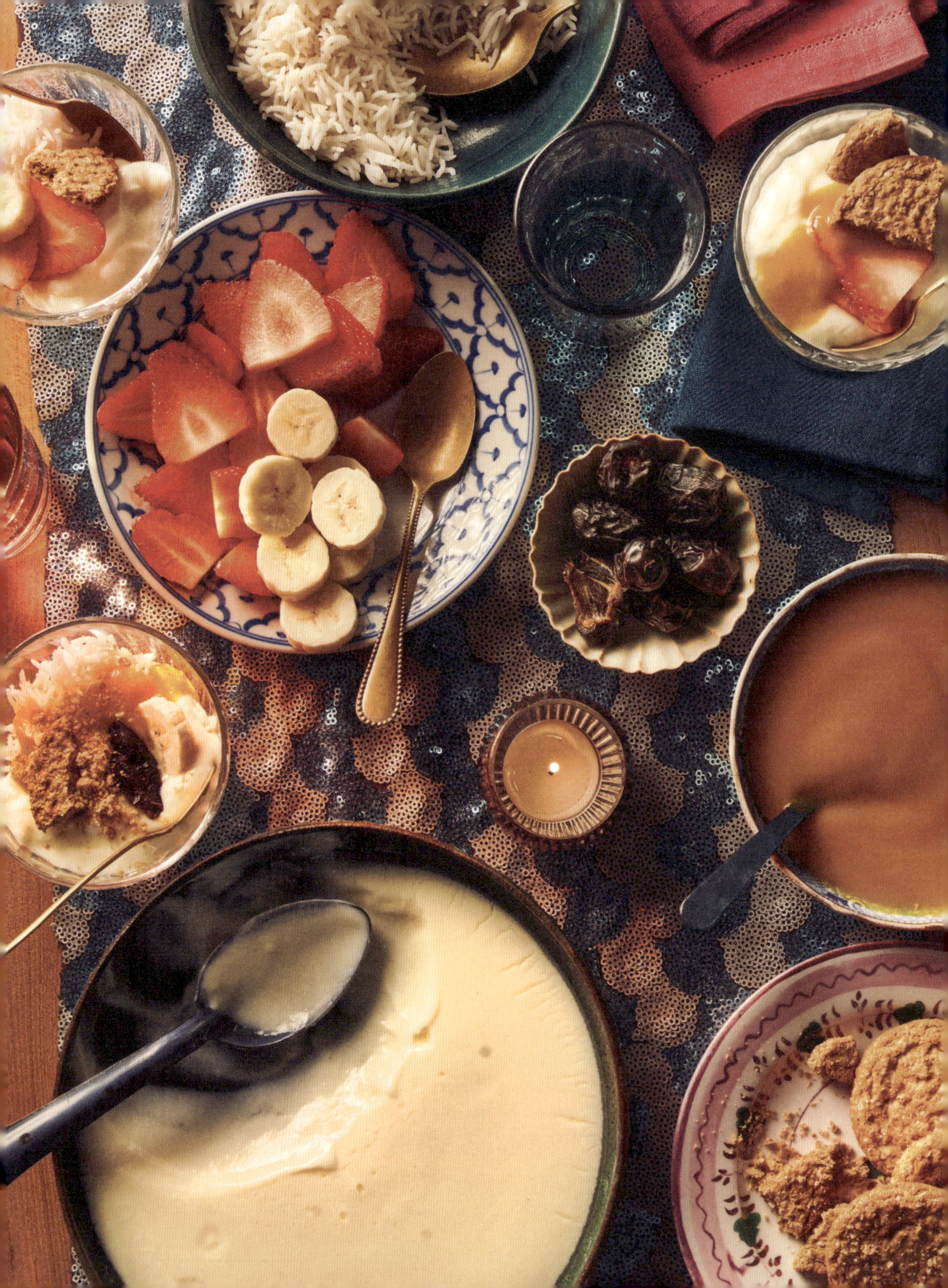

Bangladesh

MISHTI DOI
Sweet yoghurt

As yoghurts go, this yoghurt is elite. Many will think, well, why make it when you can buy it? You can buy it, but it will never be as good as when you make it from scratch. It's richer, creamier and sweeter, making it the perfect after-dinner dessert. We like to serve it with mango, banana and other fruit or, if you are hungry, you can eat it with hot rice.

Serves: 6–8

Start by making the yoghurt. Put the milk in a pan and bring to the boil. Leave to simmer for about 1 hour, or at least until the mixture has halved in liquid. Set aside and cool the milk for about 10 minutes.

Add the sugar and mix till the sugar has dissolved. Add the live yoghurt and whisk in well so everything is really well combined.

Preheat the oven to just 40°C. We are creating a warm environment for the yoghurt to set. Have a dish large enough for the mix to sit in an even layer.

Strain the mix through a sieve straight into the dish. Bake in the oven for 1½ hours. As soon as it has set, take out of the oven and pop into the fridge overnight.

To serve, take a dollop of the yoghurt, add a few spoonfuls of mango pulp and then sprinkle over some strawberries, bananas and crumbled biscuits.

For the yoghurt
1 litre whole milk
180g caster sugar
200g live yoghurt

For the mango
450g tin of mango pulp
strawberries

To serve
bananas
biscuits

Lebanon

DOLMAS, BATTATA HARA AND BABA GHANOUSH
Stuffed Vine Leaves, Spiced Potatoes and Aubergine Dip

Serves: 6–8

I love Lebanese food because of how different it is to the types of foods we grew up with. The spicing isn't complicated and the flavours really shine. I love making dolmas as much as I like eating them. Perfect for a picky dinner with the battata hara and baba ghanoush, this is such a lovely way to break a fast.

Start by making the dolma filling. Put the uncooked rice along with the lamb mince, dried oregano, diced onion, chopped parsley, salt and tomato purée in a large bowl. Get your hands in and mix everything really thoroughly, so the mixture is as even as it can be.

Preheat the oven to 180°C. Take a large casserole dish and grease the inside with some oil.

Take your vine leaves and with the widest end closest to you and the vein side up, add about a tablespoon of the mince mixture, fold over both sides and then the base, roll into fat cigar shapes and add to the casserole dish. Do this till you have finished all the vine leaves, or till you have finished all the mince. Pack them in side by side and on top of one another.

Make the sauce by putting the passata, garlic, salt and water in a jug. Pour all over the dolmas. Cover in foil, add a weighted pan or a mortar on top and bake in the oven for 45 minutes.

While they bake, make the battata hara. Pour the oil into a large non-stick pan. As soon as the oil is hot, add the garlic and fry till golden.

Add the cubed potatoes and fry over a high heat so you get some fried marks on some of the edges. Keep frying, but with a lid on, for 10 minutes – just enough time for the potatoes to become tender. As soon as they become tender, take the lid off and crisp the potatoes up on a high heat.

➜

For the dolmas
180g basmati rice
375g lamb mince
3 teaspoons dried oregano
2 onions, very finely diced
small handful of fresh parsley, finely chopped
1½ teaspoons salt
1 tablespoon tomato purée
oil, for greasing
250g vine leaves

For the sauce
400g carton of passata
2 cloves of garlic, minced
½ teaspoon salt
150ml water

For the battata hara
100ml oil
4 cloves of garlic, minced
500g potatoes, peeled and cut into 2cm cubes
1 teaspoon salt
2 teaspoons chilli flakes
1 teaspoon paprika
1 lemon, juice only
small handful of fresh coriander, for sprinkling

For the baba ghanoush
3 large aubergines
3 cloves of garlic, peeled
1 lemon, juice only
4 tablespoons tahini
3 tablespoons olive oil
pinch of salt

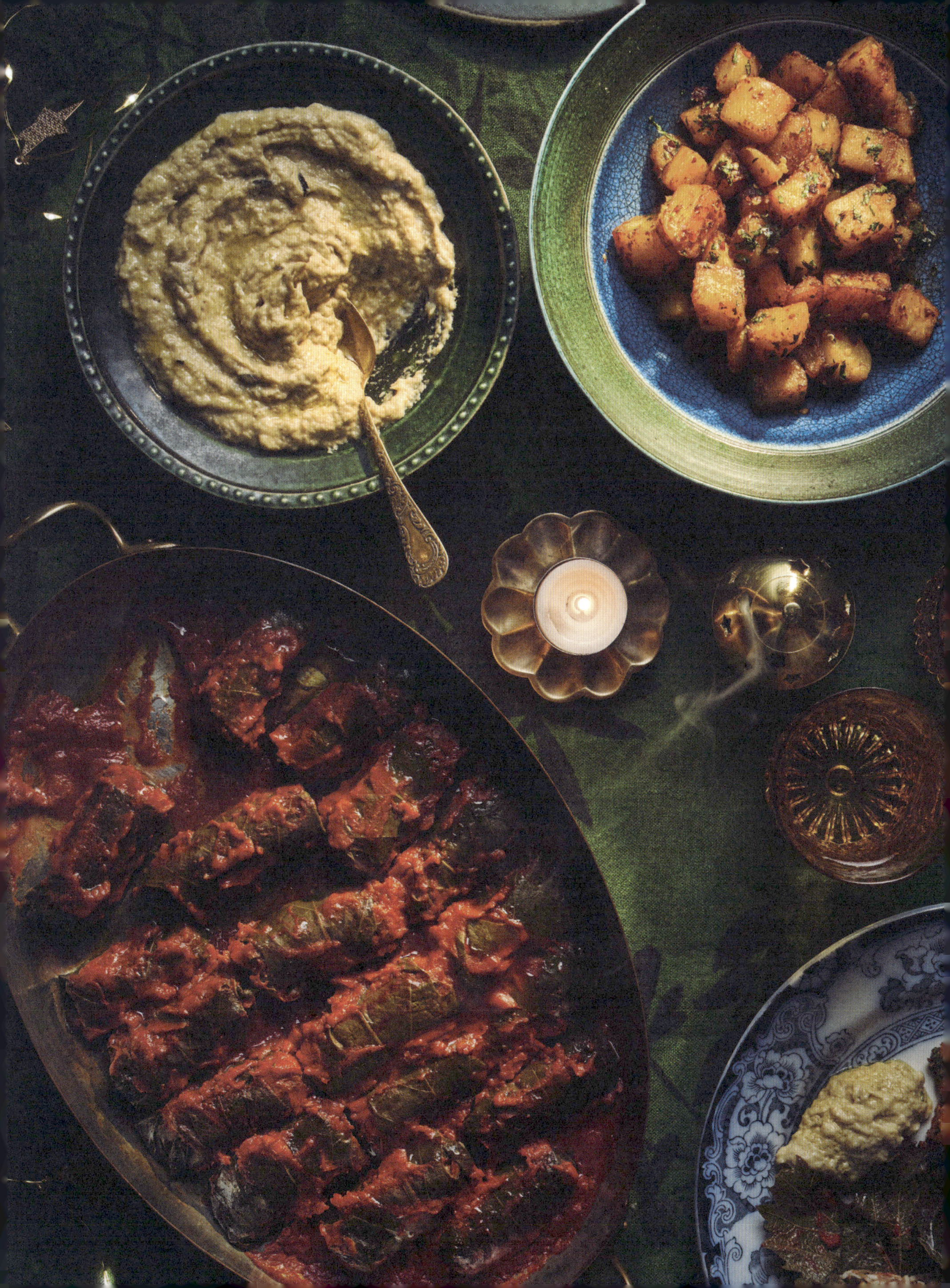

Lebanon

Add the salt, chilli flakes and paprika and mix it all through. Squeeze the lemon juice in, add the coriander and it is ready. If the crispy potatoes stick to the pan, just leave to cool for a few moments and they'll come away cleanly without breaking up.

Now start on the baba ghanoush by turning on the grill or getting a gas hob on its highest heat. Pierce the aubergines and grill under a hot grill or over the hob until totally black and the flesh is very soft. Remove the flesh from the blackened skin and put the flesh into a food processor, along with the garlic, lemon juice, tahini, olive oil and salt. Blend to a smooth paste and transfer to a serving dish with an extra drizzle of oil.

Take the dolmas out of the oven, uncover and leave to sit for 10 minutes before tipping out on to a large dish and serving with the battata hara and baba ghanoush.

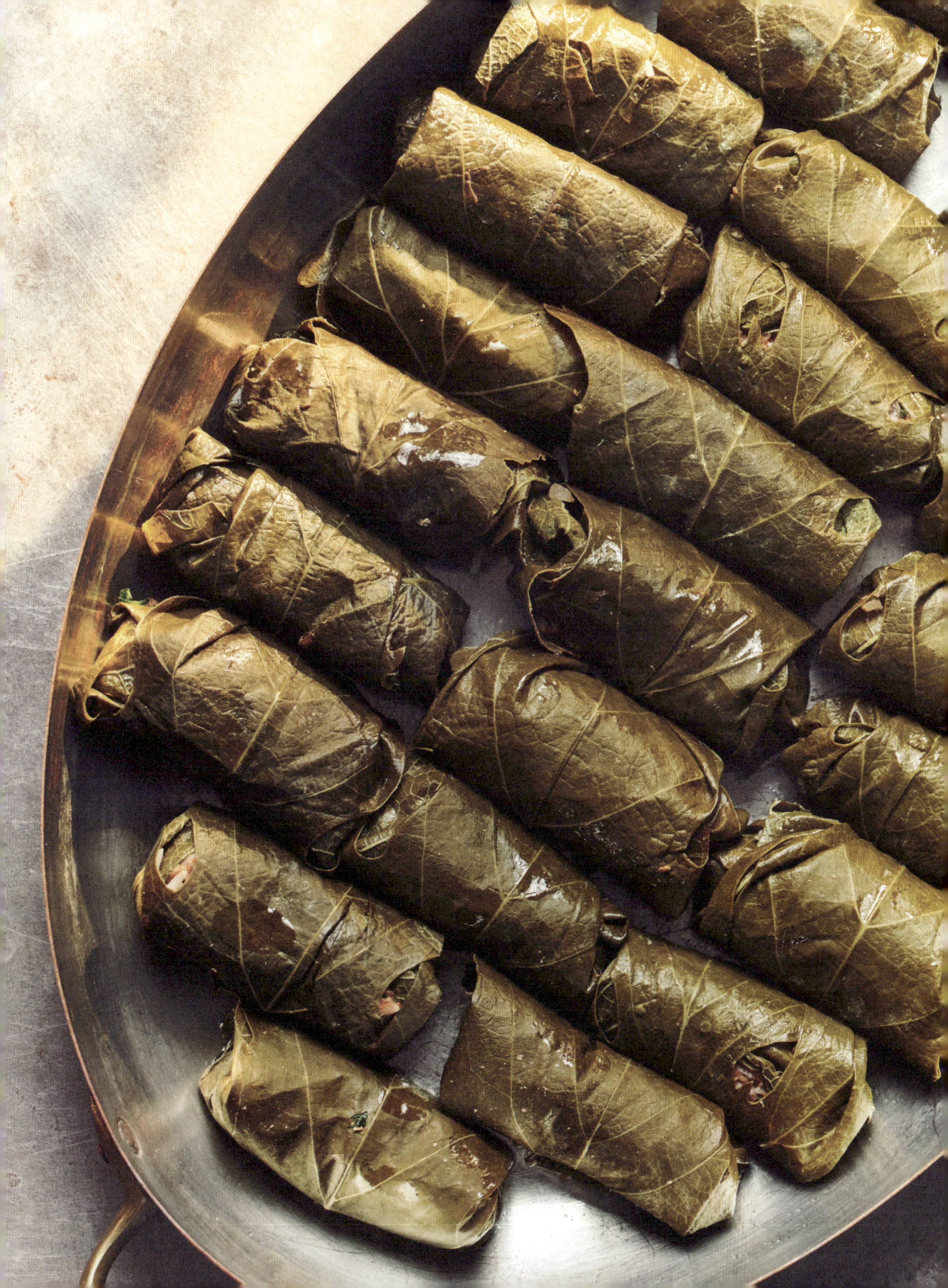

Lebanon

ZNOUD EL SIT
Filo Filled with Custard

These parcels are just joy wrapped in filo. The creamy interior is like a thickened custard, which works really well with the crunchy filo and sugar syrup. Lots of textures and flavours all at once.

Start by making the filling. Pour the whole milk into a pan. Put the cornflour in a bowl, add 5 tablespoons of milk from the pan and mix together, then add the cornflour mixture back into the pan. Add the fine semolina, ground cardamom and sugar and whisk through.

Put the pan on a medium heat and keep whisking the whole time till the mixture is really thick. Take off the heat, transfer to a flatter dish and allow it some time to cool completely.

Have your pastry ready, the oven preheated to 180°C and a medium baking tray ready to place the parcels on when they are filled.

Make up the glue by putting the plain flour in a bowl with the water and mixing till you have a gloopy mixture.

Take one sheet of filo, leaving the sheets you're not working with under a damp tea towel. Place one-sixth of the cooled milk filling into the centre and fold the long sides over the filling. Fold over the long end closest to you and roll over till you have a small, square parcel. Brush the ends with the flour glue and set aside on the tray. Once you have done all six, butter all over. Bake in the oven for 20 minutes.

Meanwhile, make the syrup by putting the caster sugar, water, lemon juice and rose extract in a pan. Bring to the boil and leave to simmer for 10 minutes till the sugar has dissolved.

As soon as the filo parcels come out of the oven, pour the syrup all over. Sprinkle over the pistachios and zest the orange over them while they are all still hot. Serve up with a huge dollop of ice cream.

Makes: 6 parcels

For the filling
500ml whole milk
5 tablespoons cornflour
1 tablespoon fine semolina
½ teaspoon ground cardamom
100g caster sugar

For the pastry/glue
270g pack of filo pastry, ready rolled (6 sheets)
5 tablespoons plain flour
5 tablespoons water
150g butter, melted

For the syrup
100g caster sugar
100g water
½ lemon, juice only
1 tablespoon rose extract

To finish
50g pistachios, roasted and roughly chopped
1 orange, zest only

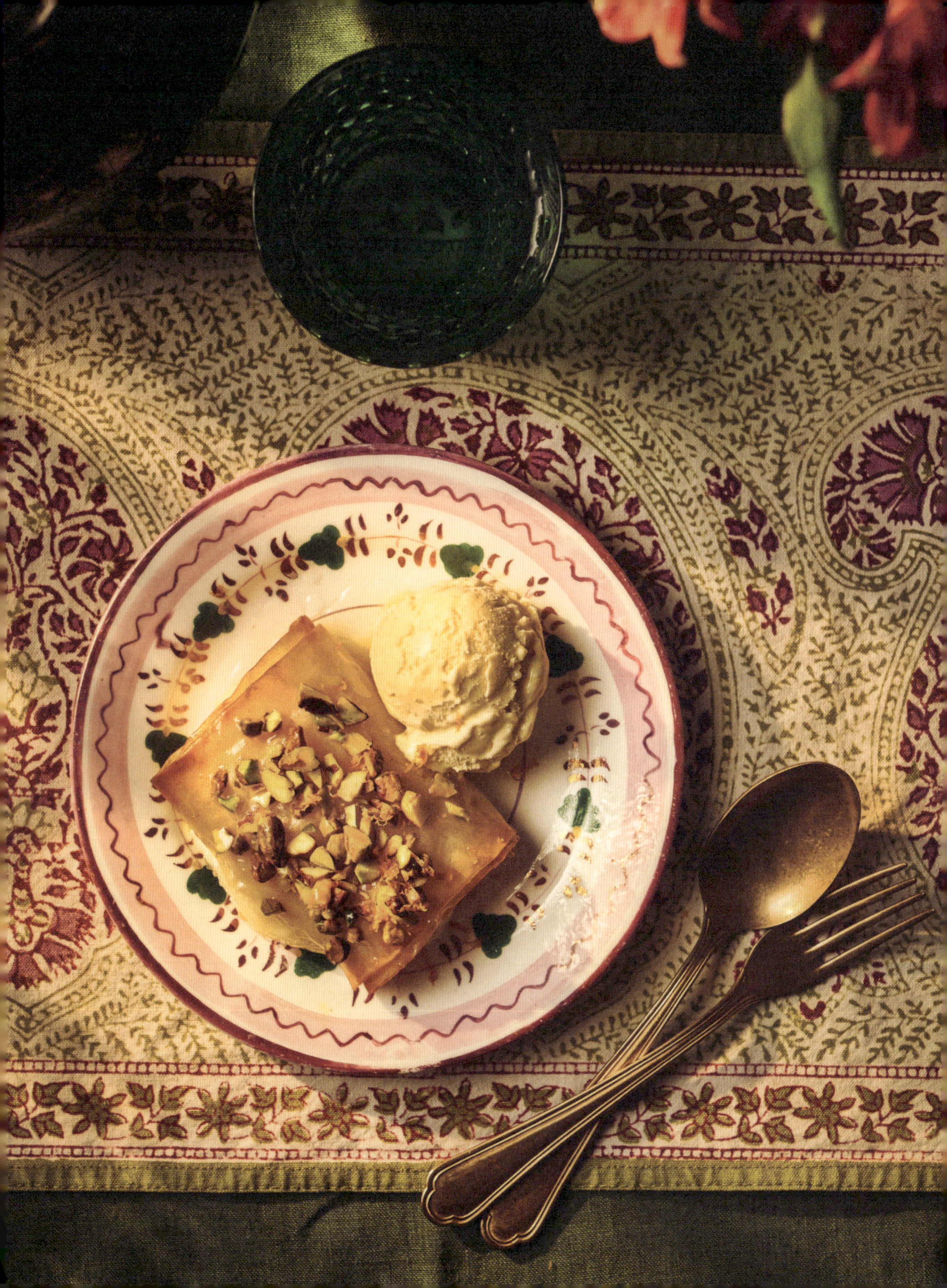

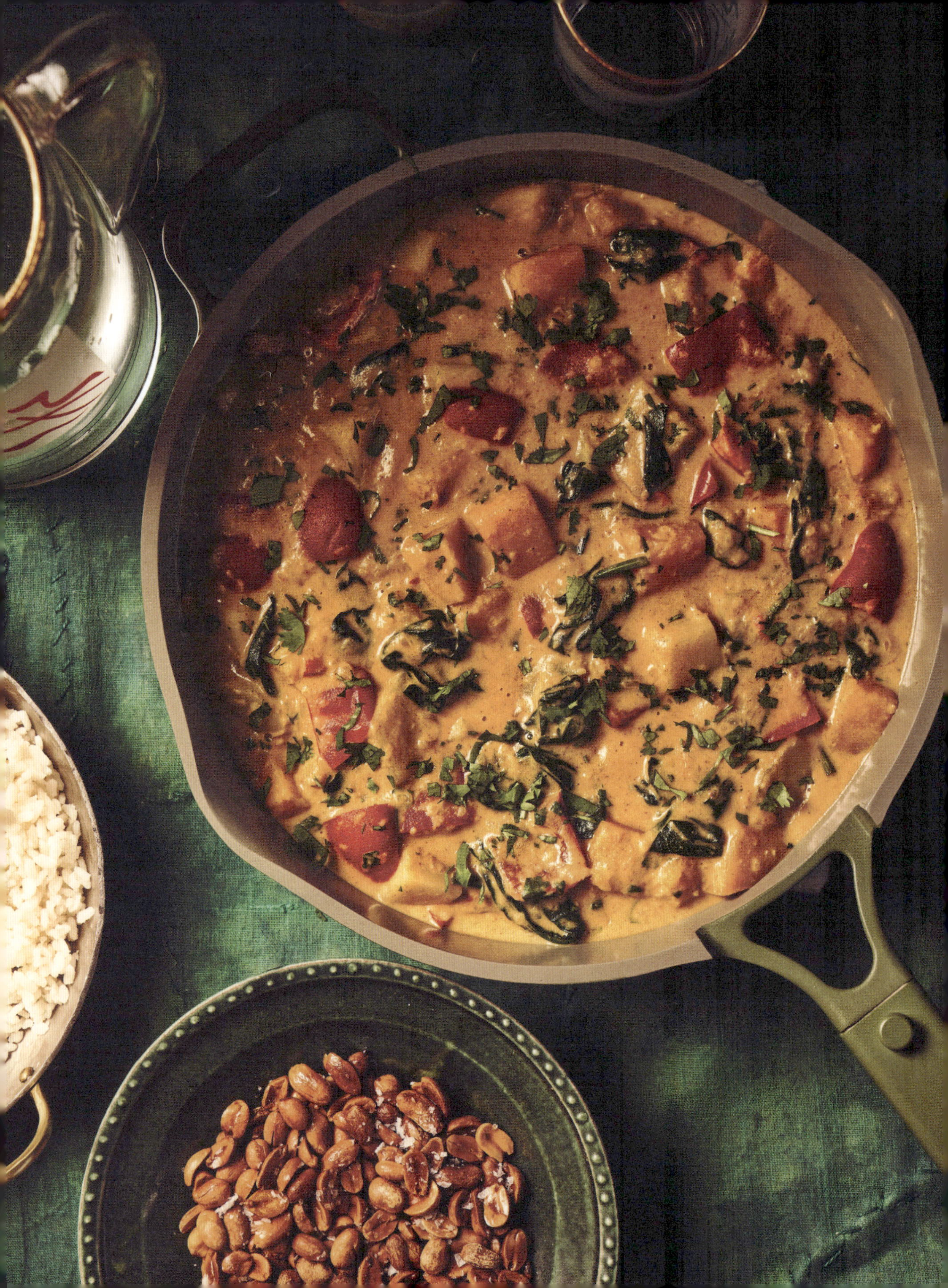

Thailand

VEGETABLE PEANUT CURRY
with Sticky Rice

Since discovering that my family ancestry links to Thailand, it is the cuisine that sits right beside my Bangladeshi cooking. I am always learning and experimenting with Thai recipes. Of all the curries, this vibrant peanut vegetable curry is one of my favourites to make and share with my family, especially during Ramadhan.

Before we do anything, let's start by sorting out the sticky rice. By the time that is cooked, we will have this curry made.

For the sticky rice, you need to make sure you wash it really well till the water runs clear. You can use the hot tap water to remove the starch. When it runs clear, drain the rice in a colander that has very small holes so the rice grains don't escape.

Leave the rice to drain, then pop a pan on the hob that is big enough to suspend the colander at its rim. Pour some hot water into the base, bring the water to the boil and leave to simmer.

Put the colander in the pan, making sure the water doesn't touch the rice grains. Pop on a lid that fits the top of the colander and leave the whole thing to steam for 1 hour 30 minutes. Occasionally check that there is still hot water simmering in the base. If it is lacking, just top it up with water from the kettle.

Now let's make the paste by putting the onion, lemongrass, red chillies, garlic, ginger, fish sauce, lime juice, chilli powder, palm or brown sugar, ground cumin, coriander and shrimp paste in a food processor. Blend the whole thing till you have a smooth, even mixture. If you find it isn't shifting at all, add a small splash of water. Once that is done, set it aside.

On to the vegetables. Pour some oil into a frying pan and get the oil lovely and hot. Add the paste into the pan and cook for 5 minutes till it looks dry and is much darker in colour. Now add the smooth peanut butter and mix through.

Serves: 6

For the sticky rice
600g Thai sticky rice (found in most supermarkets)

For the paste
1 onion, roughly chopped
1 lemongrass stalk, roughly chopped
3 Thai red chillies
6 cloves of garlic
5cm piece of peeled ginger, roughly chopped
2 tablespoons fish sauce
1 lime, juice only
2 tablespoons chilli powder
1 teaspoon palm or brown sugar
1 teaspoon ground cumin
1 teaspoon ground coriander
2 teaspoons shrimp paste

For the vegetables
oil, for frying
2 tablespoons smooth peanut butter
1 whole squash, peeled and chopped into chunks (700g)
4 medium potatoes, peeled and chopped into chunks
2 red peppers, chopped into chunks
2 x 400ml tins of coconut milk
400ml cold water
100g spinach, roughly chopped

Lower the heat, get the squash, potato and red pepper in and give everything a good mix. Pour in the coconut milk and cold water and bring the mixture to the boil. As soon as it comes up to the boil, leave to simmer over a medium heat with the lid off for 30 minutes. As soon as the potatoes are tender, add the spinach in and mix through so it can wilt for 5 minutes.

To make the peanuts, pour the oil into a pan and get the oil hot. Add the peanuts and fry till golden brown. Drain on to a plate with kitchen paper and sprinkle over some salt. Be sure to use your leftover home-made peanut oil for other recipes when it has cooled down.

Now it's time to serve. Take your sticky rice and serve some curry alongside, sprinkling over the salted fried peanuts and chopped coriander.

To serve

200ml oil

150g peanuts

handful of fresh coriander, finely chopped

salt

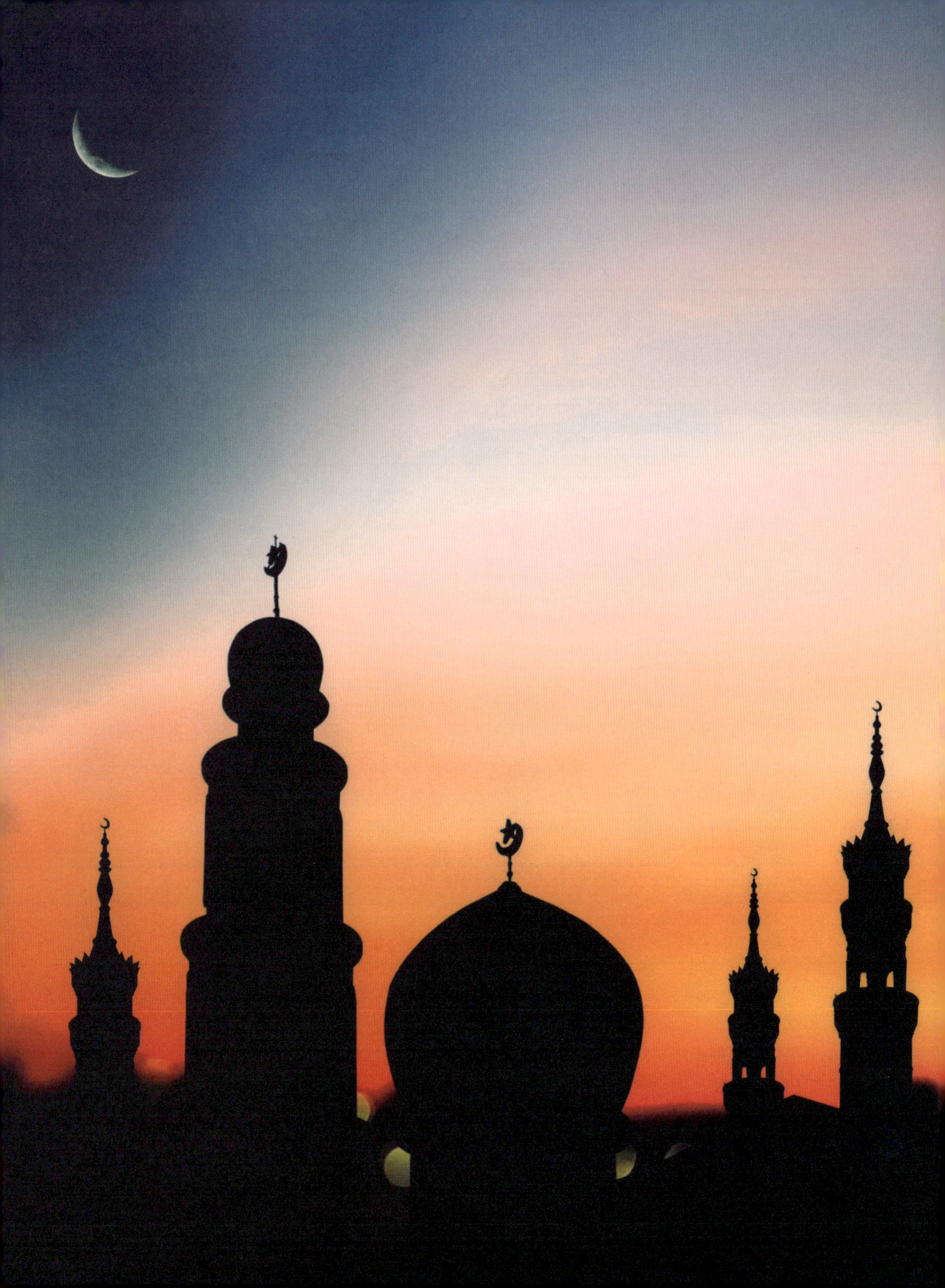

BANANA SPRING ROLLS

Bananas and coconuts play a huge role in making sweet treats, so I wanted to make a quick recipe that combines the best of both. Bananas wrapped in buttery filo, dipped in coconut and fried. Serve warm with the salted caramel and dollops of ice cream.

Makes: 6 spring rolls

For the spring rolls, get the filo pastry out and lay a sheet out flat, leaving the sheets you're not working with under a damp tea towel. Brush the surface of the entire sheet with melted butter. Place a banana on the shorter end of the pastry and roll the banana tightly all the way across till you have used up all the pastry.

Press the banana down now so you remove that domed effect and have more of a flat filo roll. You should see the banana squeeze all the way to the ends of the pastry. Lay on a baking tray and do the same with the rest of the sheets.

Put your eggs, caster sugar and whole milk in a shallow dish and whisk till everything is combined. Lay the desiccated coconut on another plate in an even layer.

Dip each banana filo roll into the egg mixture and then straight into the coconut. Set each one back on the tray.

Before you fry these, let's make the salted caramel. Put the brown sugar, golden syrup and butter in a pan and heat till the sugar has somewhat dissolved and the butter melted. Pour in the cream, mix and bring to the boil. As soon as it boils, add the salt, reduce the heat and let the salted caramel thicken over the lowest heat.

Now let's fry the banana filo rolls. Put a large dollop of butter in a frying pan and heat the butter up till frothing. Add the filo banana rolls in carefully and fry till golden, toasted and buttery. You may need to do this in batches depending on the size of your frying pan.

Take the caramel off the heat. Serve the spring rolls while still warm, with a drizzle of salted caramel and a dollop of ice cream.

For the spring rolls
270g pack of filo pastry, ready-rolled (6 sheets)
200g salted butter, melted, plus extra for frying
6 medium bananas, peeled
2 medium eggs
2 tablespoons caster sugar
1 tablespoon whole milk
100g desiccated coconut

For the salted caramel
140g soft brown sugar
2 tablespoons golden syrup
50g unsalted butter
300ml double cream
large pinch of rock salt

Mauritius

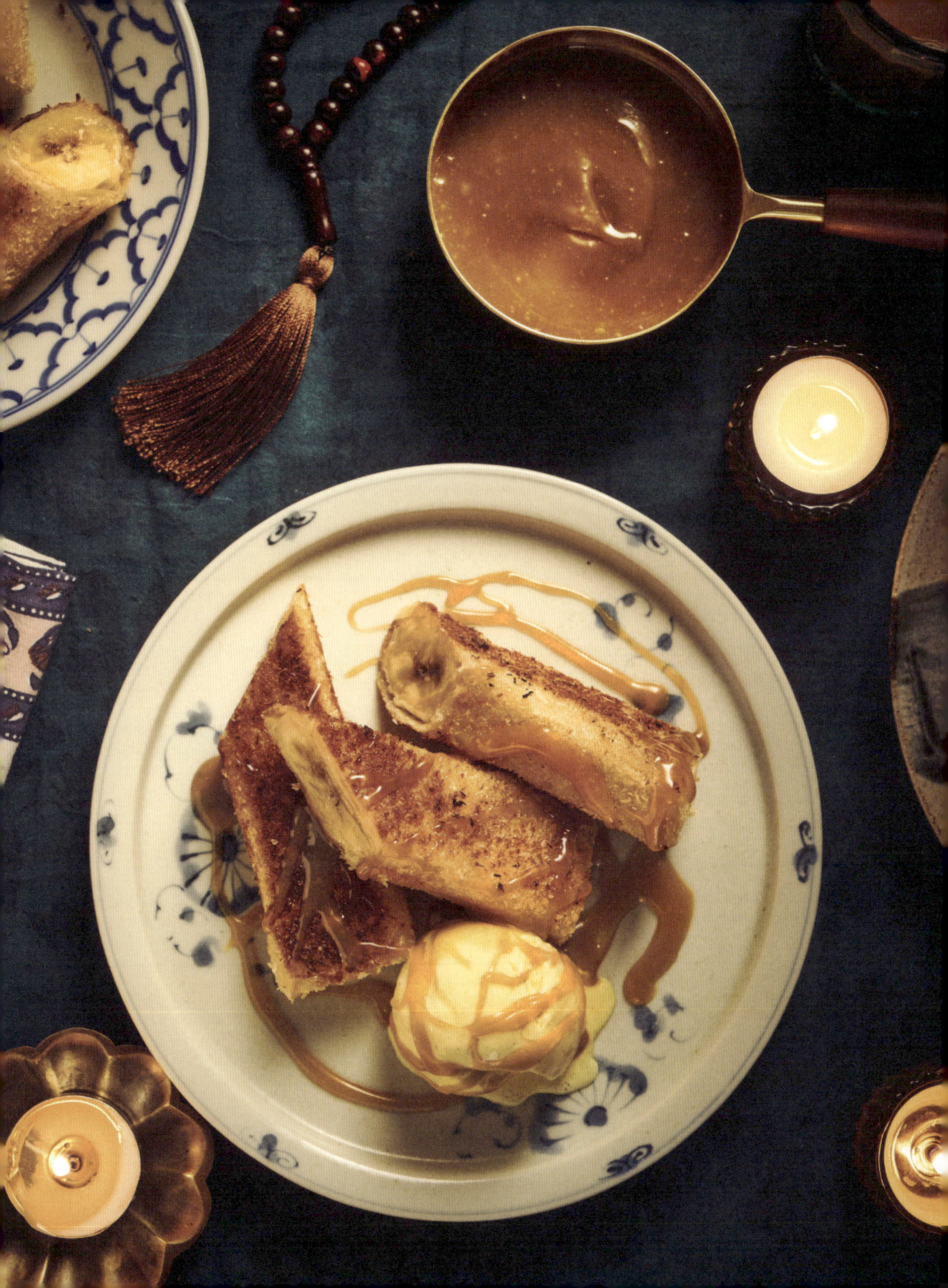

Mauritius

FISH ROUGAILLE
Fish curry

We grew up with Muslim Mauritian neighbours, who spoke French. Their cuisine was entirely different to ours and it intrigued me even as a young child. So, I wanted to share a recipe that I once tried at their house of fish rougaille, which I think you will love.

Serves: 6

Let's make a start by preparing the roti. Put the plain flour in a bowl with the salt and use your hands to mix through. Drizzle in the oil and again use your hands to combine the oil into the flour.

Make a well in the centre and pour in the hot water. Bring the dough together with a palette knife and then get your hands in and bring it together so you have no more dry, floury spots. Put the dough on a work surface and knead till the dough is smooth and shiny. Place back in the bowl, cover and leave till you are ready to make the roti.

Start on the rougaille. Heat the oil in a large pan over a medium heat. As soon as the oil is hot, add the garlic and fry till golden. Add the onion with the salt and cook till the onions are soft and brown.

Add the cumin and paprika and cook through for a few minutes. Pour in the cold water, apple cider vinegar and passata and cook for 10 minutes till the mixture is drier and less watery. Add the chunks of fish, mix through and leave covered to cook through.

Now make the roti. Divide the dough into 12 equal pieces by cutting the mound into triangles. Roll each ball out on a floured surface into an approximately 20cm round.

Brush the surface of the round with oil and sprinkle with flour. Fold two edges over into the centre. Brush the strip with oil and sprinkle with flour. Fold one third into the centre and then the other third. Turn over and what you should be left with is a neat square. Roll that out to about 15cm - it needs to be nice and thin.

Pop a non-stick frying pan on the hob and over a medium to hot heat, cook the square for 3-4 minutes on each side, brushing with oil while cooking. Repeat with the rest of the roti to make all 12.

Serve the curry with coriander and the roti.

For the roti

600g plain flour, plus extra for dusting

1 tablespoon salt

4 tablespoons oil, plus extra for brushing

300ml hot tap water

oil, for frying

For the rougaille

4 teaspoons oil

3 cloves of garlic, minced

1 onion, finely diced

2 teaspoons salt

2 teaspoons ground cumin

3 teaspoons paprika

150ml cold water

3 teaspoons apple cider vinegar

400g carton of passata

800g white fish, cut into chunks

large handful of fresh coriander, finely chopped

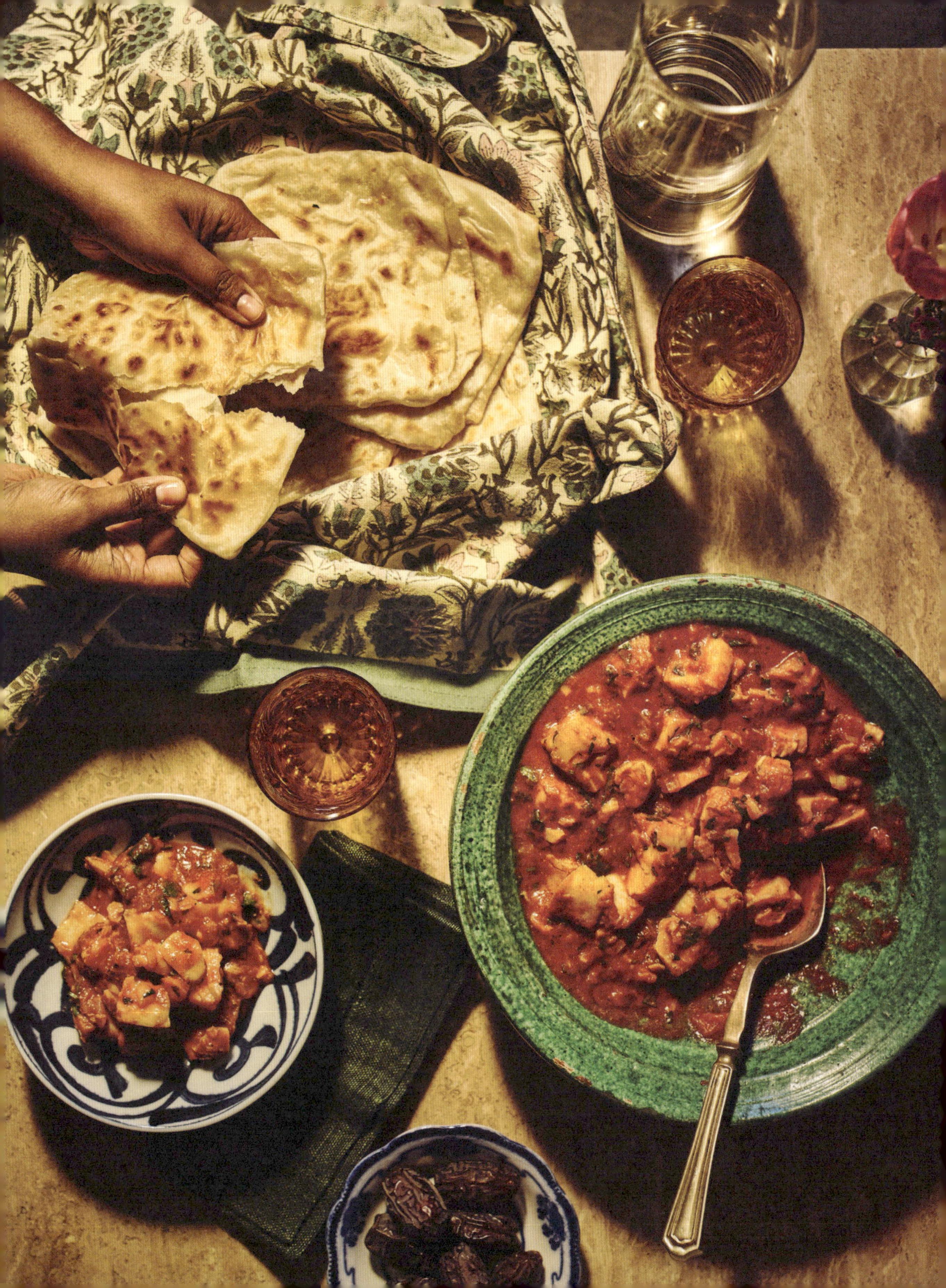

Mauritius

NAPOLITAINES

If you love icing, you will love these biscuits. Two buttery, shortbread-type biscuits sandwiched with a tart jam and then covered in a runny icing are perfect for after dinner and great to share with neighbours as an iftar offering.

Makes: 12 biscuits

Let's start by making the dough for the biscuits. Put the flour in a large bowl along with the cubed butter and rub the butter into the flour till you have a dough that comes together. Wrap the dough ball in cling film and leave to chill for at least 30 minutes-1 hour.

Preheat the oven to 180°C. Line a baking tray with some baking paper and set aside.

Between two sheets of cling film, roll the dough out to about a 5mm thickness. Use a 4½cm round cutter to cut out 24 rounds.

Bake in the oven for 12-14 minutes, till just light golden brown. Take out of the oven and leave to cool on the tray completely.

Once they are cool, sandwich two biscuits together with the jam, doing the same for all of them. You should have 12 sandwiched biscuits. Place them on a wire rack with a tray underneath to catch any spillage.

Make the icing by putting the icing sugar in a bowl with the rose water. Add the water 1 tablespoon at a time till you have an icing that is still thick enough to coat the back of the spoon. Add the gel food colouring and mix well till you have a pale pink colour.

Spoon the icing all over each biscuit till they are coated entirely, then use the bristles of a brush to splash gold lustre over each biscuit. Leave to air dry for a few hours or overnight before you eat them.

For the biscuits
250g plain flour
175g unsalted butter, cubed
seedless raspberry jam, for the filling

For the icing
200g fondant icing sugar, sifted
1 teaspoon rose water
2-3 tablespoons cold water
pink gel food colouring
edible gold lustre, to finish

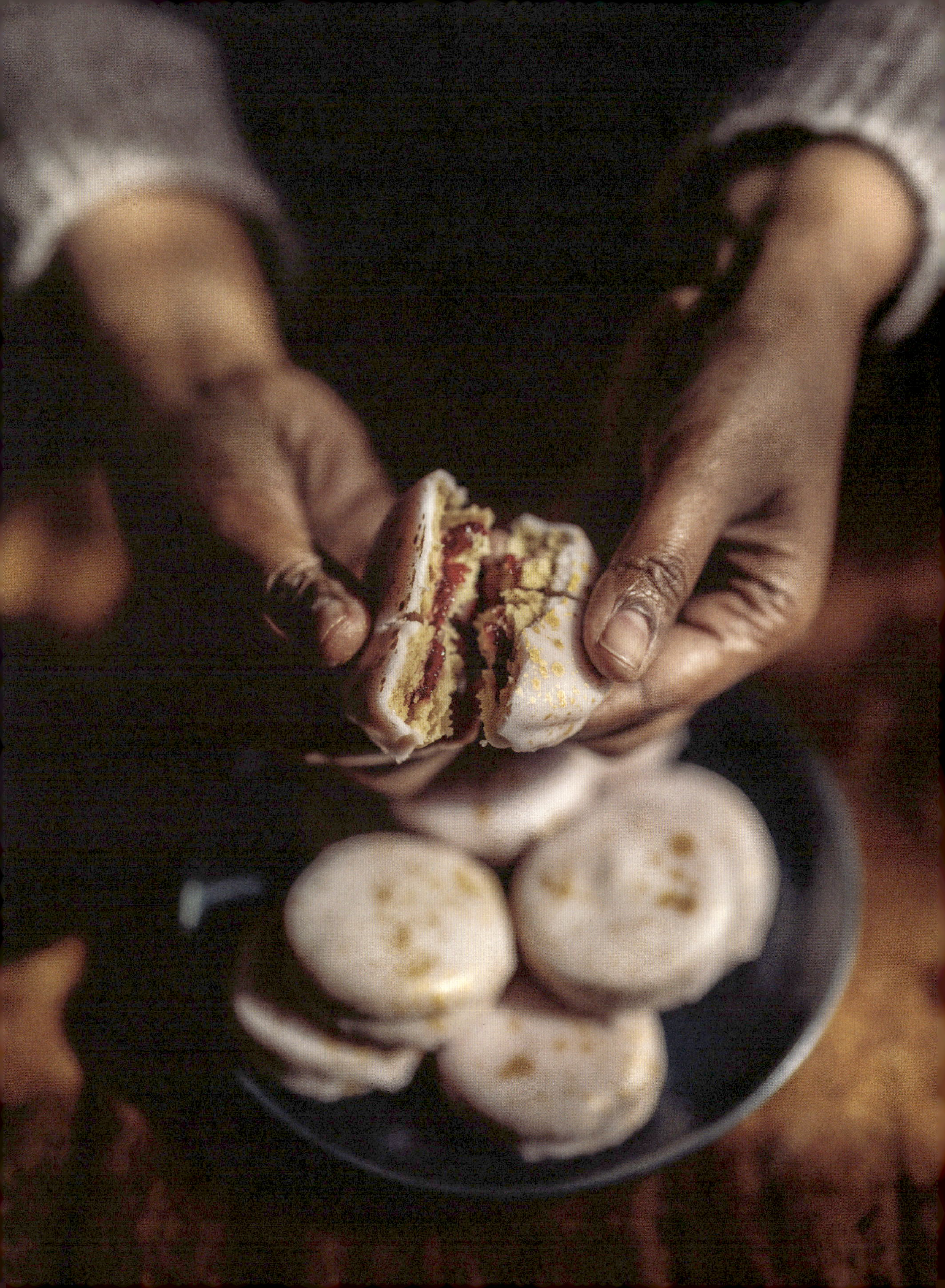

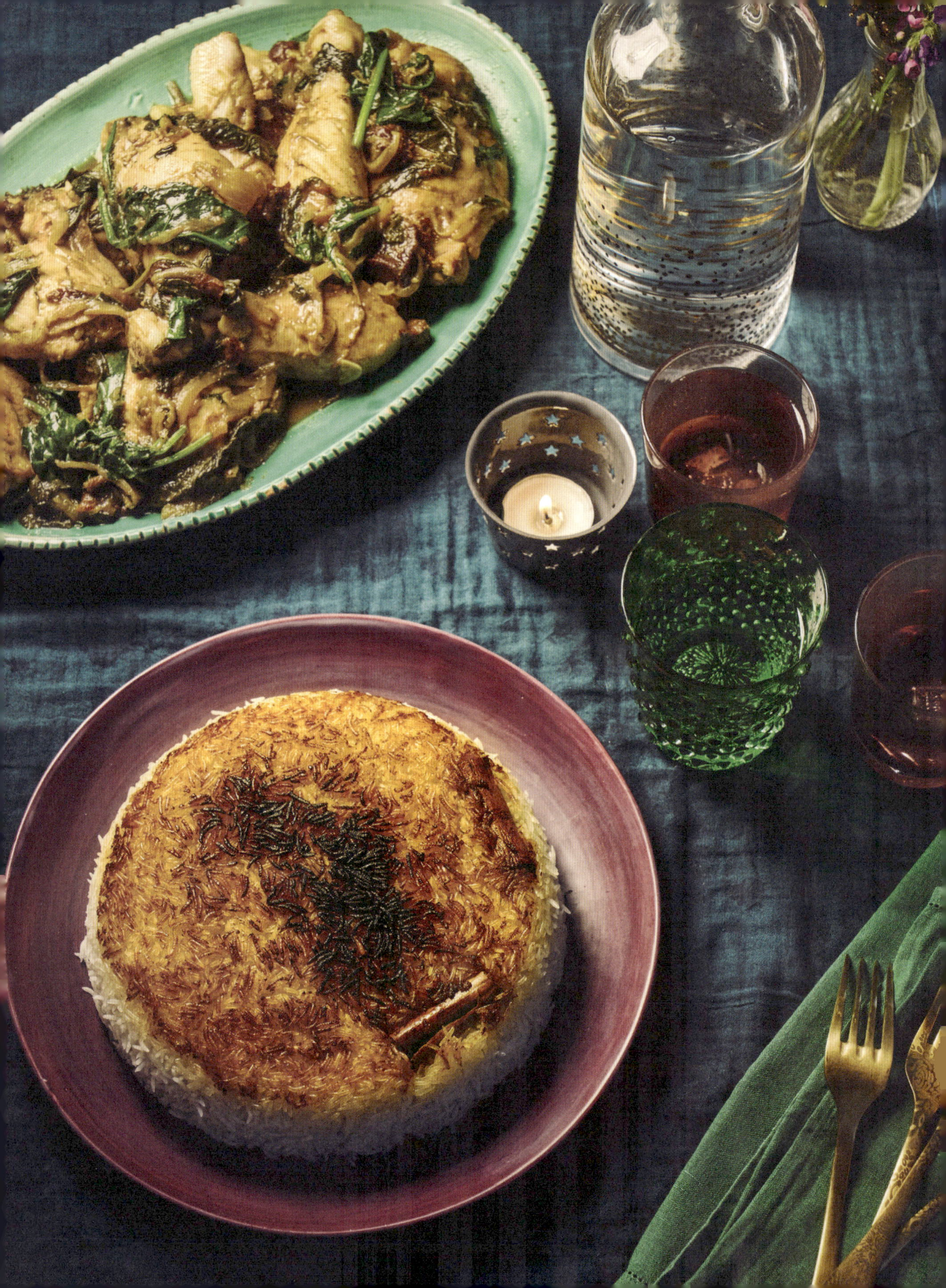

Iran

KHORESH ALOO ESFENAJ with Tahdig
Spinach Chicken with Crispy Rice

Iran is comprised of many ethnic groups and so the cuisine, Persian at heart, is made up of thousands of dishes that are influenced by neighbouring countries such as ones in Asia, as well as Greece, Russia and Turkey. This stew is easily one of the most delicious I've ever eaten. The prunes add a layer of sweetness that makes it truly a special dish.

Serves: 6

Start by making the tahdig as this will need to sit cooking for a while. Wash the basmati rice till the water runs completely clear. Put the rice in a larger than normal pan with the cinnamon stick and salt. Fill the pan with plenty of cold water, so the rice has lots of room to move around.

Bring to the boil and cook for 6 minutes. Drain the rice immediately and rinse under cold water till the rice has cooled down completely.

Find a non-stick pan the right size to fit all that rice right to the top. Put the pan on the hob over a high heat and add the salted butter. As soon as the butter is hot and melted completely, add all the cooled rice in. Don't pack it in tightly, just fill the pan. Leave the rice on a high heat for 2 minutes, then reduce the heat completely. Lay a tea towel over the top of the pan, pop the lid on and leave to steam for 45 minutes.

While the tahdig steams, let's make the khoresh aloo esfenaj. Pour the oil into a medium pan and when the oil is hot, add the garlic and fry till golden brown. Add the sliced onions along with the salt and cook till the onions are soft and golden.

Add the turmeric, cinnamon, black pepper and lemon juice and cook the spices for a few minutes before adding the water and then the chicken. Coat the chicken in the spices. Add the prunes and spinach, pop the lid on and cook over a medium heat for 30–40 minutes.

Once the rice is ready, take off the lid and tea towel and place a serving dish on top. Carefully tip it over and lift off the pan to reveal the perfectly cooked rice and the crunchy rice top. Serve with the chicken.

For the tahdig
600g basmati rice
1 large cinnamon stick
1 teaspoon salt
cold water, to cover
100g salted butter

For the khoresh aloo esfenaj
6 tablespoons oil
6 cloves of garlic, thinly sliced
2 onions, sliced
1 tablespoon salt
½ teaspoon ground turmeric
1½ teaspoons ground cinnamon
2 tablespoons ground black pepper
1 lemon, juice only
300ml water
6 chicken legs (thighs and drumsticks), skin removed and slashed
100g prunes, chopped in half
150g fresh spinach

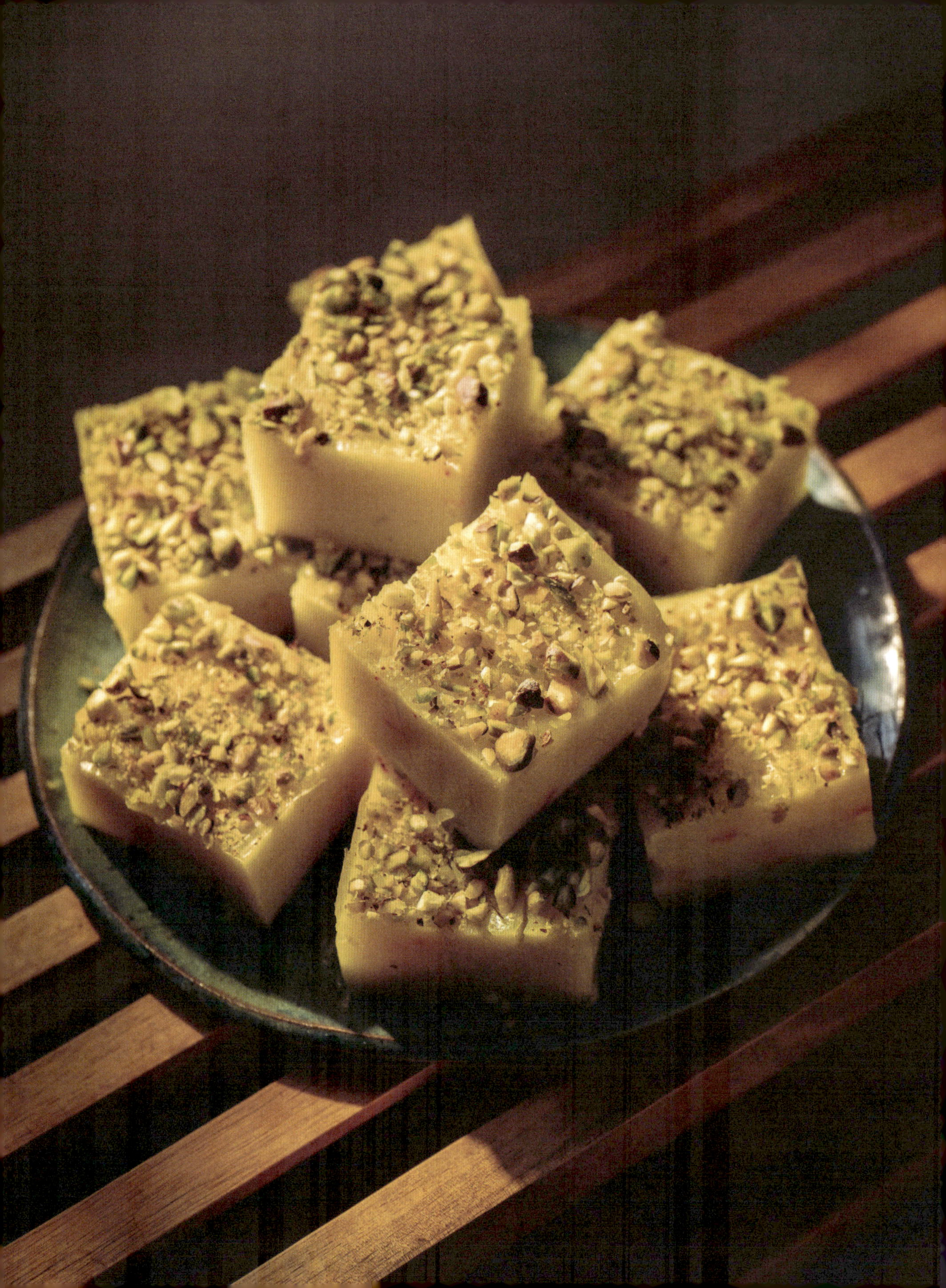

MASGHATI
Fragrant Pudding Squares

This dessert is so beautiful to look at that it's almost too difficult to eat! The cornflour creates a unique texture and the saffron imparts the most beautiful colour. If you are looking to make something truly special for dessert, this is the one.

Makes: 9 squares

Generously grease a 23cm square cake tin with melted ghee and set to one side.

Put the cornflour in a pan with the caster sugar. Pour in the cold water and whisk till everything is combined. Add the cardamom, rose extract and saffron and mix again.

Pop on to a medium to low heat and cook gently for about 8-10 minutes. You will know it is ready when you can use your spatula to make a line across the mix and the line stays visible.

Add the ghee and cook through for a few minutes. Pour the mixture into the tin and flatten on top.

Sprinkle over the roasted pistachios and leave to cool in the tin for 20 minutes, then set in the fridge for 4 hours or overnight.

To serve, tip out on to a greased board and cut into squares. I like to serve this with whipped cream on the side.

- 200g cornflour
- 400g caster sugar
- 1.2 litres cold water
- 1 teaspoon ground cardamom
- 2 teaspoons rose extract
- 1 teaspoon saffron strands, crushed
- 100g ghee, melted, plus extra for greasing
- 50g pistachios, roasted and roughly chopped

Iran

BAZIN
Steamed Dough with Meat Stew and Eggs

The cuisine of Libya is a combination of Berber, Arab and Mediterranean cuisines with influences from the Ottomans and Italy. One of the most popular Libyan dishes is bazin. It is an unleavened bread, which is so unique in its texture that I had to show you how to cook it. It makes for a very special way to eat a stew, especially if you love to eat with your hands as I do.

Serves: 6

Start by making the meat stew. Pour the oil into a pan and heat. As soon as the oil is hot, add the minced garlic to the pan and fry till golden. Add the fenugreek seeds and toast with the garlic till dark brown. Now add the diced onions, with the salt, and cook till the onions are soft. Mix in the tomato purée.

Get the shoulder of lamb in with the potatoes, the turmeric and red chilli powder. Mix together really well. Pour in the cold water and bring to a hard boil, add the eggs, leave on a medium heat, put the lid on and cook for 1 hour.

For the bazin, put the wholemeal flour and plain flour in a large non-stick pan with a lid and whisk through so it is well combined. Add the salt to the boiling water.

Make a well in the centre of the dry ingredients, pour the water into the centre and mix everything through till you no longer have any more spots of flour. Pop the lid on and leave to steam for 20 minutes on a low heat.

After 20 minutes, lightly grease the worktop and your hands and tip the dough out on to the surface. Make sure it is warm enough to handle.

Knead the dough for 15 minutes till the dough is smooth, then divide into six portions, knead into smooth balls and cling film each one, to keep them warm and soft.

Take the stew off the heat, add the dough in the centre of each plate and pour the stew around it with an egg each. Pinch mounds of the dough to scoop up the stew and enjoy.

For the stew
100ml oil
6 cloves of garlic, minced
1 tablespoon fenugreek seeds
3 onions, finely diced
1 tablespoon salt
3 tablespoons tomato purée
1kg diced shoulder of lamb
500g potatoes, peeled and diced
1 teaspoon ground turmeric
1 tablespoon red chilli powder
500ml cold water
6 hard-boiled eggs, peeled

For the bazin
1kg wholemeal flour
250g plain flour
1 tablespoon salt
1.5 litres boiling water

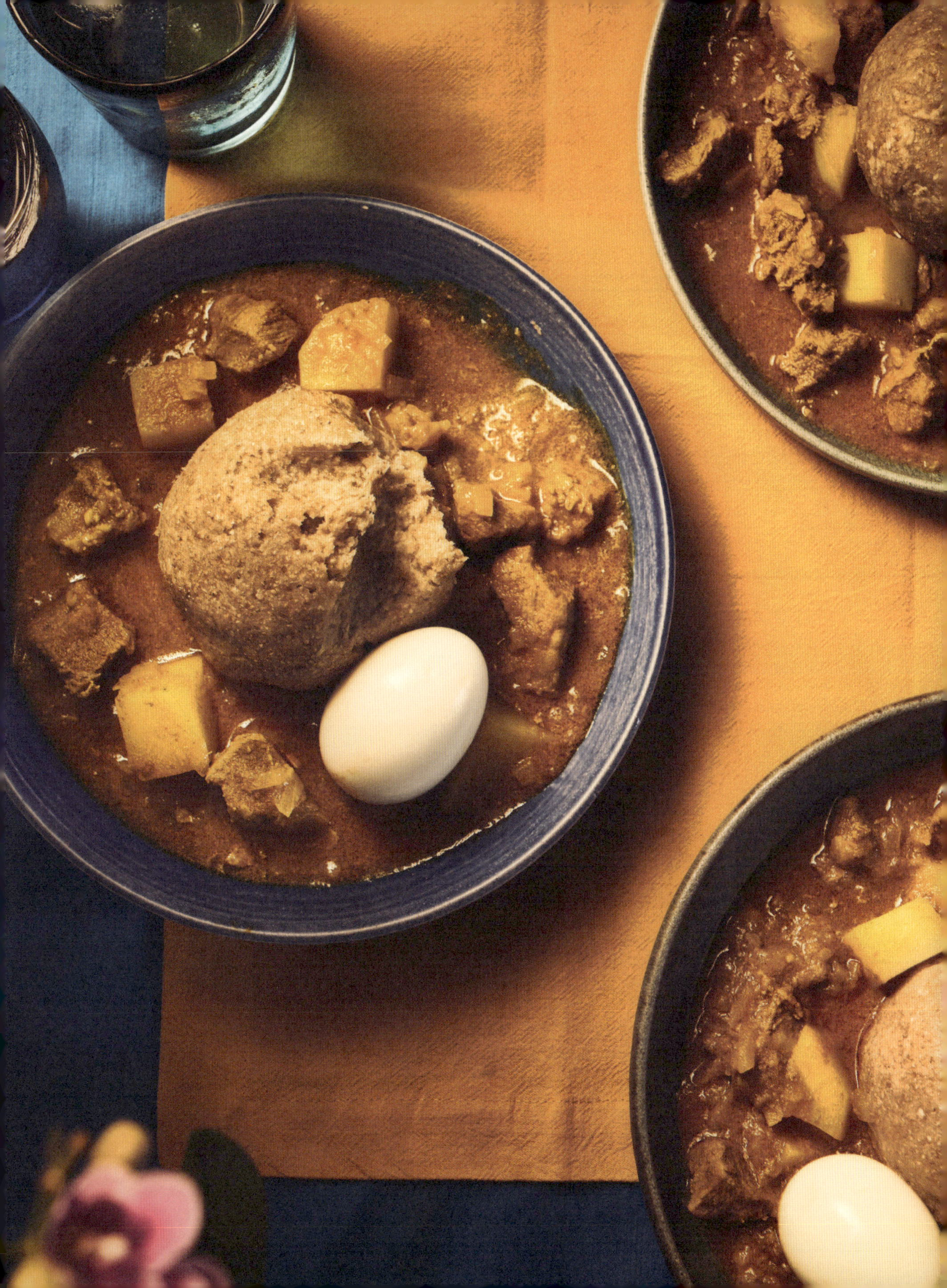

North Africa

BABOUSA
Semolina Cakes

This dessert is really simple to make and takes its syrupy influence from other Arab and neighbouring countries. Though dense in texture, the flavour is light and refreshing.

Makes: 9 squares

For the cake, start by preheating the oven to 200°C and lining the base and sides of a 20cm square tin.

Put the semolina in a bowl with the caster sugar, desiccated coconut, milk and coconut oil. Mix till you have a thick paste. Spoon into the tin and spread into an even layer. Cut nine squares so you know exactly where to place the almonds, then place an almond in the centre of each square.

Bake in the oven for 30 minutes, till a deep golden brown.

Meanwhile, make the syrup by putting the caster sugar in a pan with the cold water. Bring to the boil, then leave to simmer for 10 minutes till the syrup has thickened.

Take the cake out of the oven and then pour the syrup all over the cake. Re-cut the cake where you cut it originally. Leave to cool completely in the tin, then take out and slice. Serve with cream.

For the cake
200g semolina
100g caster sugar
100g desiccated coconut, toasted
150ml whole milk
100ml coconut oil
9 whole almonds, to decorate

For the syrup
200g caster sugar
200ml cold water

To serve
double cream

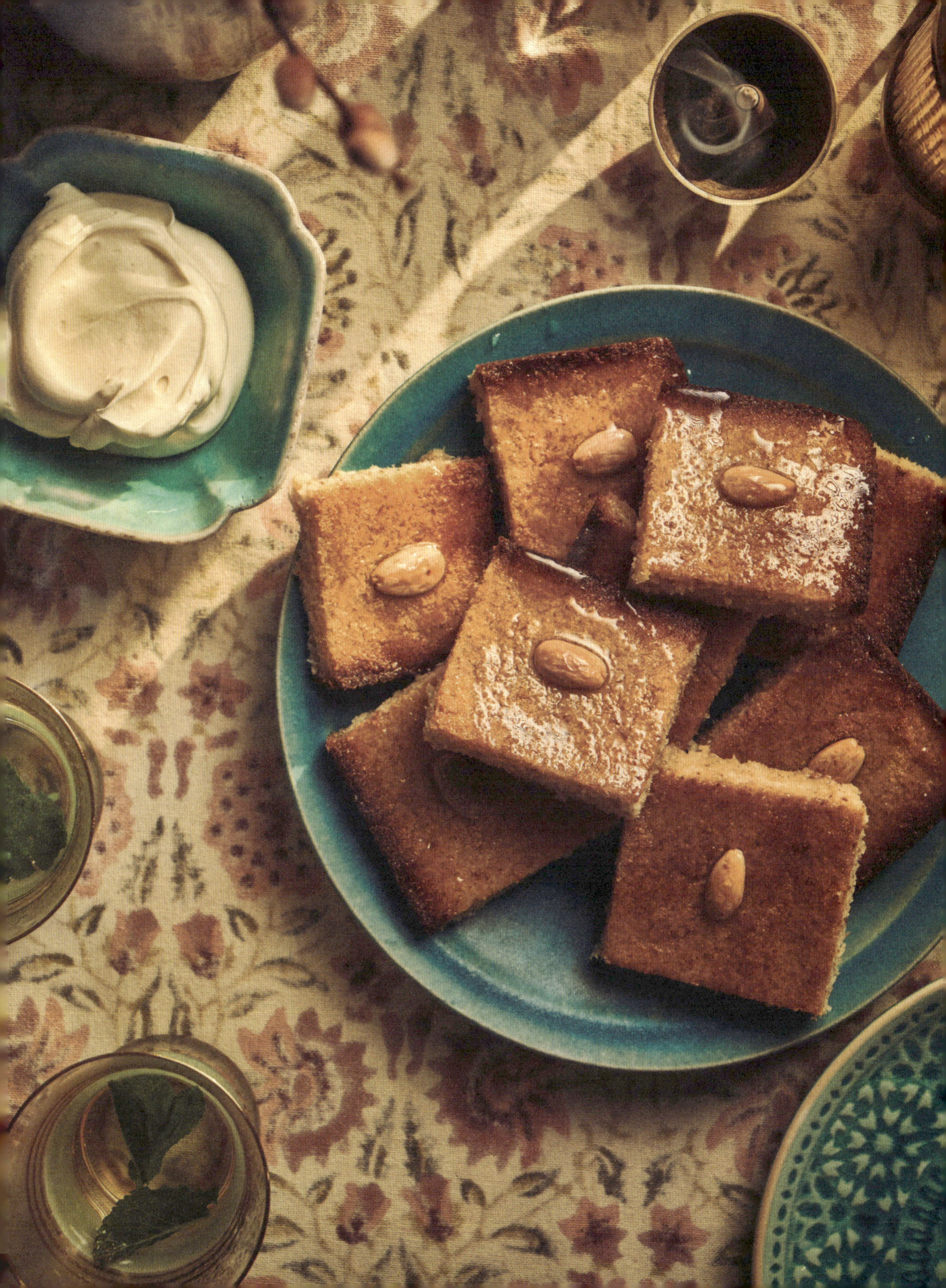

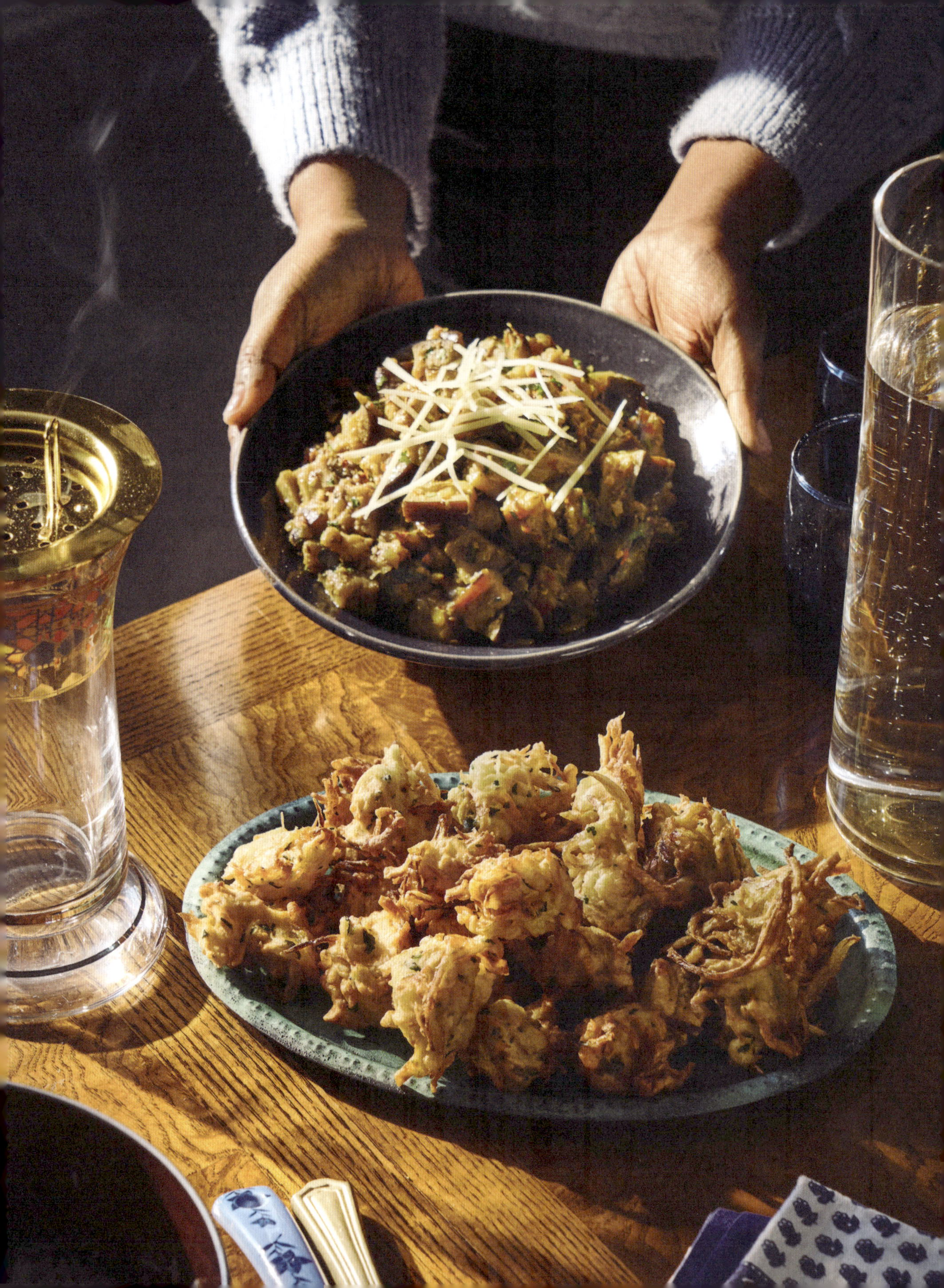

BRINJAL BHAJI
with Ghee Pulao and Aloo Pakora

I grew up surrounded by family who worked in Indian restaurants, creating dishes that satisfied the masses. But when I think about Indian cuisine, I think about recipes that are simple, like aubergines, just fried in onions and spices, and served with rice and pakora, which create a crispy contrast.

For the brinjal bhaji, start by pouring all the oil into a large frying pan that has a lid. When the oil is hot, add the cumin seeds and when the seeds start to sizzle, add in the garlic and cook till golden.

Add the diced onions into the oil with salt and cook till soft. Now add your turmeric and chilli flakes and mix through. Get the diced aubergine in and mix with all the spices. Pop the lid on and let it steam on a low to medium heat.

For the ghee pulao, put the ghee in a large non-stick pan and allow the ghee to melt on a low heat with the black cardamom.

Wash the rice till the water runs clear, drain off the water and add the rice to the ghee. Over a medium heat, cook the rice in the ghee and stir to stop it sticking. Pour in the boiling water, add the salt and bring the whole thing to a boil. As soon as every grain is visible and the water evaporated, pop a lid on and leave to steam for 30–35 minutes.

Make the aloo pakora by putting the onions in a bowl with the salt, coriander and green chillies. Mix with your hands, really squeezing to remove the moisture. Now add the potatoes and mix through by hand. Add the chickpea flour and, using your hands, bring the dough together. The mixture should clump together.

Pour the oil into a pan about two-thirds of the way up. Heat to 180°C and start to drop small clumps of the pakoras into the oil. Fry for 4 minutes, turning occasionally so they are evenly golden. Take out with a slotted spoon and drain on a plate lined with kitchen paper. Continue until the pakoras are all fried.

Sprinkle the fresh ginger and coriander all over the aubergine, fluff up the rice and serve with the pakoras.

Serves: 6

For the brinjal bhaji
150ml oil
3 teaspoons cumin seeds
8 cloves of garlic, minced
2 onions, finely diced
2 teaspoons salt
1 teaspoon ground turmeric
3 teaspoons chilli flakes
3 large aubergines, diced with skin on

For the ghee pulao
150g ghee
1 black cardamom pod
600g basmati rice
900ml boiling water
1 tablespoon salt

For the aloo pakora
2 onions, thinly sliced
1 teaspoon salt
small handful of fresh coriander, finely chopped
3 green chillies, thinly sliced
2 medium potatoes, peeled and grated
150g chickpea flour
oil, for frying

To serve
fresh ginger, cut into slivers
small handful of fresh coriander, finely chopped

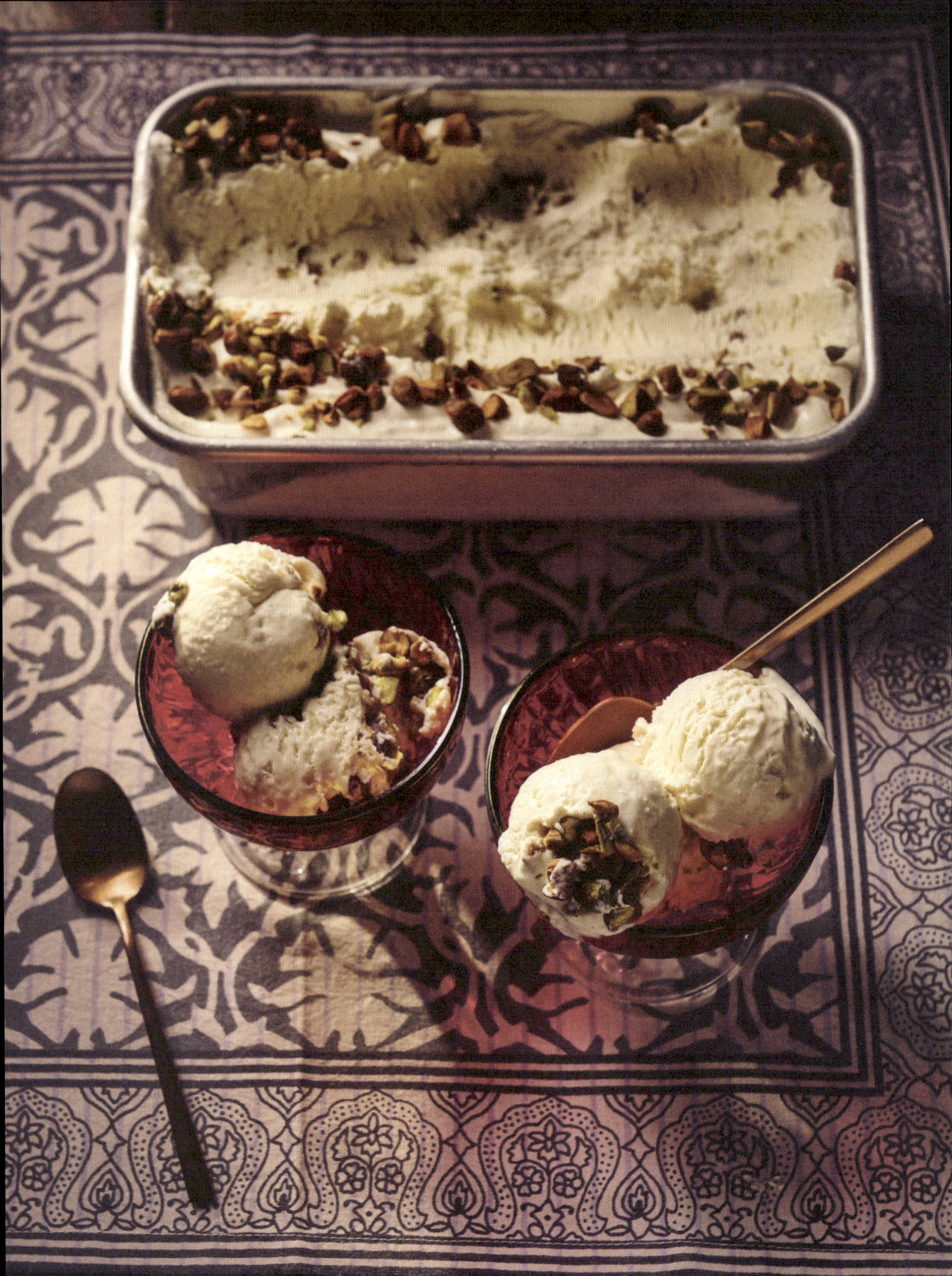

KULFI ICE CREAM

Kulfi ice cream is a superior ice cream in terms of flavour and this recipe is no exception. It has a creamy taste from the bread that goes into it, and it is a huge, huge winner in our house as a go-to dessert after iftar.

Serves: 6

Start by putting the double cream in a bowl with the condensed milk.

Take the cardamom pods and crush, remove the husks and grind the seeds down to a fine powder. Add to the cream. Whisk the whole thing to soft peaks.

Now add the breadcrumbs and whisk to stiff peaks.

Transfer half the mixture to a freezer-safe Tupperware. Sprinkle over half the pistachios. Put the other half of the mixture on top of the pistachios and sprinkle over the rest of the pistachios. Seal tight with the lid and freeze overnight.

When you are ready to serve, take out 10 minutes beforehand and then go for a scoop.

600ml double cream
397g tin of condensed milk
8 cardamom pods
1 slice of white bread, breadcrumbed to a fine crumb
200g pistachios, roasted and finely chopped

Middle East

MOUSSAKA

Moussaka is a wholesome meal that has everything you need in one dish. It is packed full of meat, vegetables and a creamy sauce and has the most delicious aroma of cinnamon.

Serves: 6

This recipe is all about the layers, so we have to make each one, then assemble the moussaka, then bake it in the oven.

Let's start off with the aubergines. Put the aubergines in a bowl and generously drizzle with the oil. Fry the rounds in batches till the aubergines are cooked and softer, but not falling apart. Set aside and get on to the beef.

Pour the oil into a medium pan and heat over a medium heat. As soon as the oil is hot, add the bay leaves and as soon as the bays start to sizzle, add the beef mince. Cook over a high heat and break the mince up as you cook it.

Now add the diced onion, garlic, tomato purée, salt, oregano and cinnamon and mix through. Cook for a few minutes, then pour in the beef stock and cook the mince till there is no more liquid left and the mixture is dry. Set this aside and get on to the potatoes.

Put the potatoes in a large pan, pour in water till the slices are submerged, then add the salt, bring to the boil and boil for just 7-8 minutes. Drian and set aside.

Now make the white sauce by putting the butter in a pan and melting. Add the flour and whisk through. Gradually pour in the milk and whisk till the mixture is thick. Take off the heat and whisk in the egg and egg yolk.

Preheat the oven to 180°C.

Get a large roasting dish and add a third of the meat into the base of the dish. Spoon half the aubergine slices on top of the mince and then half the potato on top of the aubergine. Spread the rest of the meat on top, then again with the aubergine and then the potato. Spread the white sauce all over that.

Bake in the oven for 1 hour. Take out and leave for 10 minutes before serving.

For the aubergines
3 medium aubergines, cut into 1cm thick coins
6-10 tablespoons oil

For the beef
2 tablespoons oil
2 bay leaves
800g beef mince
1 onion, diced
6 cloves of garlic, minced
2 tablespoons tomato purée
1 teaspoon salt
4 teaspoons dried oregano
2 teaspoons ground cinnamon
200ml beef stock

For the potatoes
600g potatoes, thinly sliced
water, to cover
large pinch of salt

For the white sauce
50g salted butter
50g plain flour
600ml whole milk
1 large egg
1 egg yolk

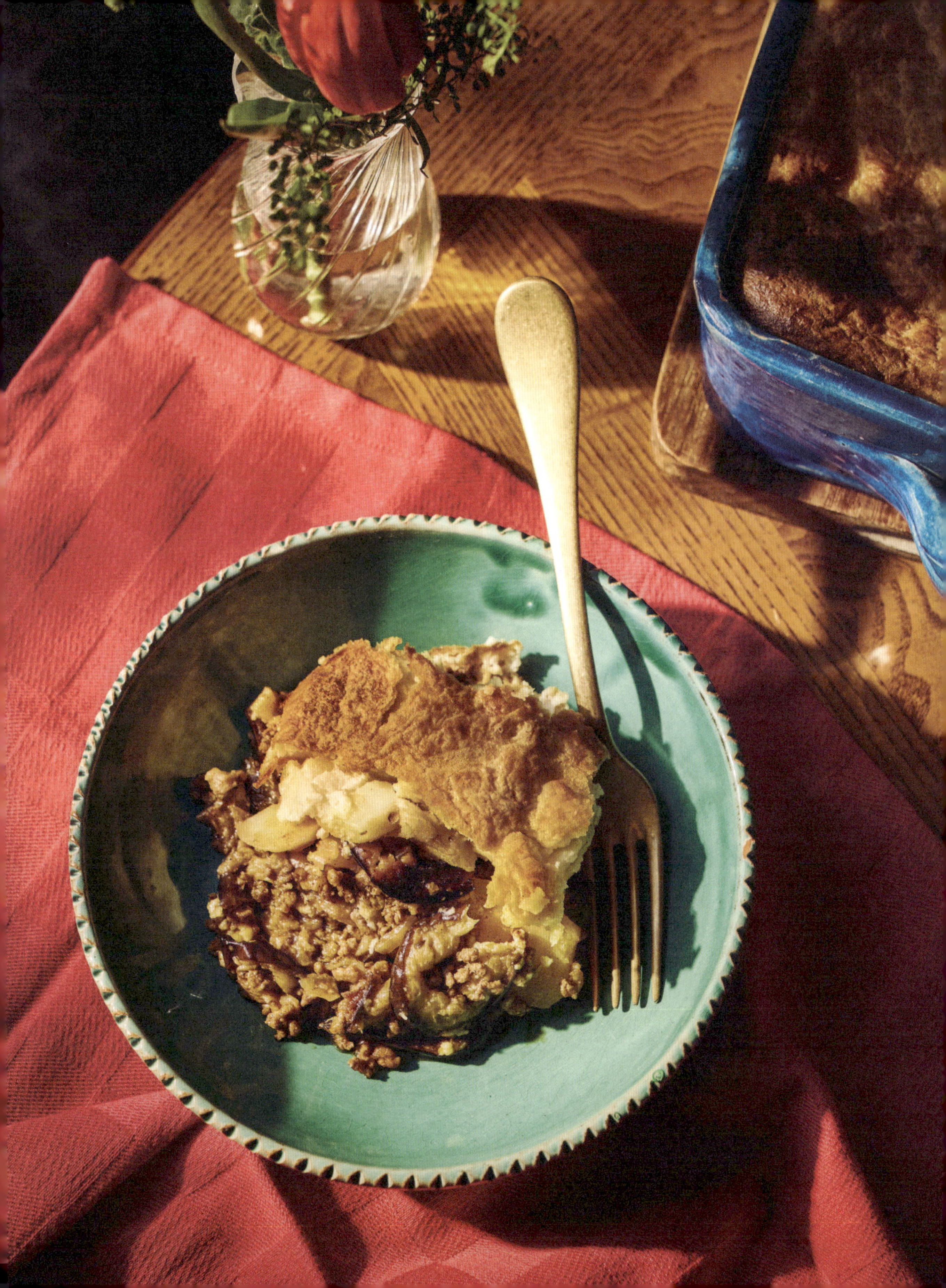

ATAYEF BIL ASHTA
Marscarpone-filled Pancakes

These are as beautiful to make as they are to look at and are even more of a delight to eat. Tender pancakes, pinched to create a space ready to fill with sweetened cream and pressed into pistachios, these will please the crowds, the family, the neighbours, everyone!

Start by making the pancakes. Put the flour in a bowl with the baking powder and caster sugar, whisk to combine and create a well in the centre. Pour in the eggs, milk and melted butter. Whisk till you have a smooth, even batter.

Take a non-stick pancake pan and heat over a medium heat. Brush the pan with a light amount of butter and spoon in 2 tablespoons of the batter, making as many pancakes as you can fit without crowding the pan. Cook over a medium to low heat till the tops are dry and the pancakes aren't wet or runny.

Take the pancakes off the pan one by one and while they are still warm, pinch only one half together at the seams to create a semi-circled pocket. Repeat with all of them and wait for them to cool completely.

For the cream filling, put the mascarpone in a bowl with the orange blossom extract, icing sugar and orange zest. Mix really well and pop into a piping bag. Pipe the mixture into the cavity of the pancakes and, using a palette knife, scrape to create a flat edge, removing any excess.

Dip the exposed ends with the cream into the pistachios. Repeat with all of them. Before serving, drizzle with honey.

Makes: 12–15 pancakes

For the pancakes
200g self-raising flour, sifted
½ teaspoon baking powder
50g caster sugar
3 medium eggs, lightly beaten
200ml whole milk
25g salted butter, melted
butter, for frying

For the cream filling
250g mascarpone
1 teaspoon orange blossom extract
2 tablespoons icing sugar
1 orange, zest only

To finish
100g pistachios, roasted and finely chopped
runny honey

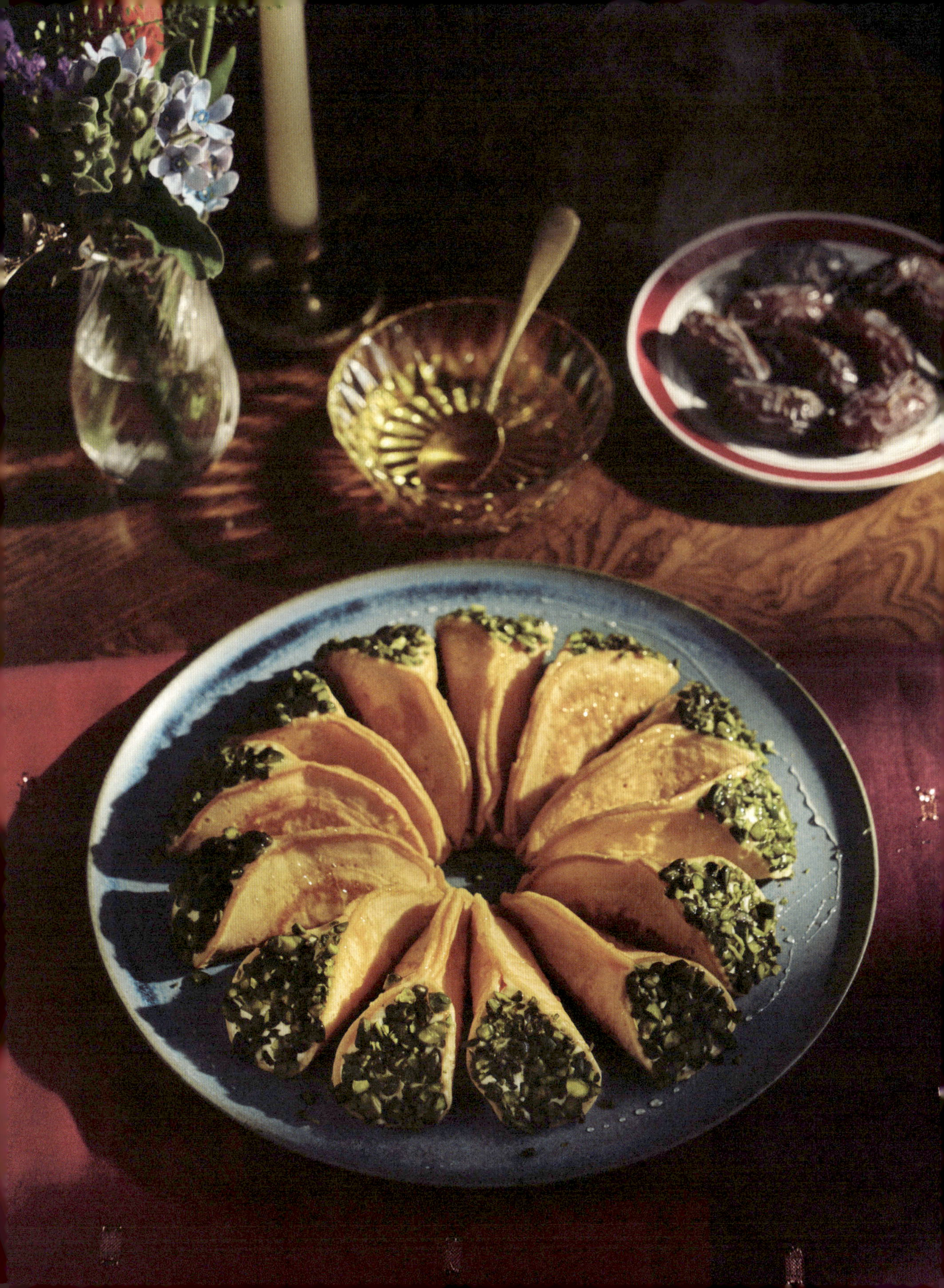

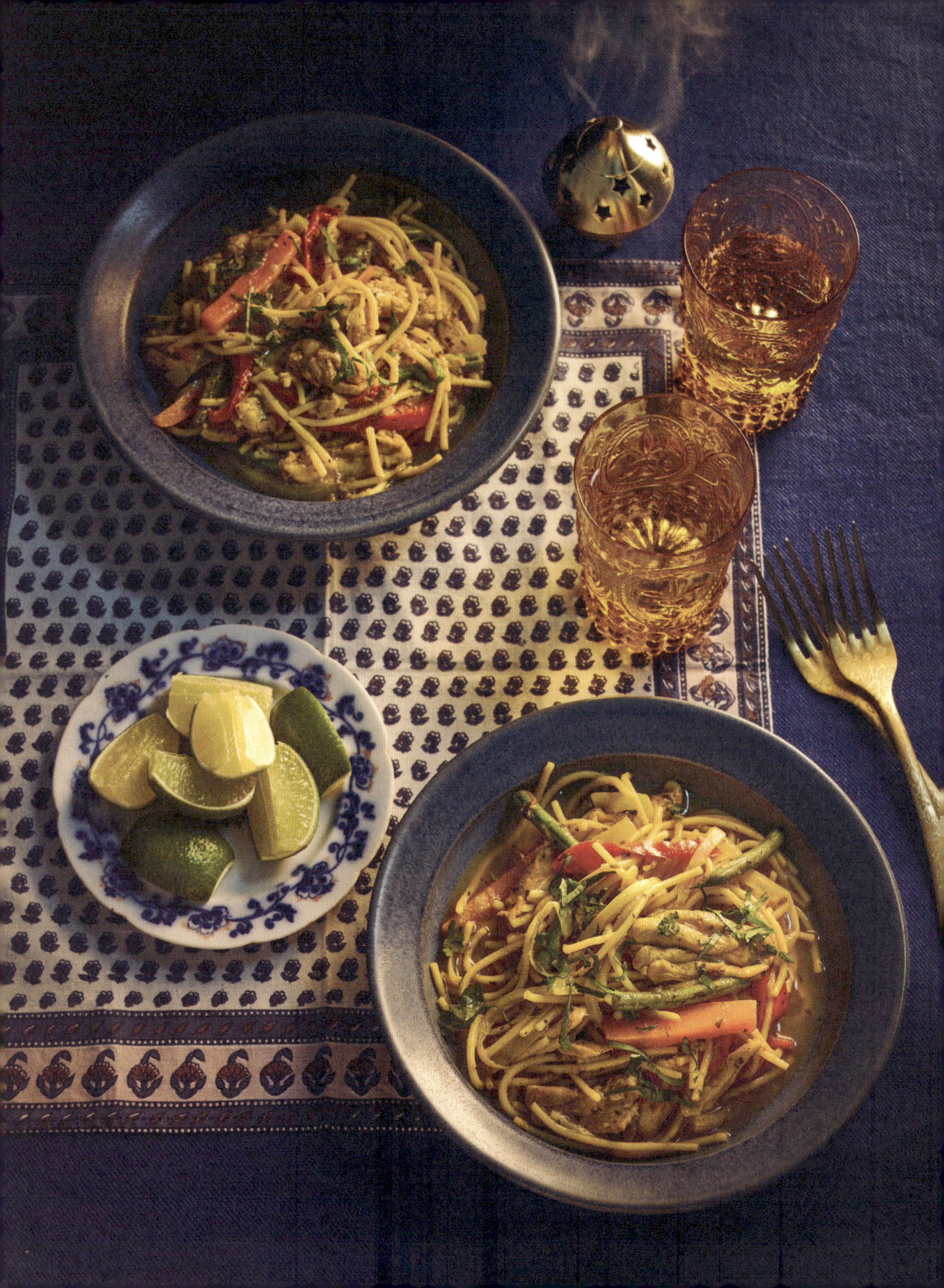

Nepal

THUKPA
Chicken Noodles

I learnt that my bloodline leads us to Nepal and when I visited the country, I felt a deep closeness to the people and the cuisine. Apart from the most amazing rice and lentils, the thukpa is just out of this world, so I've got my own recipe down for everyone to enjoy at home.

Serves: 6

Start by making the paste. Put the garlic, ginger, green chillies, cumin seeds, black peppercorns, coriander and tomato in a processor and blitz to a smooth paste.

Place a large pan over a medium heat. Pour the oil into the pan and when the oil is hot, add the asafoetida – it will fizz a little. Give it a mix and then add in that paste.

Cook the paste for a few minutes till the paste is dry. Add the chicken thighs, along with the turmeric and salt, and cook the chicken through. Now add the red pepper, green beans, white cabbage and carrot and mix to combine well.

Pour in the chicken stock or water, bring the whole thing to a rapid boil and let it boil for about 10 minutes. Now add the broken spaghetti pieces, allow it to boil for another 10 minutes and then leave to simmer for 30 minutes with the lid on.

Serve in bowls, sprinkling over the fresh coriander and serving with lime wedges on the side.

For the paste

3 cloves of garlic, peeled
2–3cm piece of peeled ginger
4 green chillies
1 tablespoon cumin seeds, roasted
1 tablespoon whole black peppercorns
small handful of fresh coriander with the stalks
1 tomato, roughly chopped

For the thukpa

3 tablespoons oil
½ teaspoon hing (asafoetida)
500g boneless chicken thighs, cut into strips
½ teaspoon ground turmeric
3 teaspoons salt
1 red pepper, thinly sliced
100g green beans, cut into 2–3cm pieces
100g white cabbage, shredded
1 carrot, cut into thin 2–3cm strips
1 litre chicken stock or water
200g spaghetti, broken into 5cm pieces

To serve

handful of fresh coriander, finely sliced
lime wedges

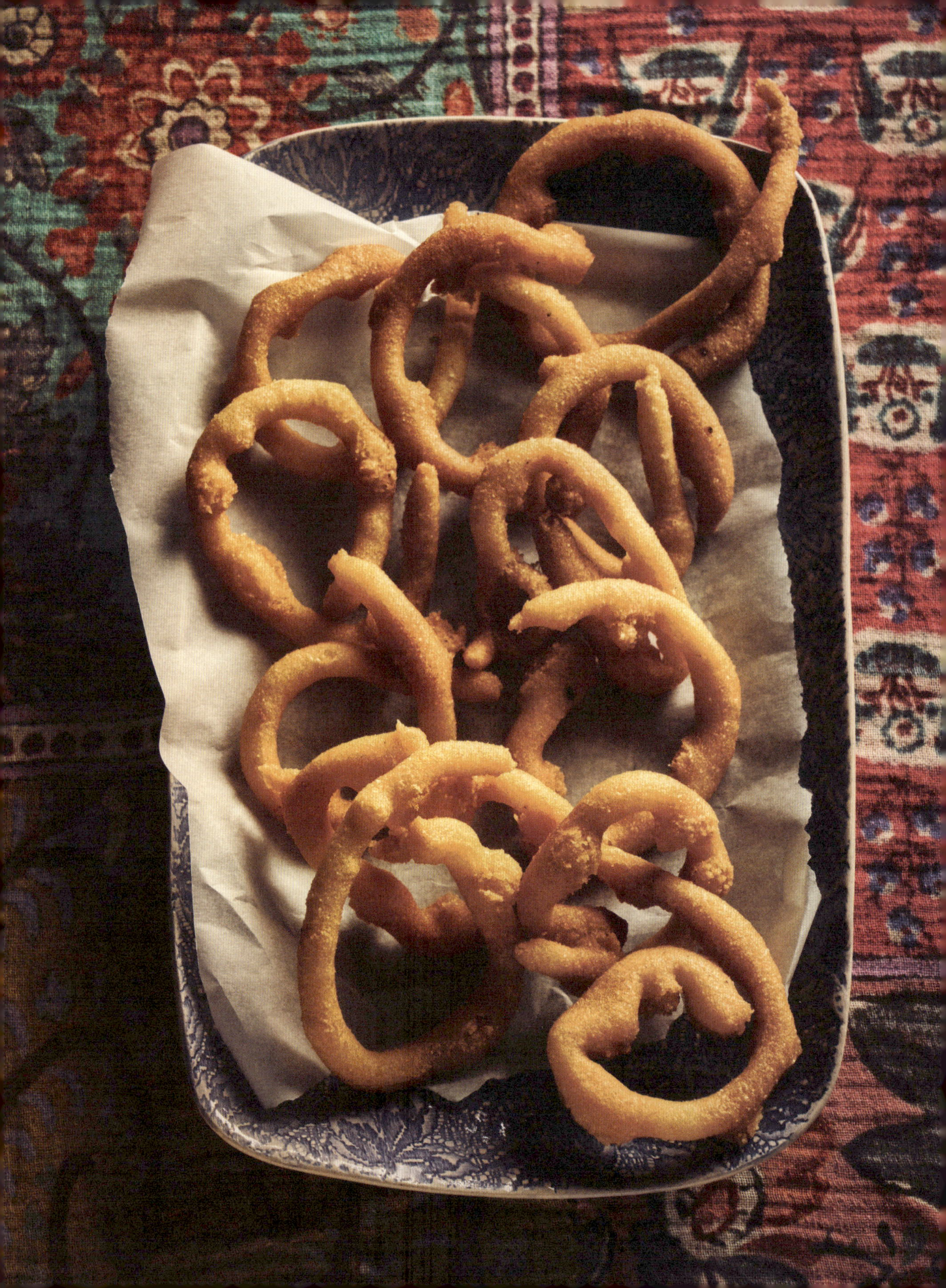

SEL ROTI
Sweet Rice Churros

I ate these at a street market where everything is made at shin level, so to get in and amongst, you had to kneel down and fully immerse yourself. These rotis were etched on my mind and I make them often now, not just during Ramadhan. They are aromatic with the soaked, slightly fermented rice and they are just so subtly sweet, crunchy all the way around yet soft in the

Makes: 10 roti

Start by soaking the basmati rice overnight. Drain the rice and leave to sit and drain further for 1 hour.

Put the rice in a blender jug along with the melted ghee, caster sugar, baking powder and cold water. Blitz enough to create a grainy paste. Set aside for 1 hour, covered.

Take a large pan and pour in the oil about two-thirds of the way up.

Heat the oil to 180°C. Have a baking tray lined with kitchen paper to hand.

Put the mixture into a piping bag and pipe one large circle into the oil. They tend to stay at the bottom, but after a minute of frying and with enough time to establish a strong shape, encourage the circle up off the base of the pan. Fry till golden, using chopsticks to turn the roti over.

Take out, then make the rest. These are best served warm.

500g basmati rice
50g ghee, melted
110g caster sugar
1 teaspoon baking powder
100ml cold water
oil, for frying

Cambodia

LEMONGRASS AND GINGER CHICKEN
with Lort Cha *(Noodles)*

This chicken dish is rich in flavour and so balanced and aromatic. Served with the noodles, it is a recipe you will for sure come back to after Ramadhan is over.

Put the garlic, salt, ginger, onion, lemon peel and juice, lemongrass, red chillies and cashews in a food processor, along with a splash of water, and blend to a paste.

Place a medium pan on the stove with a splash of oil. Heat the oil, get the paste in and cook for a few minutes. Add the chicken thighs into the pan and cook for a few minutes. Pour in the coconut milk and water and cook on a high heat, then cover and simmer for 25 minutes.

Now make the lort cha by putting the noodles in a large bowl and breaking them up into small pieces. Cover the noodles till submerged with boiling water, then drain after 10 minutes.

Meanwhile, make the sauce by putting the fish sauce, soy sauce, lime juice and honey in a bowl. Mix and set to one side.

Heat a non-stick wok over a high heat, add the oil to the wok and the garlic and fry for a few seconds till brown. Add the beansprouts and spring onions and cook for a few minutes, till just charred.

Make a well in the centre, move all the veg around the side of the pan, add a little extra oil to the centre and drop the beaten egg in there, frying until well scrambled.

Mix and add the noodles, mix through again, then add the sauce and cook through for a few minutes. Drizzle with chilli sauce.

Take the chicken off the stove, squeeze over the lime juice, sprinkle over the coriander, and serve alongside the lort cha.

Serves: 6

For the lemongrass and ginger chicken
6 cloves of garlic
2 teaspoons salt
8cm piece of peeled ginger
1 onion, roughly chopped
1 lemon, peel and juice
2 lemongrass stalks, roughly chopped
4 Thai red chillies
100g cashews, toasted
oil, for frying
12 chicken thighs
400ml coconut milk
200ml water, plus a splash for the paste
a squeeze of lime juice
fresh coriander, to serve

For the lort cha
350g egg noodles
boiling water, to cover
1 tablespoon fish sauce
1 tablespoon soy sauce
½ lime, juice only
2 teaspoons honey
3 tablespoons oil, plus extra for the egg
2 cloves of garlic, minced
100g beansprouts
50g spring onions, sliced
2 medium eggs, lightly beaten
chilli sauce, to drizzle

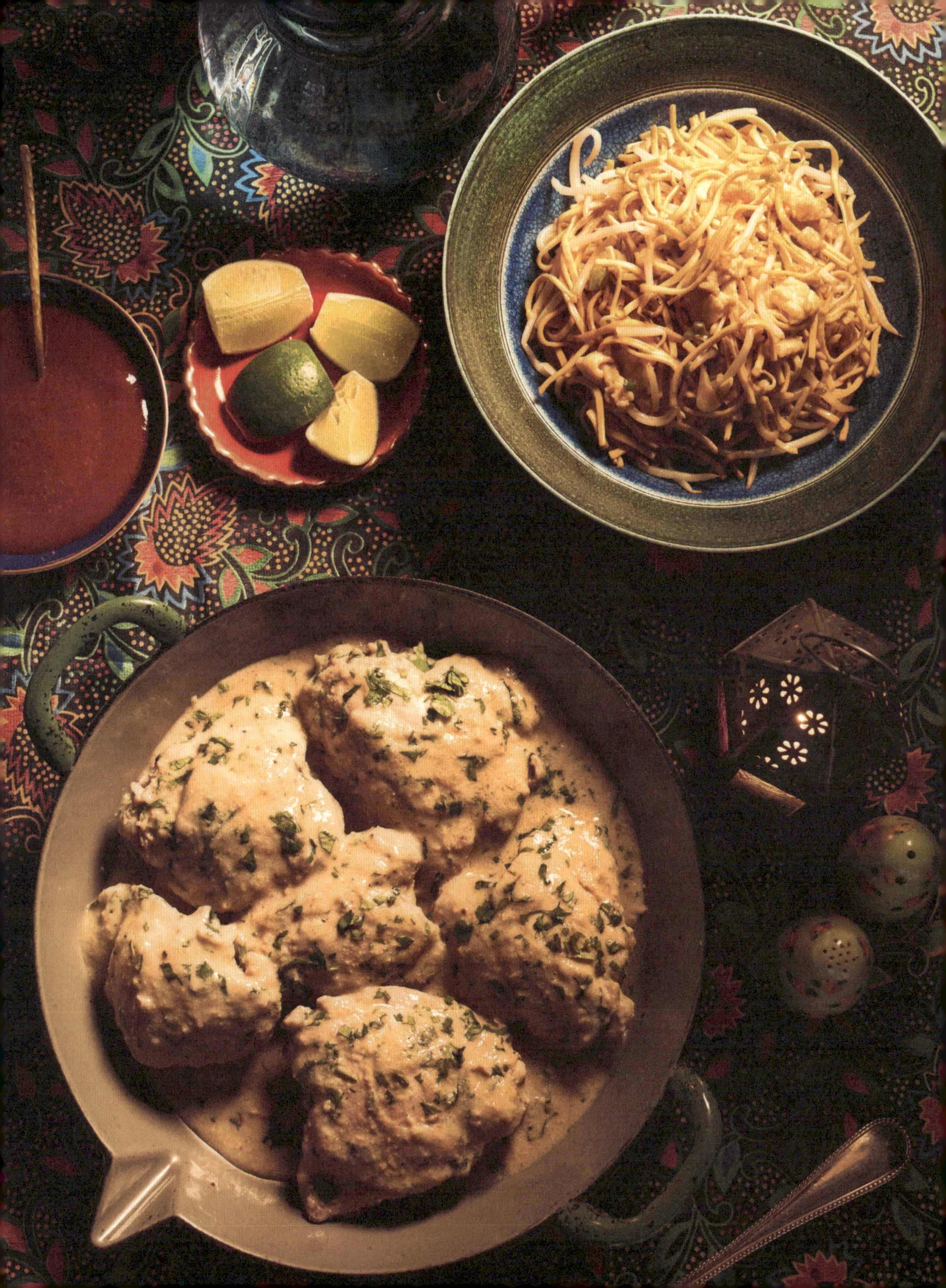

Cambodia

NAM VAN
Sweet Noodles

If you are looking for something fun to look at and eat, you will love this. With tons of different textures, this is a great dessert to enjoy chilled after a hearty meal.

Serves: 6

We need to make all the layers separately. Let's start with the tapioca layer. Bring 2 litres water to the boil in a pan and add the tapioca pearls. Cook for 1 hour.

Tip the tapioca into a sieve and run under a cold tap till the gloopy liquid is removed and you are left with the translucent balls. Divide the mixture between two bowls. Add a few drops of red colouring to one and orange to the other, mix well and pop into the fridge.

For the noodle layers, bring a pan of water to the boil with the food colouring and then add the noodles. Cook for 6-8 minutes till the noodles are just cooked but not too soft. Drain and rinse under a cold tap.

Transfer into a bowl, add a tiny amount of oil and mix through to stop the noodles from sticking. Set aside in the fridge.

For the basil seed layer, add the basil seeds to the milk and set aside for the seeds to plump up and the mixture to thicken. Leave it in the fridge to chill.

For the sweet milk, pour the coconut milk into a jug with the condensed milk and mix well. Pop into the fridge.

To serve, start layering with the tapioca red layer and orange layers, then in with the green noodles, put the basil seeds on top, then top with the sweet milk. Give it all a good mix and use a spoon or a large straw to enjoy.

➜

For the tapioca layers
2 litres water
300g large tapioca pearls
red gel food colouring
orange food colouring

For the noodle layer
boiling water, to cover
green gel food colouring
150g vermicelli noodles, broken into smaller strands
oil, for the noodles

For the basil seed layer
7 tablespoons basil seeds (tukmaria) or chia seeds
300ml whole milk

For the sweet milk
400ml tin of coconut milk
½ x 397g tin of condensed milk

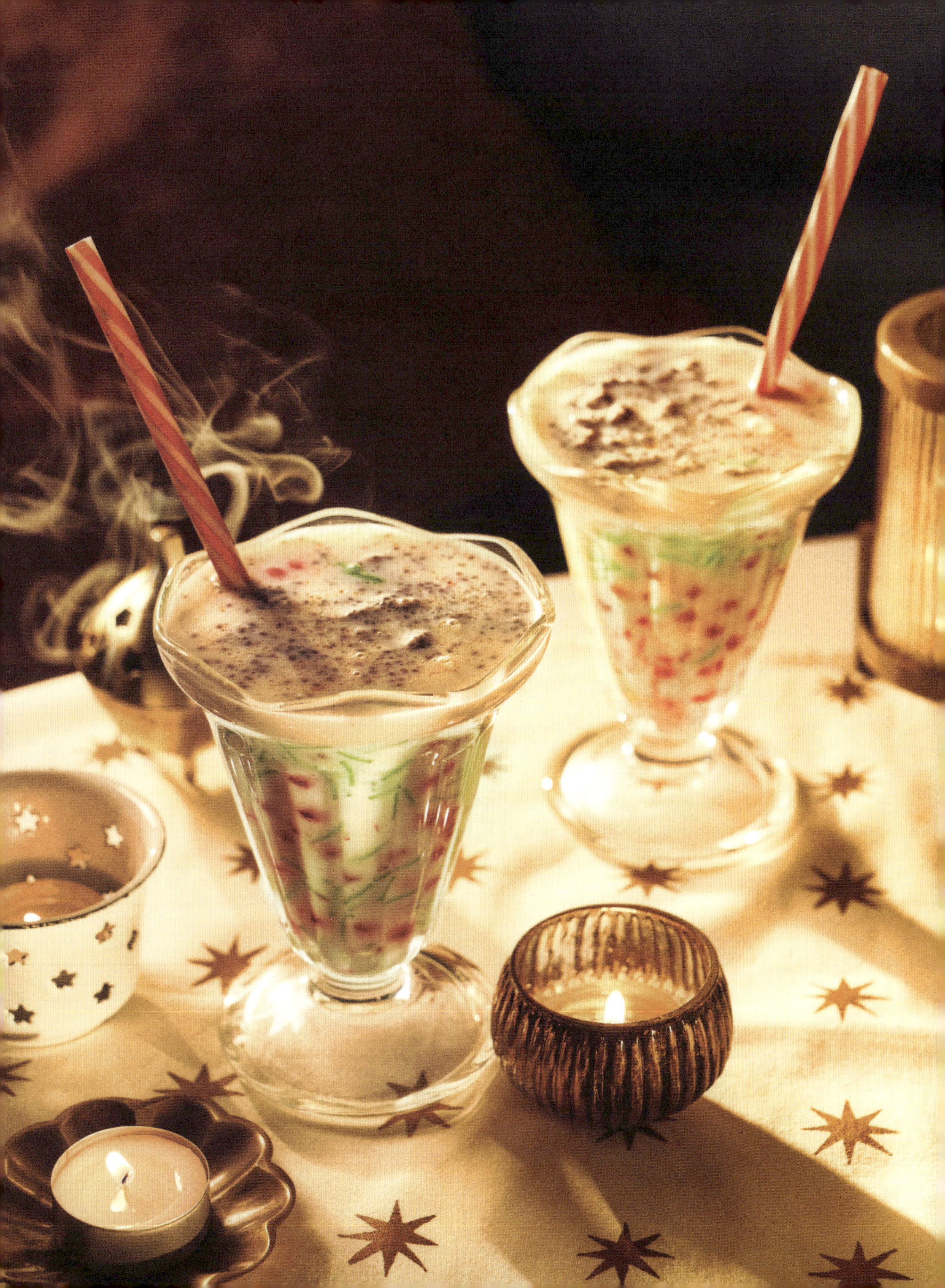

TIP: *This is the kind of dessert that is best served very chilled, so ideally make the layers the night before and take out of the fridge when you are ready to serve it.*

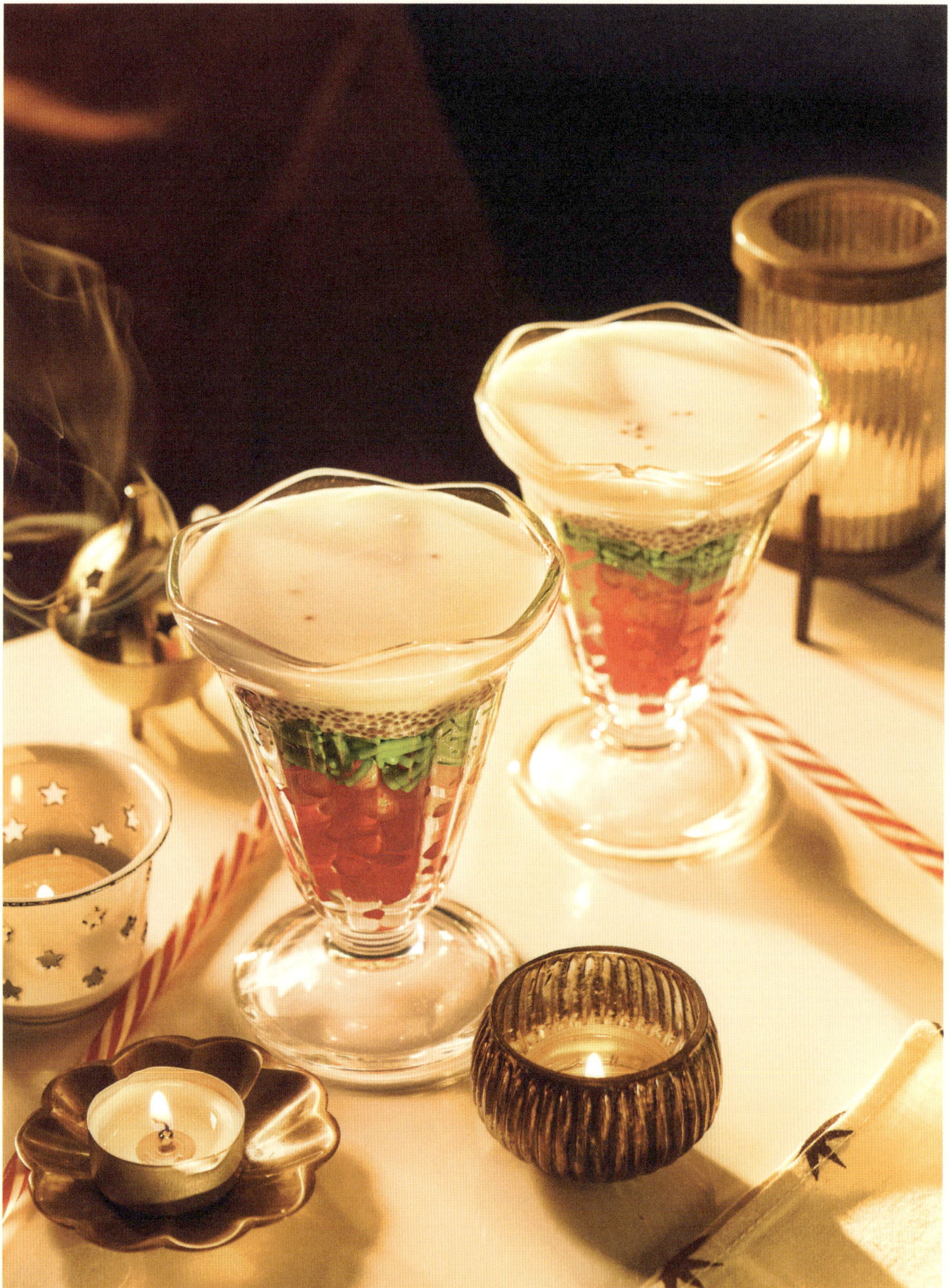

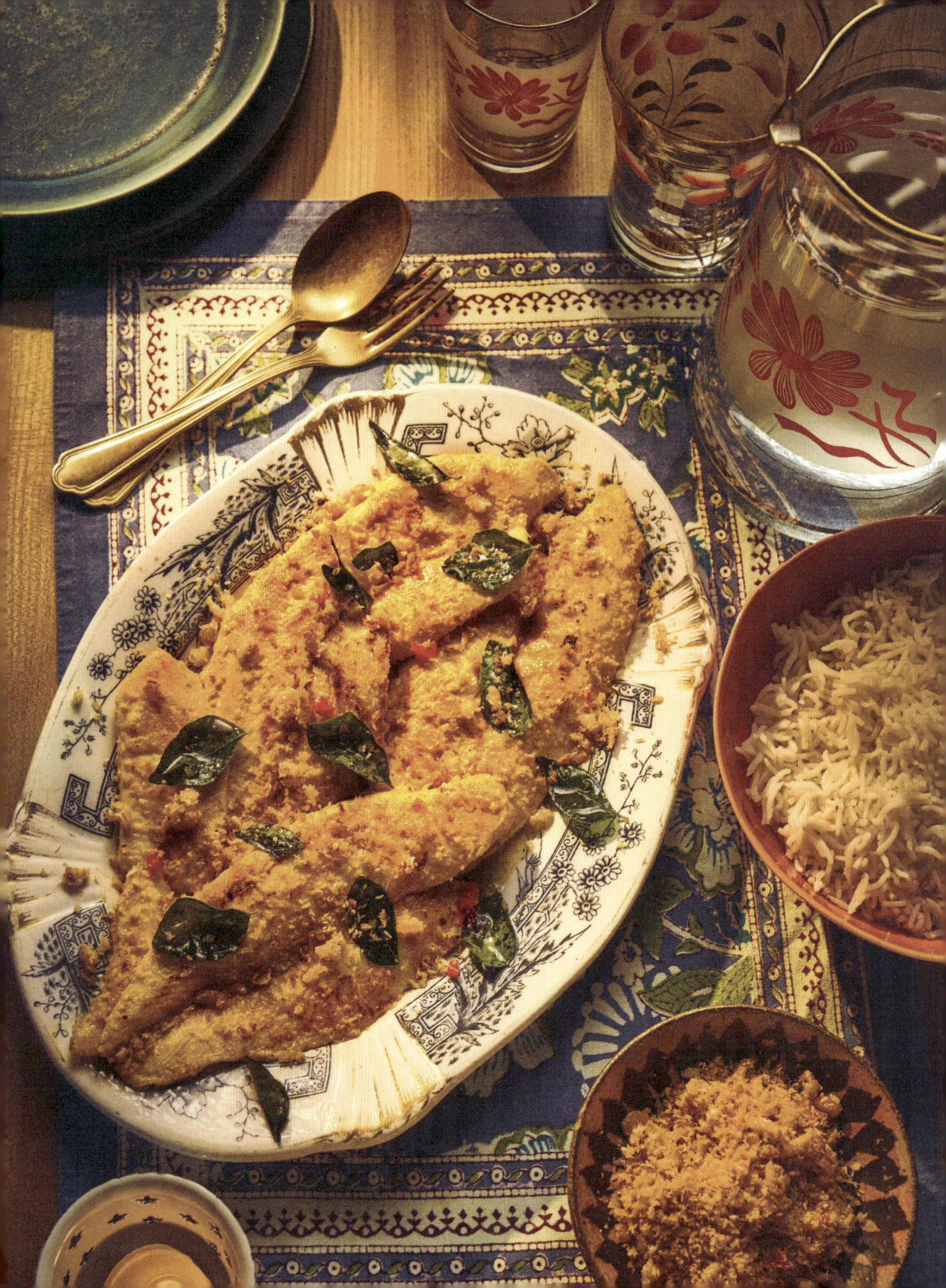

SRI LANKA AMBUL FISH
with Rice and Kuni Raal *(Spicy Shrimp Topping)*

If you like Sri Lankan food and flavours, you will love this fish. It is the perfect combination of tangy, creamy and lightly spiced.

Serves: 6

Start by prepping the ambul fish. Put the yoghurt in a large bowl with the garlic, turmeric, salt, ground black pepper and chilli powder and mix till you have an even colour. Add the tilapia fillets and make sure each fillet is covered in the marinade. Cover and set aside while you make the rice.

Make the rice by first washing it till the water is crystal clear, then drain the rice and put in a medium pan along with the cloves. Pour in the cold water and salt and pop the pan over a high heat. Stir occasionally to stop the rice sticking to the base. As soon as the rice comes to the boil and the water has evaporated, lower the heat and get the lid on. Leave to steam for 15 minutes.

Let's fry the fish. Get a large non-stick pan on the hob and pour in enough oil to lightly cover the base. As soon as the oil is hot, add the fillets in, cooking in batches (I can normally cook two at a time). Fry for 4 minutes on one side and 1 minute on the other.

Once you have fried them all and laid them out on a serving dish, add a little extra oil if there isn't a lot left in the pan and fry the curry leaves till they sizzle and pop. As soon as you can smell the aromas, pour over the fish, oil and all.

Take the rice off the heat and make the quick kuni raal by putting the dried shrimp in a food processor with the coconut, fried onions, garlic and red chillies and blitz to an even consistency.

Serve the kuni raal with the rice and fish.

For the ambul fish
250g plain yoghurt
8 cloves of garlic, minced
1 teaspoon ground turmeric
1 teaspoon salt
2 teaspoons ground black pepper
3 teaspoons red chilli powder
6 tilapia fillets
oil, for frying
10 fresh/dry curry leaves

For the rice
600g basmati rice
10 cloves
600ml cold water
1 tablespoon salt

For the kuni raal
200g dried shrimp
2 tablespoons desiccated coconut, toasted
50g fried onions
3 cloves of garlic, minced
4 red chillies, thinly sliced

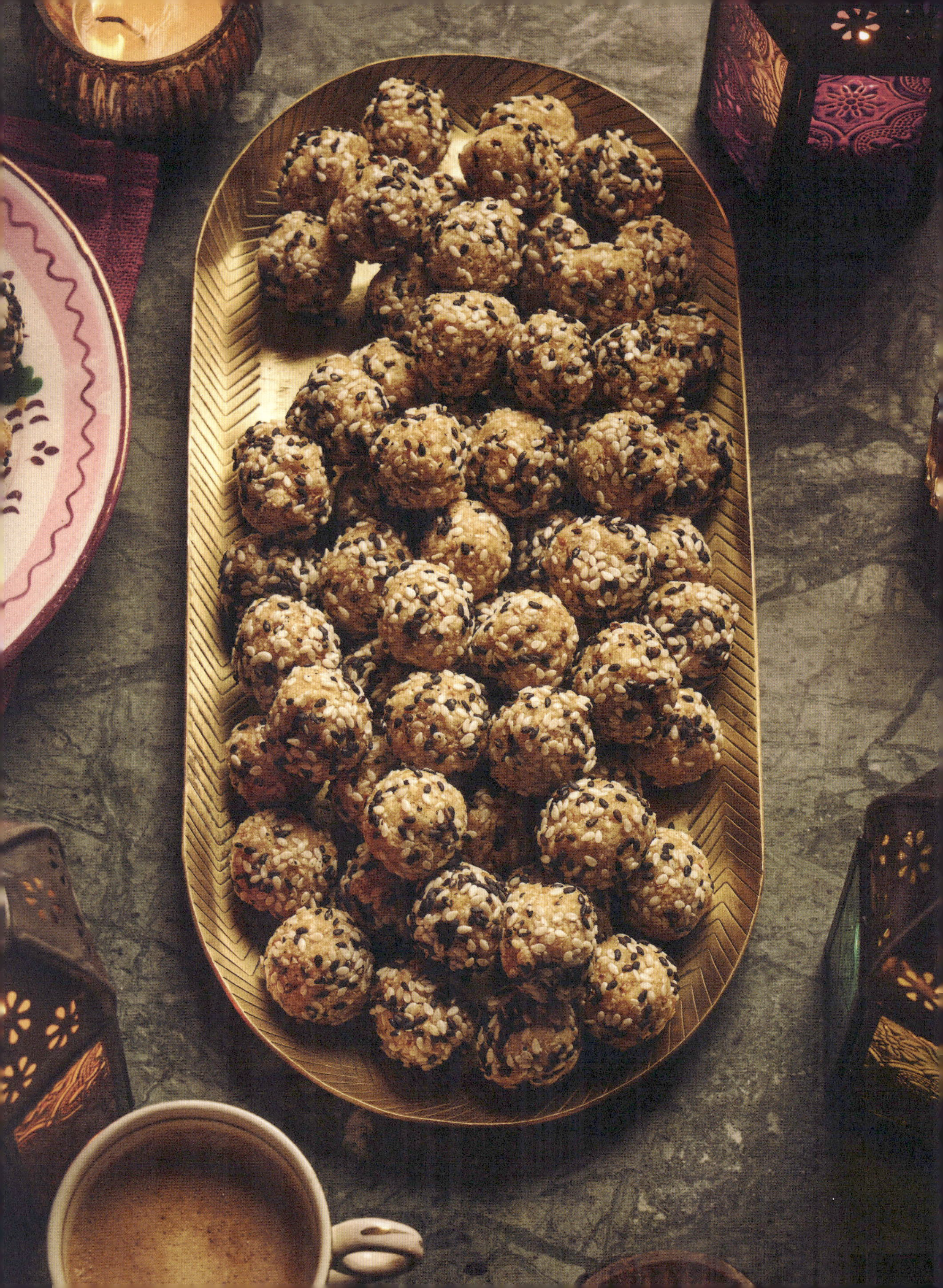

Sri Lanka

THALA GULI
Sesame Balls

These are the simplest, easiest little balls of deliciousness. With just a few ingredients, you can make these bites of nutty goodness, which will give you a sweet hit whenever you need.

For the balls, start by toasting the sesame seeds to a deep golden colour. Put in a bowl. Do the same to the desiccated coconut and add to the bowl. Leave to cool completely.

Place the mixture in a food processor along with the jaggery, golden syrup and salt. Blend till a dough is formed.

Take out and transfer to a bowl. Take small mounds, ½ teaspoon each, and make balls.

On a plate, mix the black and white sesame seeds, roll each ball in sesame and set aside. Repeat with all of them and they are ready.

Makes: 66 balls

For the balls
180g sesame seeds
70g desiccated coconut
140g jaggery, grated
130ml golden syrup
pinch of salt

To decorate
25g black sesame seeds
25g white sesame seeds

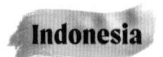

BEEF RENDANG
with Rice

If you do anything this Ramadhan, make a beef rendang. It is spiced, tangy and rich in every way. Served with rice and a frilly egg, this is everything and more.

Serves: 6

For the paste
1 lemongrass stalk
2 onions, roughly chopped
8 cloves of garlic, peeled
8cm piece of peeled ginger, roughly chopped
3 red chillies
1 tablespoon coriander seeds, toasted
1 teaspoon ground turmeric
1 teaspoon ground cinnamon
4 lime leaves
1 tablespoon dark soy
1 teaspoon salt
200ml oil

For the meat
1kg diced boneless beef
4 tablespoons tamarind
400ml tin of coconut milk

For the rice
600g basmati rice
900ml cold water

To serve
oil, for frying
6 medium eggs
toasted coconut flakes
fresh coriander, finely sliced

Start by making the paste. Put the lemongrass, onion, garlic, ginger, red chillies, coriander seeds, turmeric, ground cinnamon, chilli flakes, lime leaves, dark soy and salt in a blender jug. Pour in the oil and blend it all to a really smooth paste.

Put a medium non-stick pan on the hob and place over a medium to high heat. Pour in the contents of the jug and cook for 10 minutes or so, till the mixture is darker and starts to come away from the sides.

As soon as it does, add the diced beef and cook in the fragrant mixture till the beef has browned all over and is cooked all the way through. Now add the tamarind, mix through and pour in the coconut milk. Bring the whole thing to a boil and then leave to simmer.

Meanwhile, make the rice by washing the uncooked rice under cold water till the water runs clear. As soon as it does, drain and add to a pan. Pour in the cold water and bring the rice to a boil, stirring occasionally to stop the rice from sticking to the base of the pan. Once the rice has boiled and there is no longer any water left, lower the heat completely, put the lid on and leave to steam for 15 minutes.

Now check on the beef. The whole thing should no longer be watery – it should be thicker and the sauce should cling to the meat.

To serve, pop some oil into a non-stick frying pan and fry the eggs one at a time till frilly around the edge and runny and warm in the centre. Serve the rice with the rendang and a sprinkling of coconut flakes and coriander.

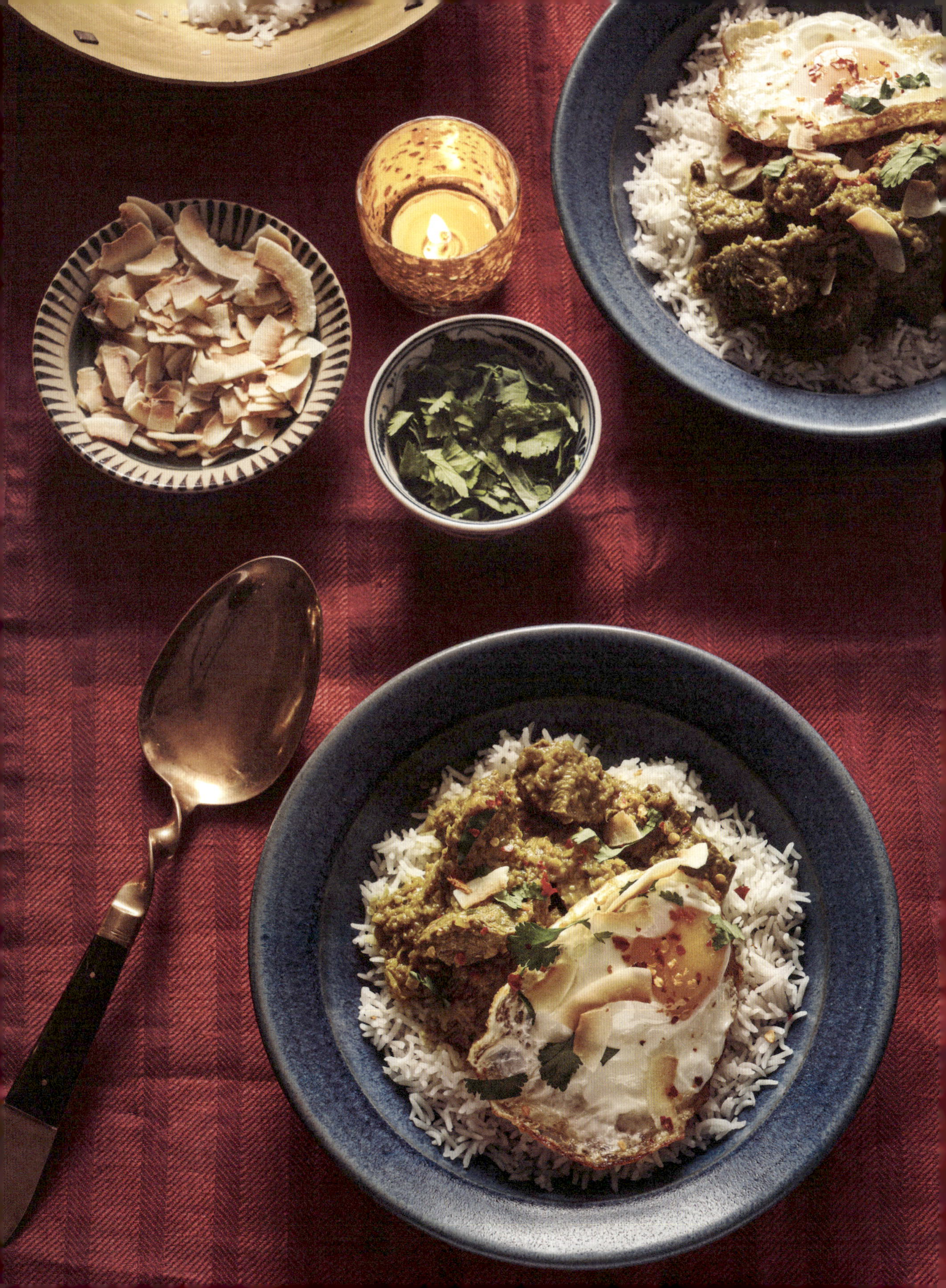

KUE PUKIS
Sweet Yeasted Half Circles

Indonesia

These little semi-circle cakes start their life off as a very unassuming yeasted batter. But you will be pleasantly surprised at how easy they are to make and how delicious they are to eat.

Makes: 24 cakes

Start by making the batter. Put the flour in a bowl and make a well in the centre. Pour the coconut milk into the centre with the eggs, yeast, lukewarm water, salt and sugar. Whisk till everything is well combined. Cover and set aside in a warm place for 2 hours.

Meanwhile, preheat the oven to 180°C and generously grease the inside of a 12-hole muffin tin.

Pour the batter in about halfway up the muffin holes and bake for 10-12 minutes, till they are golden brown. Take out and leave to cool for 5 minutes before popping them out to cool completely. Cut each one in half to create semi-circles.

Melt the chocolate, take each semi-circle and dip into the chocolate straight edge down, then dip straight into the sprinkles.

Set aside on some baking paper for the chocolate to set.

For the batter
130g strong bread flour
80ml coconut milk, room temperature from a tin
3 medium eggs, lightly beaten
7g fast-action yeast
6 tablespoons lukewarm water
½ teaspoon salt
1 teaspoon caster sugar
butter, for greasing

For the chocolate
150g milk chocolate
75g sprinkles

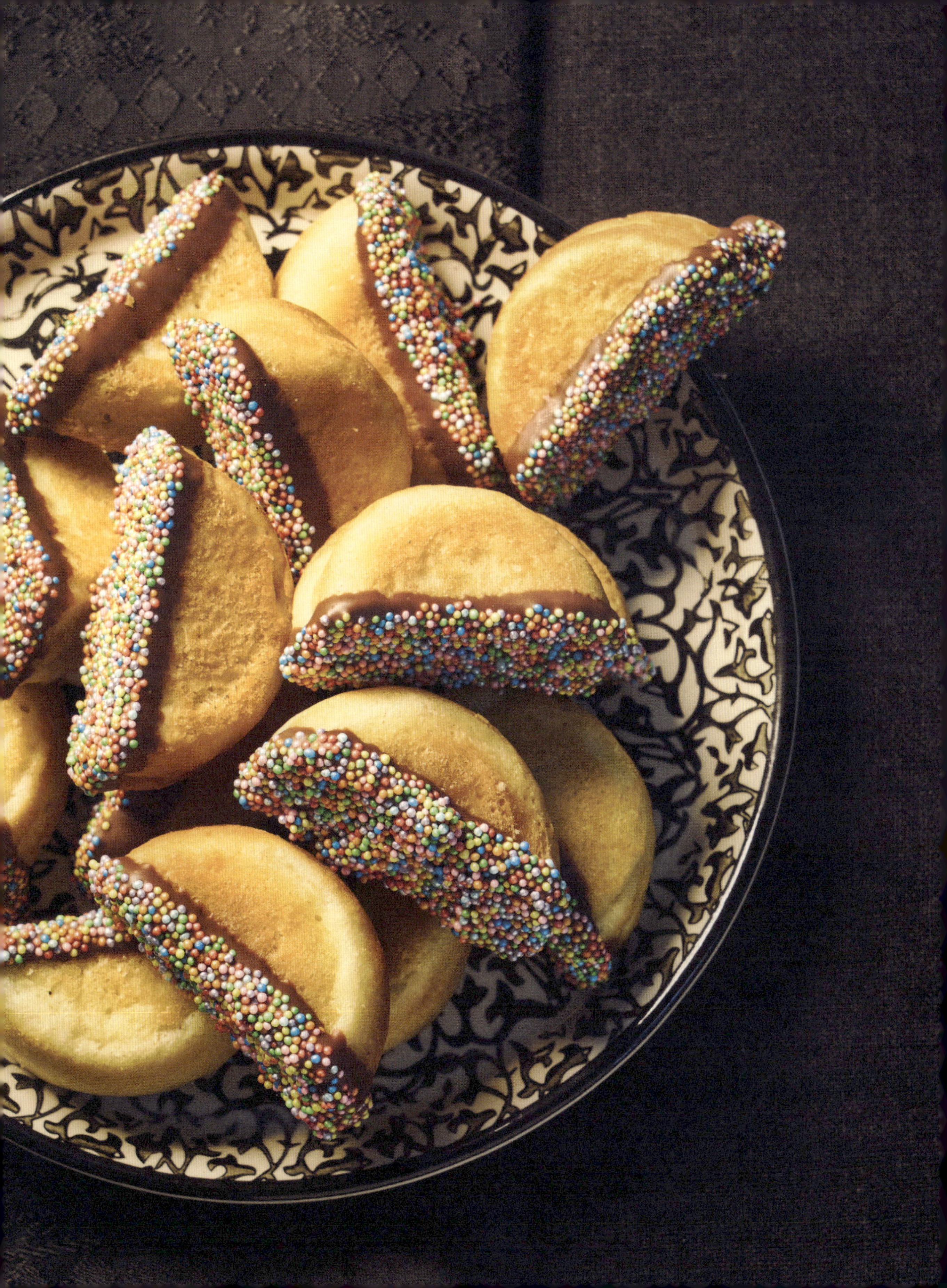

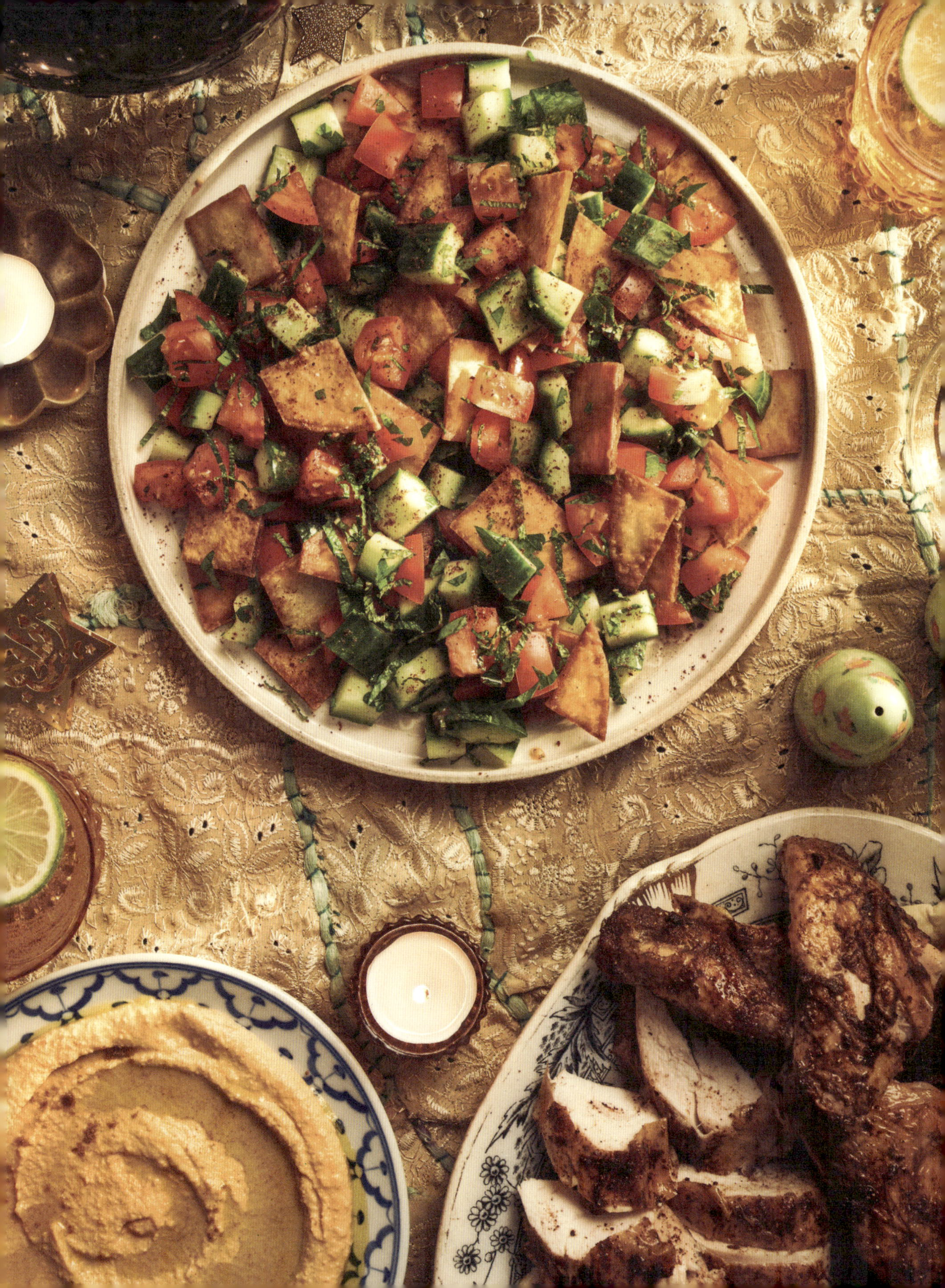

DJEJ MASHWEE
Roast Chicken with Fattoush and Hummus

Syrian food is bursting with flavour and colour, so much so it was hard to pick my favourites. Here we have spicy roasted chicken served with pittas, fattoush and, of course, smooth, creamy hummus.

Preheat the oven to 180°C.

Start by marinating the chicken. Take the whole chicken and pop into a roasting dish. Pour the oil and lemon juice into a bowl and add the garlic, salt and Lebanese 7-spice. Mix and pour over the chicken. Rub the chicken with the seasoned oil, making sure to get under the skin. You can do this step ahead of time and leave the chicken to marinate overnight or cook it straight away.

Roast the chicken in the oven for 75 minutes.

For the fattoush, pour the oil into a frying pan and bring to a medium heat. Have a plate ready lined with some kitchen paper.

Sprinkle in the tortillas in batches and cook till they are golden brown. Drain on the paper and keep doing this till you have fried them all. Sprinkle generously with salt and set to the side.

Put your diced tomatoes in a bowl with the cucumber, parsley and mint and, using your hands, get everything really well mixed.

Make the hummus by putting the drained chickpeas in a blender jug. Add the lemon juice, garlic, cumin, tahini, olive oil, paprika and a sprinkling of salt. Blend till the mixture starts to come together. Drop the ice in and blend till smooth.

Pour the hummus on to a platter and spread out. Drizzle over with some extra olive oil and ground cumin and it is ready to eat.

Add the crisp tortillas to the cucumber and tomato and mix through. Sprinkle over the sumac generously.

Take the chicken out of the oven and leave for 15 minutes before removing the legs, wings and slicing up the breast. Present on a platter. Warm up your pittas and you are ready to devour with the fattoush and hummus.

Serves: 6

For the djej mashwee
1.4kg whole chicken
100ml oil
1 lemon, juice only
8 cloves of garlic, minced
1 teaspoon salt
3 tablespoons Lebanese 7-spice

For the fattoush
oil, for frying
2 large tortillas, cut into small squares
pinch of salt
4 tomatoes, diced
1 cucumber, deseeded and diced
large handful of fresh parsley, thinly sliced
large handful of fresh mint, thinly sliced
sumac, for sprinkling

For the hummus
2 x 400g tins of chickpeas, drained
4 tablespoons lemon juice
3 cloves of garlic
2 teaspoons ground cumin, plus extra for sprinkling
4 tablespoons tahini
8 tablespoons olive oil, plus extra for drizzling
2 teaspoons paprika
salt
2 ice cubes

To serve
6 pittas

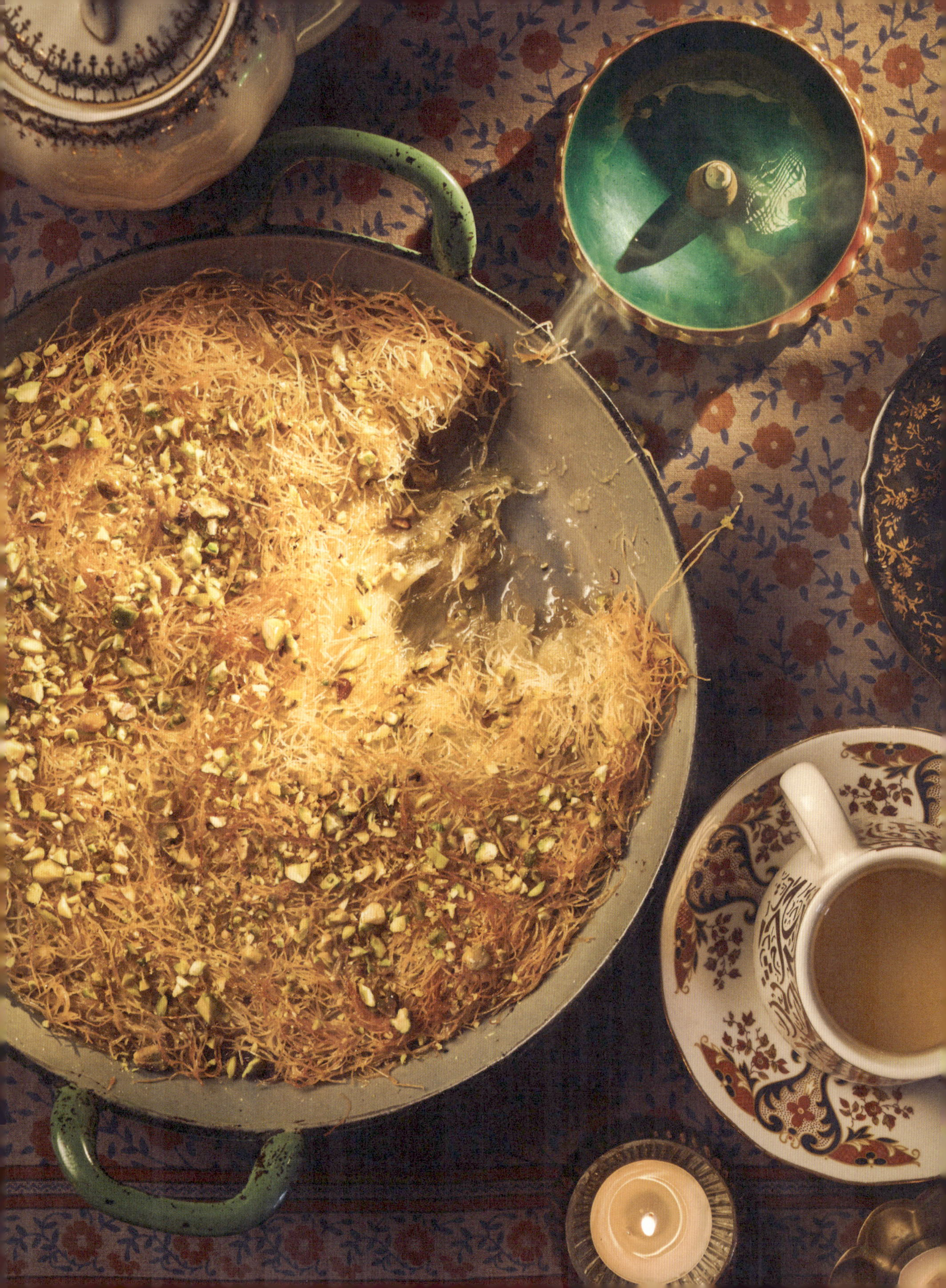

KUNEFE
Sweet Crispy Cheese

I tried this a long time ago and could not believe that there was mozzarella in a dessert, but we better believe it! Crunchy, shredded pastry with a stringy, oozy cheesy filling, all doused in a sweet syrup. It is mind-blowingly good.

Serves: 8

Preheat the oven to 180°C.

Start by putting the kataif pastry in a bowl. Break it up and take it apart, tearing the shredded pastry with your hands. Sprinkle over the melted browned butter and make sure the pastry is coated.

Take a small 20cm round shallow cake tin and arrange half the pastry in the base in an even layer. Sprinkle in your shredded cheese right on top.

Take the rest of the pastry and place on top of the cheese, covering it completely. Bake in the oven for 20 minutes.

Meanwhile, make the syrup by putting the sugar, water and orange blossom water in a pan and bringing to a boil. As soon as it has boiled, reduce and let the syrup simmer on a low heat for 10 minutes.

Take the kunefe out of the oven. Sprinkle over the pistachios and while it's still hot, drizzle the syrup all over. Leave to sit for a few minutes before cutting into eight pieces and serving.

For the kunefe

300g kataif pastry

200g salted butter, melted and browned

250g shredded mozzarella

For the syrup

400g caster sugar

400ml water

4 tablespoons orange blossom water

50g pistachios, roasted and chopped

Bengal

SHUKTO with Luchi
Veg Curry with Crisp Roti

This curry is unique in that the vegetables are fried for extra flavour and cut into large pieces, making for a really great texture in the curry. Traditionally you would use vegetables that are native to the region, but I have gone for veg that we have readily available. These are gorgeous eaten with the fried luchi.

Serves: 6

Let's start by making the luchi dough. Put the flour in a bowl with the salt and oil and use your hands to mix through. Make a well in the centre and pour in the water. Use a spatula to start mixing the water in with the flour and then eventually get your hands in and bring the dough together. Tip the dough out and knead till the dough is smooth and shiny. Cover with a damp tea towel and leave to rest for 30 minutes while you make the shukto.

Add the courgette, aubergine, plantain, sweet potato, radishes and beans to a large non-stick frying pan. Drizzle in the oil and mix. Start to fry to get as much colour on them as possible. Keep frying and turning till they are just browned. Take off the heat and set aside.

Put the mustard oil and ghee in a large non-stick pan and heat. As soon as they are hot, add the poppy seeds, mustard seeds and Bengali five spice and as soon as the whole spices start to pop, add the ginger and turmeric and cook very gently with the salt.

Now add all the vegetables and mix through. Pour in the water, bring the whole thing to the boil then leave to simmer, pour in the cream and leave for 35-45 minutes on a medium heat.

Now back to the luchi. Divide the dough into 12 equal balls. Bring a frying pan with about 5cm of oil to a medium heat. Have a colander at the ready, with a plate underneath.

Roll out the dough balls to about 15cm each. Gently drop one in and let it fry and puff up. Cook for 3 minutes on one side and 3 minutes on the other. Drain upright in the colander. Continue till you have fried them all.

Take the shukto off the heat and you are ready to enjoy.

For the luchi

600g plain flour
1 tablespoon salt
6 tablespoons oil
300ml hot tap water
oil, for frying

For the shukto

3 courgettes, quartered lengthways and halved down the middle
1 large aubergine, cut into 8 wedges, wedges halved
1 large green plantain, peeled and cut into 2cm coins
2 sweet potatoes, peeled and cut into 8 wedges, wedges halved
200g red radishes
200g green beans, topped, tailed and halved
150ml oil
4 tablespoons mustard oil
1 tablespoon ghee
1 tablespoon poppy seeds
2 tablespoons mustard seeds
1 teaspoon Bengali five spice
2 tablespoons ginger paste
1 teaspoon ground turmeric
2 teaspoons salt
1 litre cold water
300ml double cream

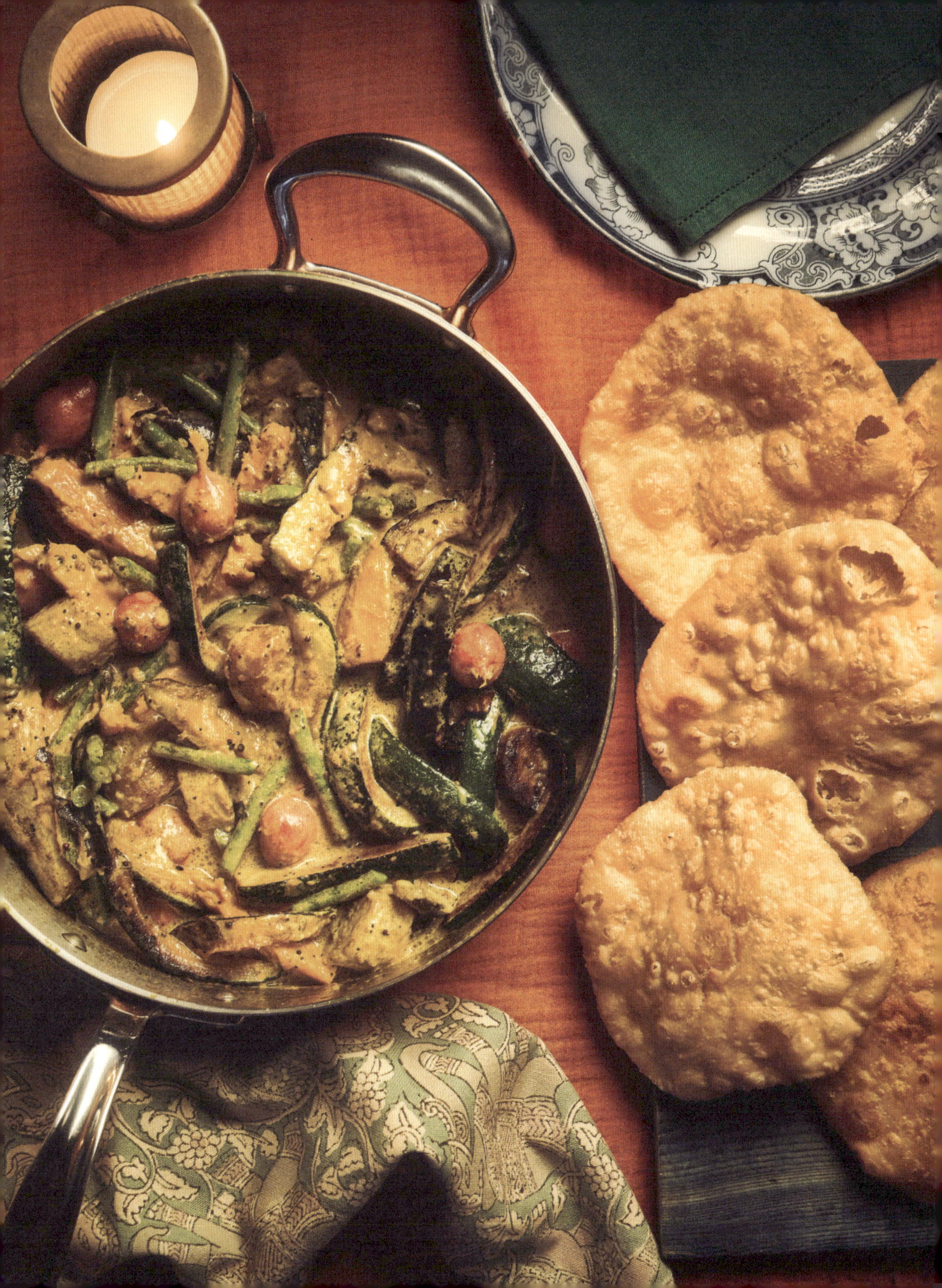

SONDESH
Fudge

These sweet sondesh are traditional and are worth making as a treat to enjoy or to give away. They are sweet and creamy and perfect with a tea.

Makes: 6

Start by heating the milk in a large pan. As soon as the milk has bubbled once, take if off the heat, add the lemon juice and mix through. You should see the curds separate from the whey.

Leave to sit for 10 minutes.

Strain through a colander lined with muslin. Leave to hang and drain for 2 hours. Put in a bowl with the icing sugar and mix through.

Place a non-stick frying pan on the hob and add the curds to cook, stirring all the time, till the mixture starts to leave the sides of the pan.

Remove from the heat, spoon on to a tray and leave to cool till warm enough to handle. Divide into 6 equal balls.

Flatten the balls slightly and press an almond into each one. Leave in the fridge for 1 hour before they are ready to eat.

1 litre whole milk
5 tablespoons lemon juice
100g icing sugar
whole almonds, to decorate

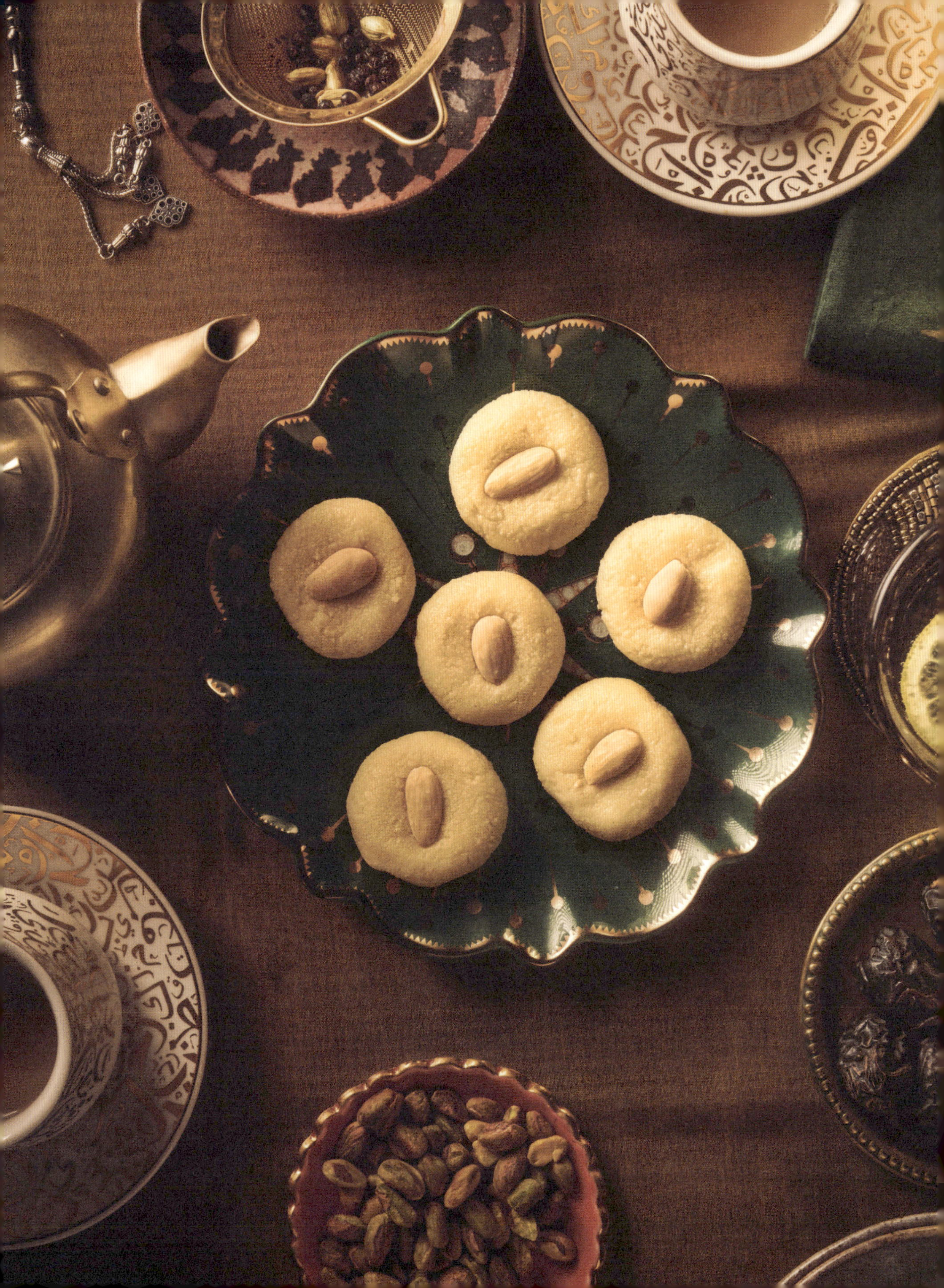

JOLLOF RICE, EGG STEW, FRIED PLANTAINS AND SLAW

I love jollof rice and there are so many recipes, variations and different ways of making it. Here, I have taken all the elements I love. Aromatic, tomatoey and subtly hot in spice, it's perfect with the fried plantain, egg stew and slaw.

Let's start by making the jollof rice. Pour the oil into a large non-stick pan and heat over a medium to high heat. Add the onions and salt and cook till golden brown and the onions are really soft. Now add the tomato paste along with the garlic and ginger pastes and mix through.

Pop the red pepper and Scotch bonnet into a food processor and blitz, then add to the onion mix and start to cook through. Now add in the dried thyme, curry powder and white pepper. Add a splash of water and cook the spices for a few minutes till you are left with a very dry base mix.

Wash the basmati till the water is crystal clear, then drain the rice. Add the rice into the spice mix over a high heat. Pour in the hot chicken stock and bring to the boil. As soon as all the rice grains are visible and the stock has evaporated, lower the heat, put the lid on and leave to steam for 20 minutes.

Let's make the egg stew. Put the tomatoes, red pepper and Scotch bonnet in a blender, blitz and set to one side.

To a non-stick frying pan add a good glug of oil. Heat the oil, add the minced garlic and cook for a few minutes till golden. Add in the onion with the salt and cook till soft. Add the pepper paste with the curry powder and thyme and cook till you have a very dry mix.

Now add your eggs and gently cook them, mixing all the time till they are velvet smooth and just cooked through.

For the slaw, put the cabbage in a bowl with the carrot, red onion and pineapple and mix everything really well. Pour in the apple cider vinegar and mix through, then add the mayo and salt and mix to bring your creamy slaw together.

Serves: 6

For the jollof rice

200ml oil
2 onions, diced
2 teaspoons salt
3 tablespoons tomato paste
3 tablespoons garlic paste
3 tablespoons ginger paste
1 red pepper, roughly chopped
1 red Scotch bonnet chilli
2 teaspoons dried thyme
2 tablespoons curry powder
1 teaspoon white pepper
splash of water
600g basmati rice
600ml hot chicken stock

For the egg stew

2 tomatoes, halved
1 red pepper, roughly chopped
1 Scotch bonnet chilli
oil, for frying
3 cloves of garlic, minced
1 onion, diced
1 teaspoon salt
2 teaspoons curry powder
1 teaspoon dried thyme
12 eggs, lightly beaten

For the slaw

½ cabbage, shredded
1 carrot, grated
1 red onion, thinly sliced
432g tin of pineapple chunks, drained, moisture removed and finely chopped

Now simply fry the plantain. Pour a splash of oil into the frying pan, get your plantains in and fry till golden on both sides and tender in the middle.

Take the rice off the hob, fluff it up and it is all ready to serve with the egg stew, fried plantains and slaw.

2 tablespoons apple cider vinegar

6 tablespoons full-fat mayonnaise

pinch of salt

For the plantains

oil, for frying

3 large plantains, peeled and cut into 1cm coins

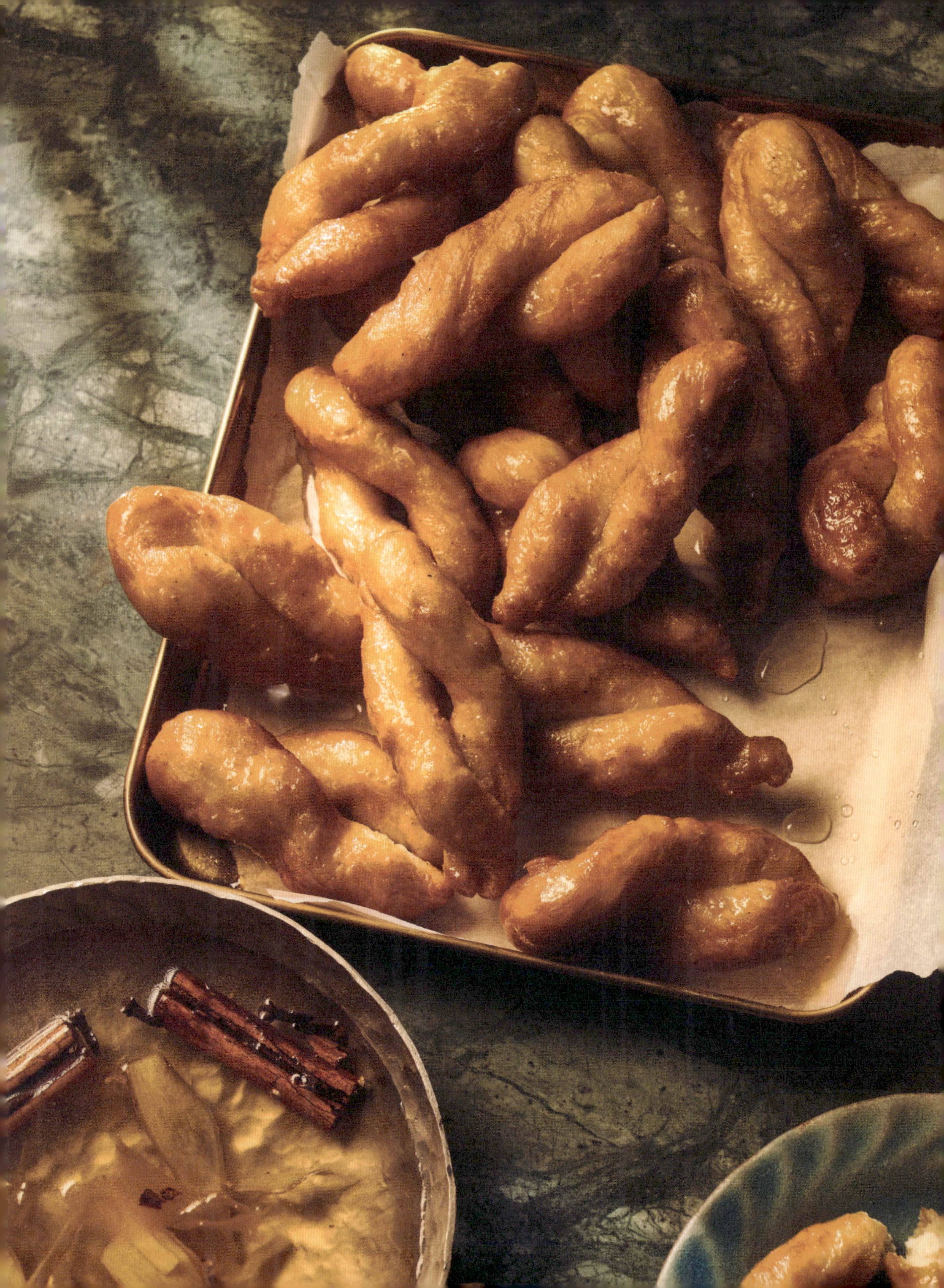

West & South Africa

KOEKSISTERS
Spiced Syrupy Doughnuts

I had these a very long time ago when I visited South Africa and I must say that the complex, syrupy taste stayed with me long enough to try and make them myself.

Start by making the syrup. To a large pan add the sugar, cold water, golden syrup, ginger, cinnamon sticks, cloves, lemon juice and peelings and the cream of tartar. Mix everything really well. Pop on to a high heat, bring the mixture to a boil and then leave to simmer for 15 minutes till thicker. Ideally make this in advance, then cool and chill in the fridge so all the flavours can infuse.

Make the dough by putting the self-raising flour in a bowl with a pinch of salt, nutmeg and baking powder. Mix it so everything is combined. Throw in the cold butter and use your fingers to rub the butter in till there are no hard lumps left.

Make a well in the centre and pour the buttermilk in, using a palette knife to bring it together. Then get your hands in and knead just till you have no soft spots and the dough is smooth. Cover with a damp tea towel and leave to rest for about 15 minutes.

After 15 minutes, uncover and divide the dough into 25 dough balls that roughly weigh 40g each. Have a tray ready with a damp tea towel at hand.

Take each dough ball and roll it out into a sausage about 20cm long. Fold in half and twist together, pinching the ends slightly. Place on the tray, cover and repeat to make all 25.

Take the syrup out of the fridge.

Pop a pan on to the hob over a high heat and fill with oil about two-thirds of the way up. Heat the oil to 160°C and start to fry the koeksisters gently on a medium heat for about 4 minutes on each side till golden all over.

Take out and while hot, add to the cold syrup and leave in the syrup for a minute, making sure to turn halfway, before popping on to a cooling rack to drain off any excess syrup. Repeat with all of them and then they are ready to enjoy.

Makes: 25 koeksisters

For the syrup

1kg caster sugar
800ml cold water
4 tablespoons golden syrup
8cm piece of peeled ginger, thinly sliced
2 large cinnamon sticks
10 cloves
1 lemon, juice and peelings
1 teaspoon cream of tartar

For the dough

600g self-raising flour
pinch of salt
½ teaspoon ground nutmeg
2 teaspoons baking powder
50g butter, chilled and cubed
375ml buttermilk

South Asia

SALMON BIRYANI
with Dahl

Biryani is a South Asian staple and I love to vary it up and use fish where I can. Salmon biryani is perfect because the salmon doesn't dry out as it sits beneath the layer of rice. Served with a simple dhal, it is a complete meal.

Start with the onions for the biryani. Into the pan that you are going to make your biryani, add the oil and ghee and heat on a high heat. As soon as the oil is hot, add the onions, separating the slices with your hands as you throw them in. Fry on a high heat till they are crispy and golden.

Line a plate with some kitchen paper and drain the onions with a slotted spoon on to the paper. Sprinkle with salt and set to the side.

Now for the salmon. Keep the same pan over a medium heat and add the onions with the salt and cook for a few minutes till the onions are golden brown and very soft. Add the ginger paste and tomatoes and cook for another few minutes. Get the turmeric, chilli powder and curry powder in and cook for a few minutes. Pour in the water and cook the spices for 5 minutes till the mixture is dry and not watery. Using a stick blender, blend the sauce to a smooth paste.

Add the salmon pieces and mix through. Cook with the lid on for 10 minutes and then move the pan to the side off the heat.

For the rice, put the basmati in a really large pan that can hold lots of water. We need the rice to have room to boil and move around in the pan. Pour in the cold water and salt, along with the cardamom pods, sticks of cinnamon, bay leaves and star anise. Pop on to the hob and bring to the boil and as soon as it boils, time the rice to boil for just 5 minutes.

When the time is up, take off the heat and drain quickly, keeping in all the aromatics. Run under cold water and cool straight away, setting aside to drain.

Serves: 6

For the onions
100ml oil
100g ghee
3 onions, finely sliced
salt

For the salmon
2 onions, finely diced
1 tablespoon salt
4 tablespoons ginger paste
6 tomatoes, chopped
1 teaspoon ground turmeric
3 teaspoons chilli powder
5 teaspoons curry powder
100ml water
500g salmon fillet joint, cut into 5cm chunks

For the rice
600g basmati rice
cold water
1 tablespoon salt
6 cardamom pods
2 cinnamon sticks
4 bay leaves
3 star anise

For the dhal
200g red split lentils, washed and soaked overnight
1 litre cold water
1 bay leaf
1 teaspoon ground turmeric
1 teaspoon salt

➜

Spoon the rice on to the salmon mix and be sure not to pat down as the rice needs room to fluff up. Sprinkle over the onions, place a tea towel on top, put the lid on and place the pan on the lowest heat. Leave to steam for 30 minutes.

Meanwhile, make the dhal by putting the lentils in a pan with the cold water, bay leaf, turmeric and salt. Bring the mixture to the boil and leave to simmer for 30 minutes, making sure to give it a whisk occasionally.

To make the tarka, pop the unsalted butter into a frying pan and heat till melted. As soon as the butter is hot, add the garlic and chilli and as soon as the garlic is golden, pour all over the lentils and mix through. Leave to simmer for another 10 minutes.

Take the biryani off the heat, sprinkle over the split chillies and some coriander and, using two large spoons, mix the biryani in the pan to bring it all together.

Take the dhal off the heat, add a final flourish of coriander and serve with the biryani.

For the tarka

100g unsalted butter
5 cloves of garlic, sliced
1 large dried red chilli

To finish

6 green chillies, split lengthways
small handful of fresh coriander, chopped

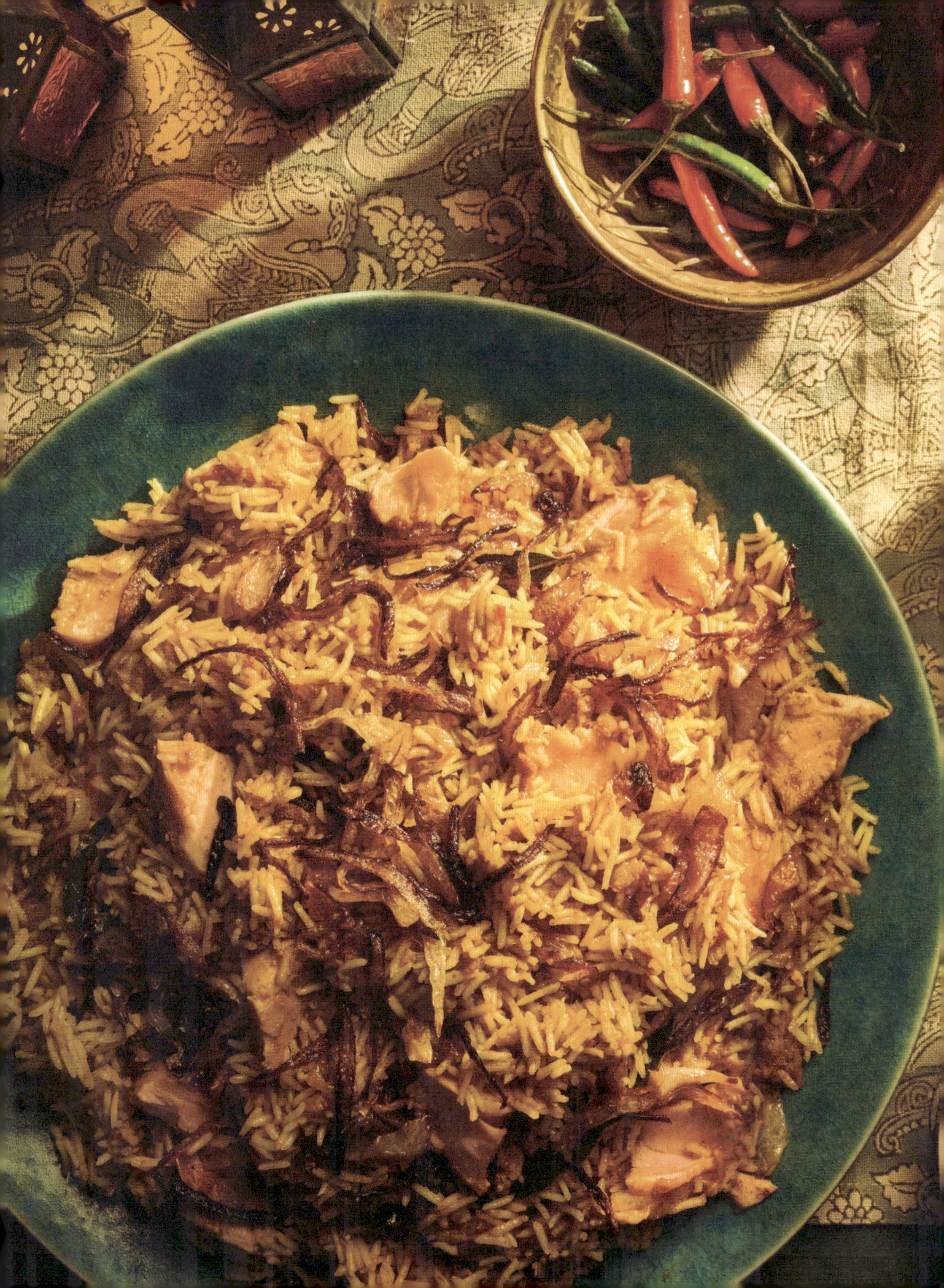

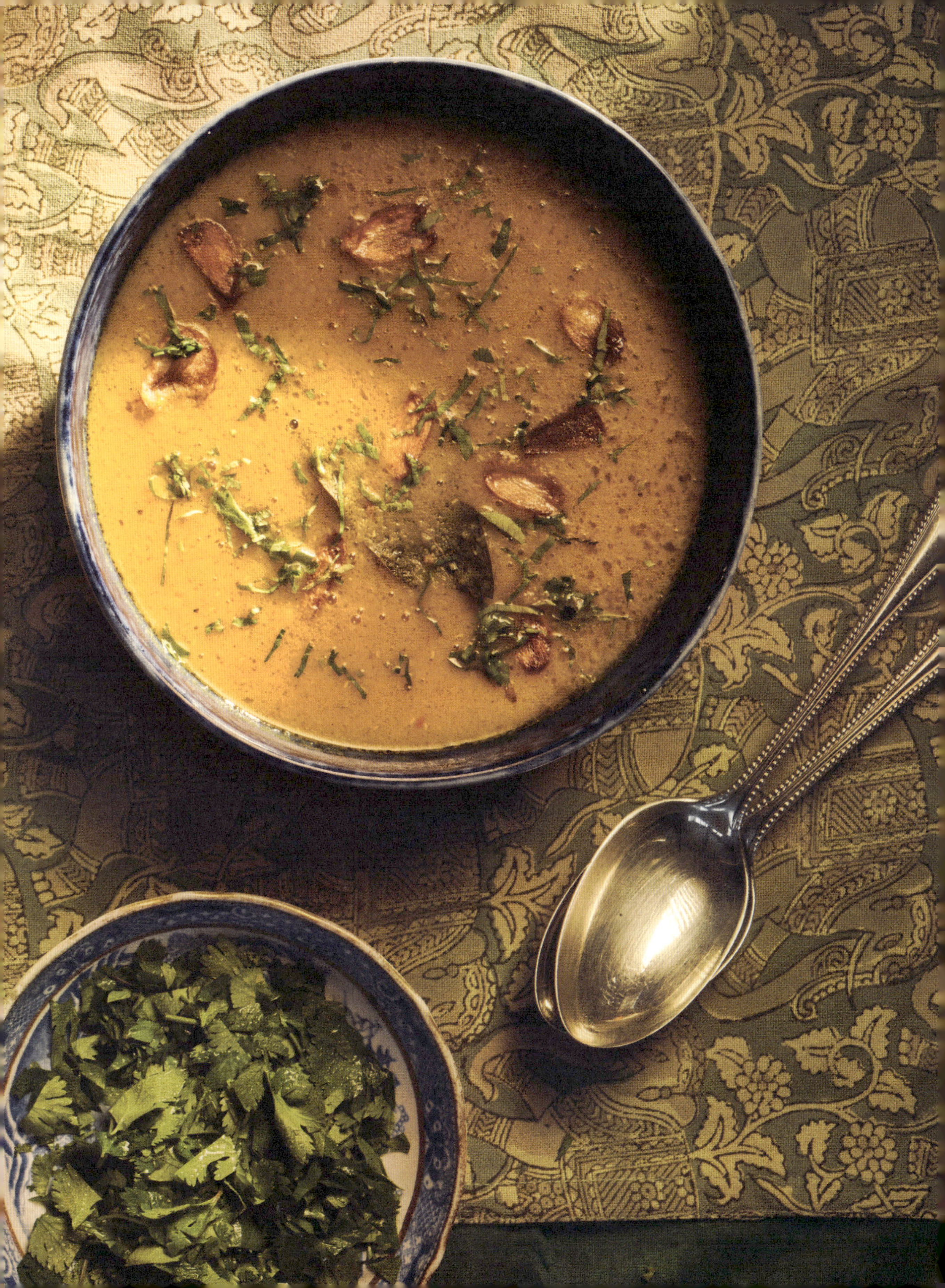

South Asia

GULAB JAMUN

These milky cake balls are deep-fried and then, while hot, dunked into a hot saffron syrup. This has to be one of the most popular desserts to buy at Indian sweet shops and now you can make it at home – and it's super easy. We love these warm with a dollop of ice cream.

Makes: 16 balls

500g caster sugar
500ml cold water
6 cardamom pods, smashed to open slightly
few strands of saffron

For the balls
100g full-fat milk powder
40g strong bread flour
½ teaspoon baking powder
50g ghee
1 tablespoon yoghurt
4–5 tablespoons whole milk
oil, for frying

Start by making the syrup. Put the caster sugar in a large pan with the cold water and give the water and sugar a mix. Throw in the cardamom pods and saffron. Place over a high heat, bring to the boil, leave to simmer for 10 minutes and then set aside.

Make the balls by putting the milk powder in a bowl with the flour and baking powder. Mix it through with your hands to combine. Add the ghee and crumble into the mixture till it has disappeared.

Now add the yoghurt and milk, a spoon at a time, mixing to create a dough that holds its shape. Roll out 16 equal-sized balls, making sure that they are tightly packed with no cracks.

Pop a pan on the hob with oil two-thirds of the way up and heat the oil to 150°C. Have a plate ready, lined with kitchen paper.

Add the balls to the oil in batches and fry for about 7 minutes till a deep golden brown, then drain.

Add the balls into the syrup, mix through and leave to soak for 3 hours in the fridge or overnight. These are best served warm with a dollop of ice cream.

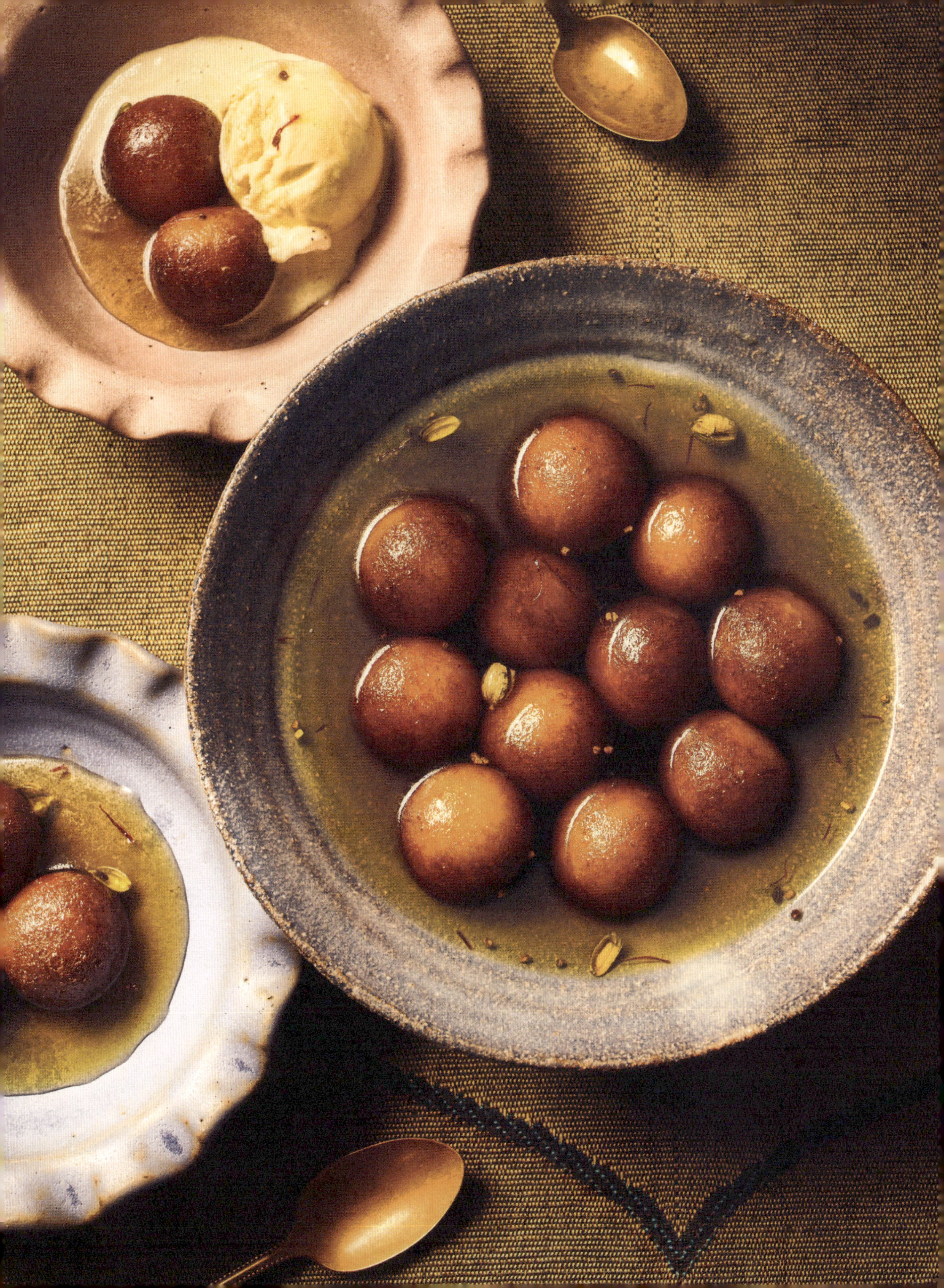

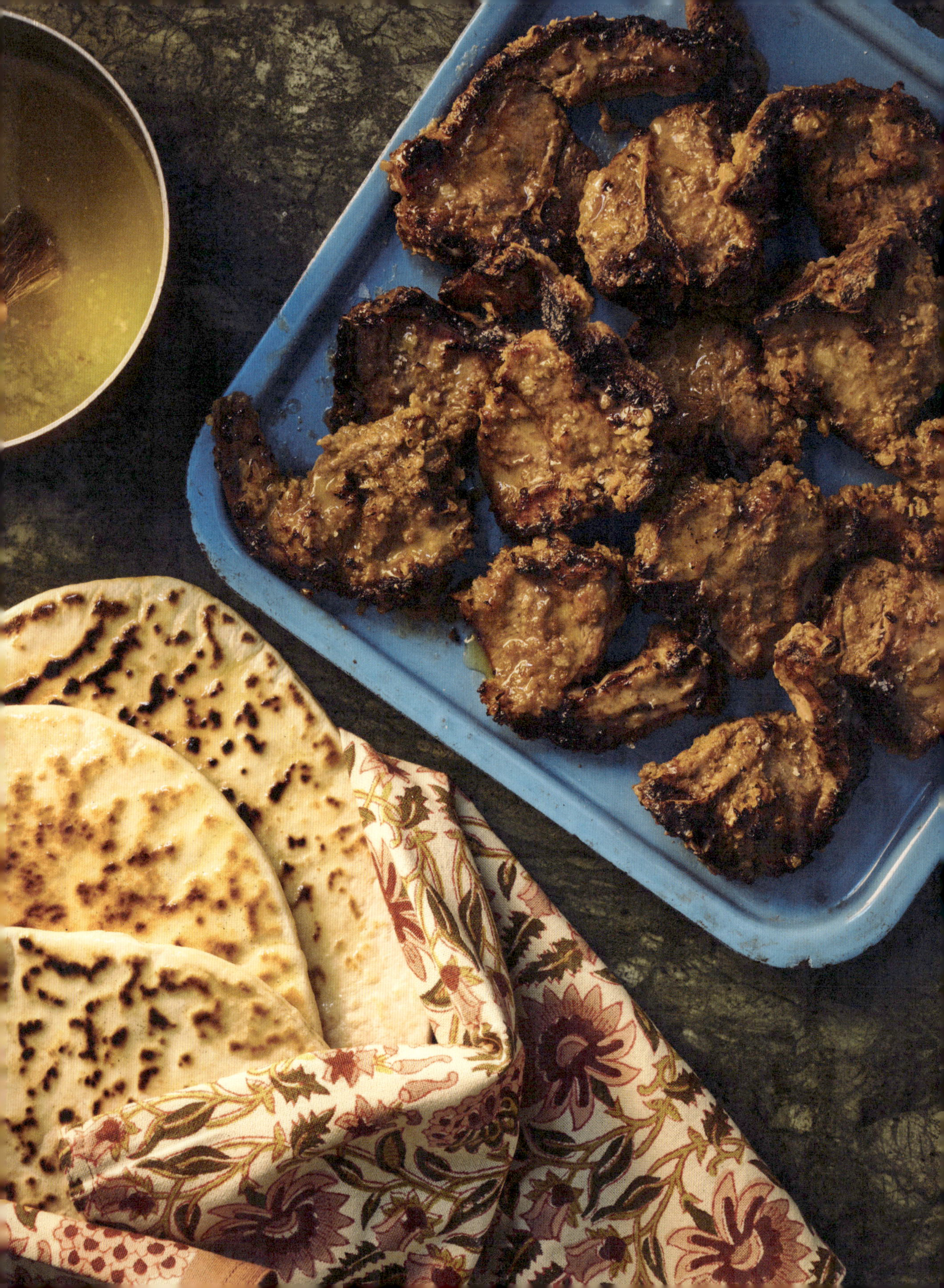

Pakistan

LAMB CHOPS
with Naan

I grew up around Pakistani families and we were used to eating plates of food that would come our way over the fence just before sunset. Often it was delicious naan, so I have a great recipe. To go with them here are my simple lamb chops, which are flavourful and tender.

Serves: 6

First take the lamb chops and use a meat hammer to gently hammer out the flesh of the chops so they are thinner. Set them aside on a large tray.

Pour the oil into a medium bowl along with the salt, onion, garlic and ginger pastes, the coriander and cumin seeds, the garam masala and the chilli powder. Give the whole thing a good mix and then smother all over the chops. Make sure every bit is covered. This lends itself to being marinated overnight but can equally be done on the day. Set aside and make the naan dough.

For the naan, put the plain flour in a bowl with the sugar, salt and baking powder and use your hands to combine. Make a well in the centre, pour in the milk and bring the dough together, kneading till you have a smooth dough. Leave to rest for 15 minutes, covered under a damp tea towel.

After 15 minutes, divide the mixture so that you have six equal balls of dough. Roll out to about 3mm thin.

Pop a non-stick pan on the hob over a medium to low heat and dry-fry a piece of dough for 3 minutes on each side, till they are puffy and light. Take off the pan, brush both sides with the melted butter and make the other five.

Put the grill on a high heat and grill the lamb chops in one layer for 5 minutes. Take them out, turn them over and grill for another 5 minutes.

Take the lamb out and serve alongside the warm naan.

For the chops
2kg lamb chops
250ml oil
2 tablespoons salt
3 onions, puréed
3 tablespoons garlic paste
3 tablespoons ginger paste
3 teaspoons coriander seeds, toasted and crushed
3 teaspoons cumin seeds, toasted and crushed
4 tablespoons garam masala
2 tablespoons chilli powder

For the naan
600g plain flour
2 teaspoons sugar
1 teaspoon salt
1½ teaspoons baking powder
360ml whole milk
melted butter, for brushing

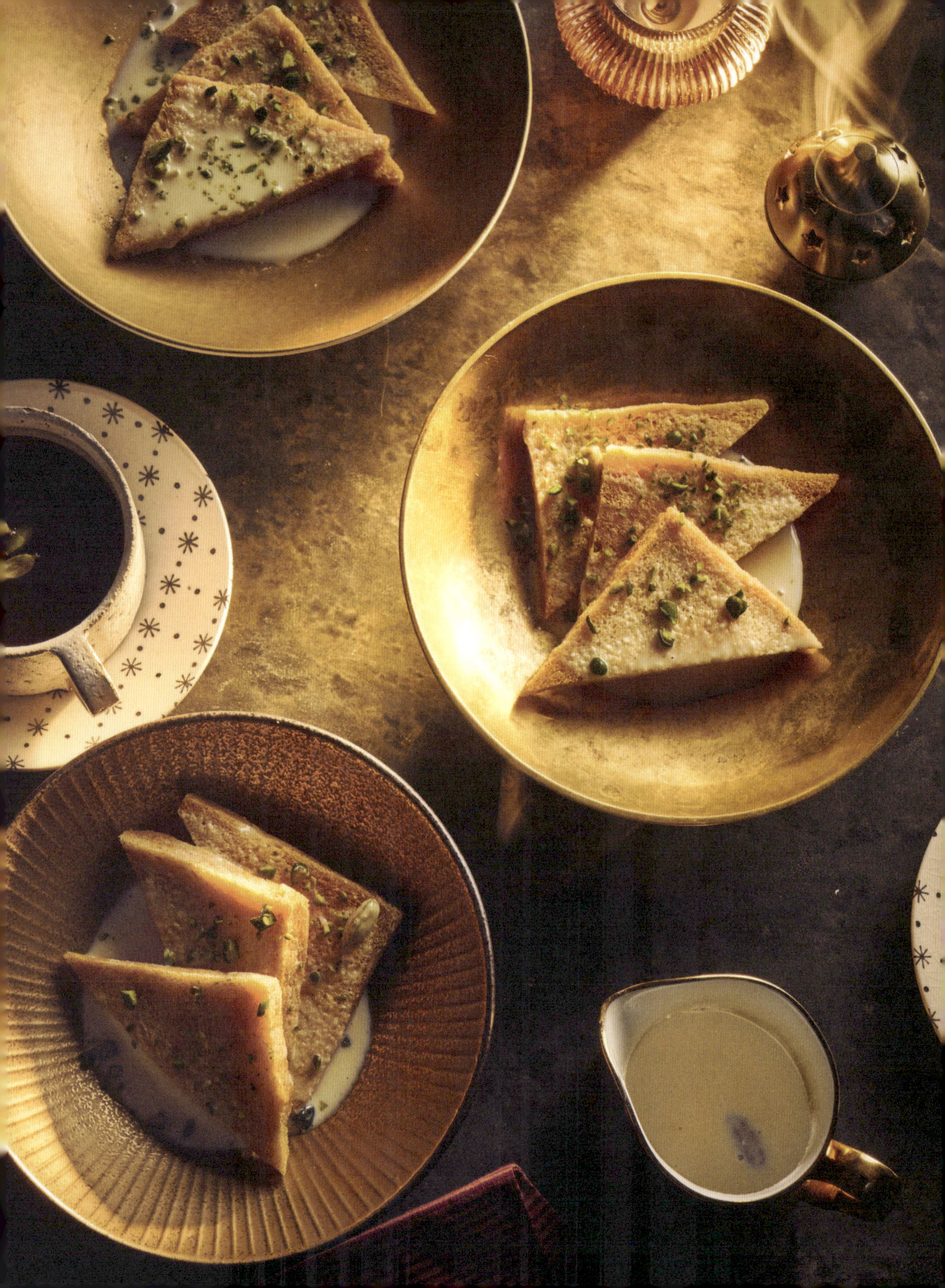

SHAHI TUKRA

Bread fried in ghee and then soaked in a cardamom and saffron milk.

Serves: 6

Start by cutting the crusts off the bread and then cut each slice into two triangles. Repeat with all the bread and then generously butter both sides with the ghee and set the triangles on a large baking tray in an even layer.

Pour the condensed milk into a pan with the whole milk, cardamom pods and saffron. Bring to a boil and then leave to simmer till just a little thicker and reduced by a quarter.

Preheat the oven to 180°C.

Pop the tray of bread into the oven and allow the slices of bread to bake till golden – this will take about 10-15 minutes – and be sure to turn the slices over so they crisp up on both sides.

Take the bread out of the oven, arrange three on each plate, pour over some of that sweet milk, sprinkle over the pistachios and it is ready to enjoy.

9 slices of white bread
180g ghee
397g tin of condensed milk
500ml whole milk
4 cardamom pods, crushed
few strands of saffron
50g pistachios, toasted and roughly chopped

Yemen

MUTTON MANDI
with Carrot Rice and Zhug

Serves: 6

These ribs are full of delicious fat and flavour, just what you need after a whole day of fasting. Served with the carrot rice, it needs the zesty zhug to finish the dish off. Everything about this is balanced and bountiful.

For the mutton, start by pouring the oil into a pan with the cinnamon sticks and onions. Cook the onions with the salt till they are a light golden brown. To the pan add the green chilli paste, garlic paste, ginger paste, cumin seeds, ground cumin, ground black pepper, garam masala and chilli flakes and mix them in with the onion.

Add the ribs now, mix through and cook the meat till golden all over. Pour in the water, bring to the boil and boil for 10 minutes, then pop the lid on and simmer for 1 hour 30 minutes.

Make the carrot rice by putting the salted butter in a medium non-stick pan. As soon as the butter has melted, in go the cardamom pods, stick of cinnamon and cloves. As soon as they begin to sizzle, add the onion and salt and cook till the onion is soft. Get the carrots in and cook over a high heat for a few minutes, then reduce the heat and pop the lid on to allow the carrot to cook through for 10 minutes.

Wash the basmati till the water is crystal clear, then drain the rice. Take the lid off the carrots, add the rice, mix in and cook for 3 minutes over a high heat. Pour in the boiling water and bring the whole mixture to a boil till the water has mostly evaporated. Put the lid on, lower the heat and steam for 15 minutes.

Make the zhug by putting the coriander, parsley, green chillies, black pepper, cumin seeds, coriander seeds, garlic and lemon juice in a food processor and blending till you have a roughly chopped mixture. Take out and decant into a bowl. Pour the oil over the mixture and stir through.

Take the mutton off the heat and make sure it is tender. Remove the rice from the heat and fluff it all up. Serve everything with the zhug on the side.

For the mutton

100ml oil
2 large cinnamon sticks
2 onions, blended to a purée
1 tablespoon salt
3 tablespoons green chilli paste
2 tablespoons garlic paste
2 tablespoons ginger paste
1 tablespoon cumin seeds
1 tablespoon ground cumin
2 tablespoons ground black pepper
2 tablespoons garam masala
2 tablespoons chilli flakes
1.5kg mutton ribs
500ml water

For the carrot rice

150g salted butter
3 cardamom pods
1 cinnamon stick
4 cloves
1 onion, diced
1 tablespoon salt
3 carrots, grated
600g basmati rice
600ml boiling water

For the zhug

large handful of fresh coriander
large handful of fresh parsley
4 green chillies
1 teaspoon ground black pepper
1 teaspoon cumin seeds
1 teaspoon coriander seeds
3 cloves of garlic, peeled
1 lemon, juice only
250ml olive oil

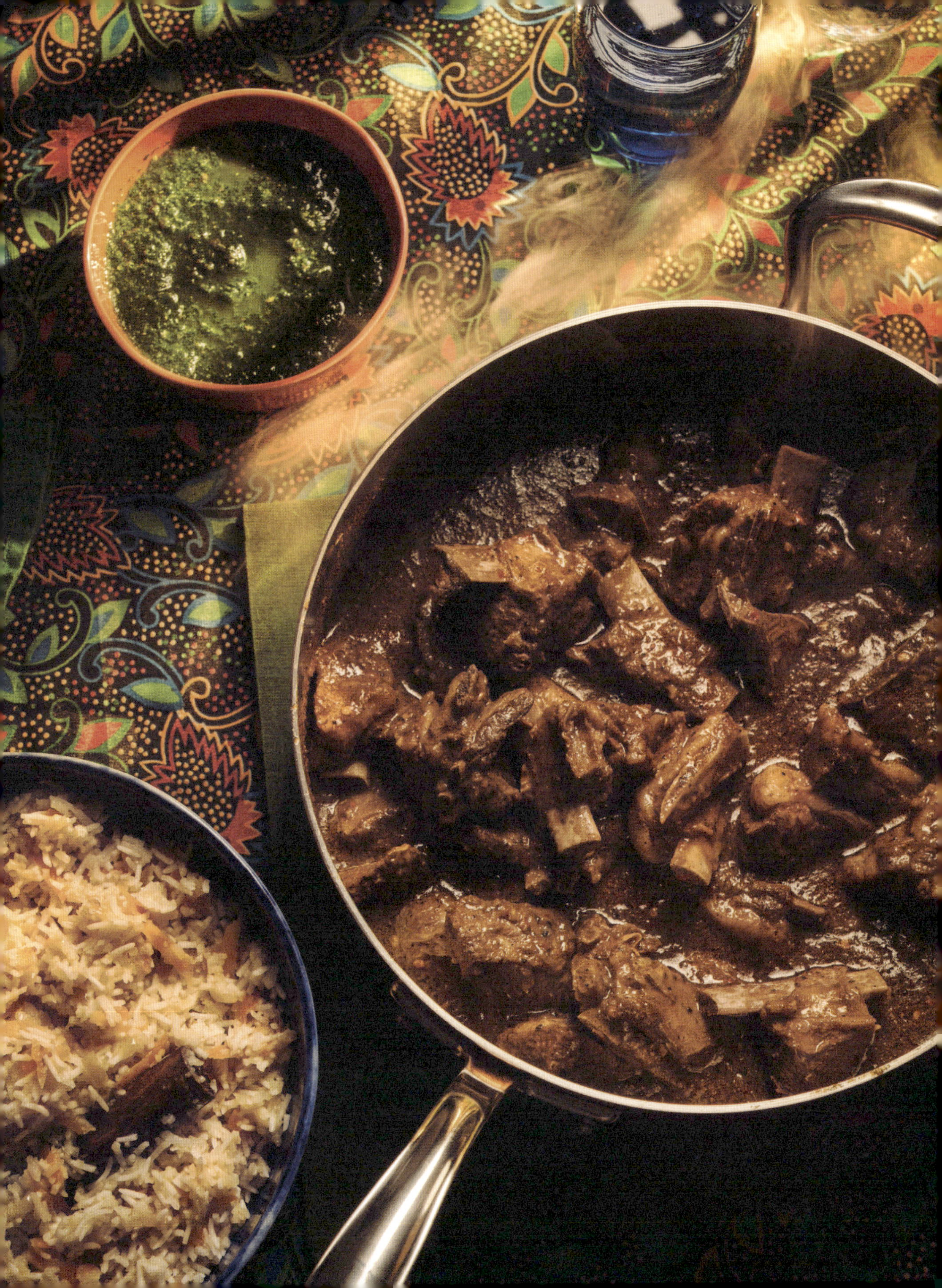

Yemen

KHALIAT NAHAL
Sweet Cream-cheese-filled Doughballs

If you like salty and sweet, you will love these sweet buns filled with cream cheese and finished with a brushing of salty sesame egg yolk wash and a sweet glaze.

Makes: 13 balls

Start by making the dough. Put the strong bread flour in a bowl with the salt, caster sugar and yeast. Use your hands to combine the dry ingredients.

Add the softened butter to the dry mix and, using your fingertips, rub the butter in till you have no more lumps of butter. Make a well in the centre and add the egg along with the lukewarm milk, using your hands to bring it together. Knead the dough on a lightly floured surface till it is stretchy and pliable. Cover and leave in a warm spot till the dough has doubled in size.

Make the filling by putting the cream cheese in a bowl with the sugar and flour. Mix together and pop into the fridge.

Once the dough has doubled, knock it back and make 13 dough balls. Each dough ball should be around 72g in weight.

Line and grease a baking tray and set to the side.

Flatten each dough ball, roll it out to about 10cm and fill with 1 teaspoon of the cream cheese mixture. Encase the filling with the dough and pop on to the baking tray. I like to arrange these to form a circle. Do the same with the rest and be sure to leave some space between them to give them room to grow.

Cover with greased clingfilm and leave to prove for another hour in a warm place. You will know they are ready when you poke them and the indentation comes up very slowly and remains.

Preheat the oven to 180°C.

Make up the egg wash by putting the egg in a bowl with the teaspoon of cold water and the salt. Brush the tops of the buns generously all over. Sprinkle over the sesame seeds and bake for 25 minutes.

While the buns bake, make the glaze by adding the sugar to the

For the dough
500g strong bread flour
½ teaspoon salt
50g caster sugar
14g fast-action yeast
100g salted butter, softened
1 medium egg, lightly beaten
240ml lukewarm whole milk

For the filling
125g full-fat cream cheese
20g caster sugar
1 teaspoon plain flour

For the egg wash
1 egg yolk
1 teaspoon cold water
pinch of salt
sesame seeds, for sprinkling

For the glaze
50g caster sugar
25ml cold water
big pinch of saffron

water in a small pan along with the saffron. Mix well, then bring to the boil and leave to simmer for just 10 minutes or so.

As soon as the buns come out of the oven, brush on the delicious sweet glaze. Leave to cool for 30 minutes before lifting out of the tin and enjoying.

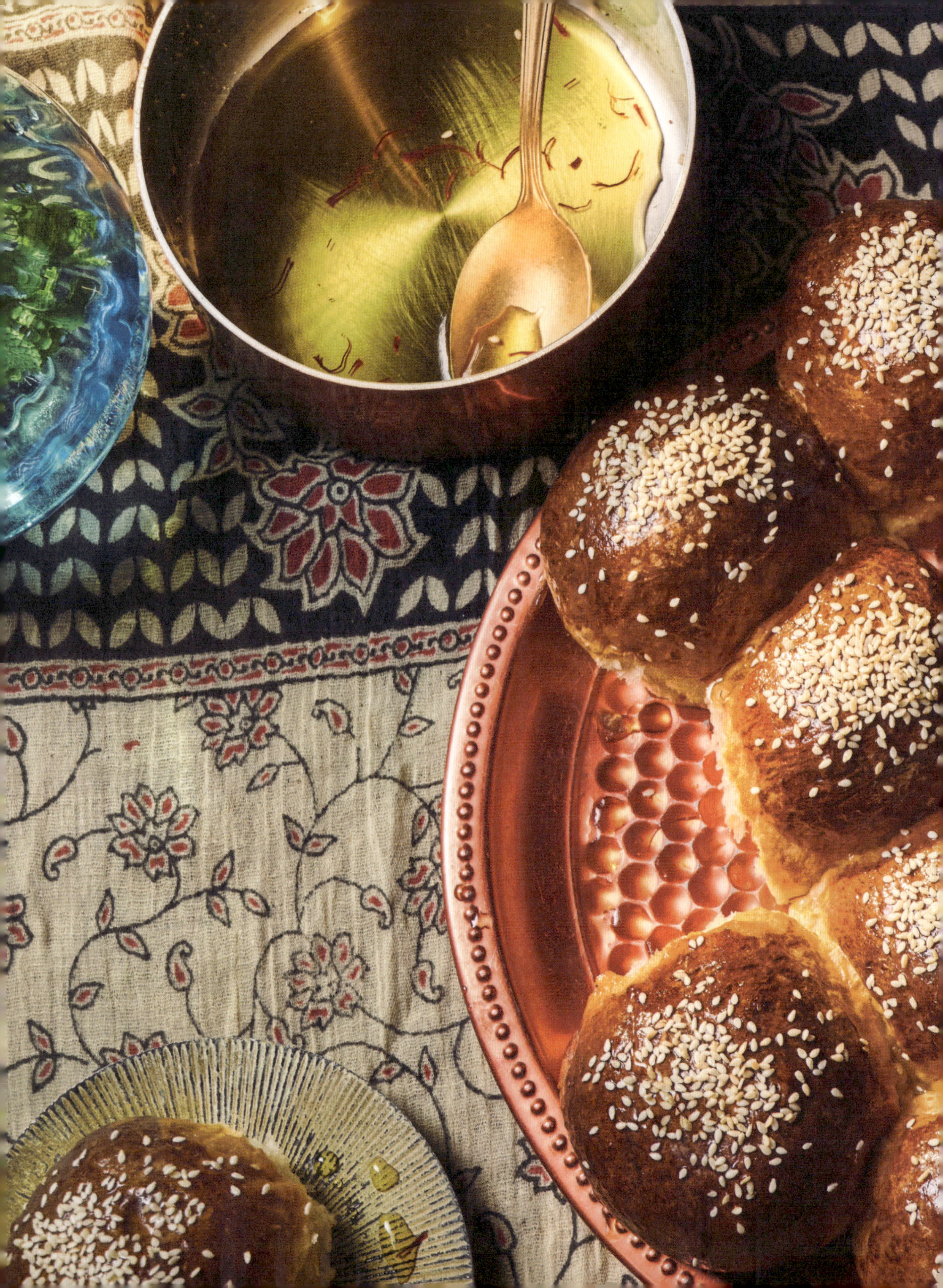

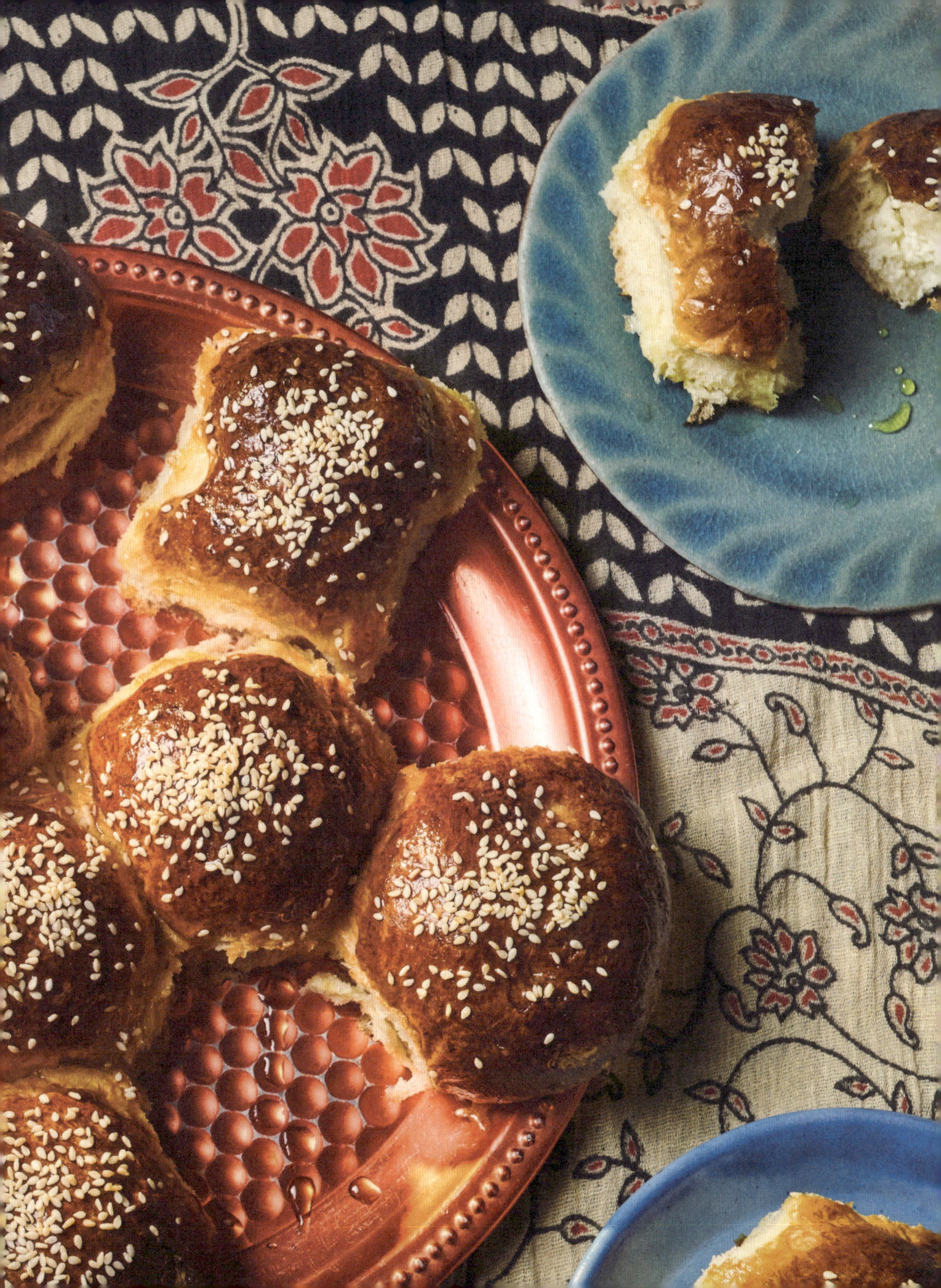

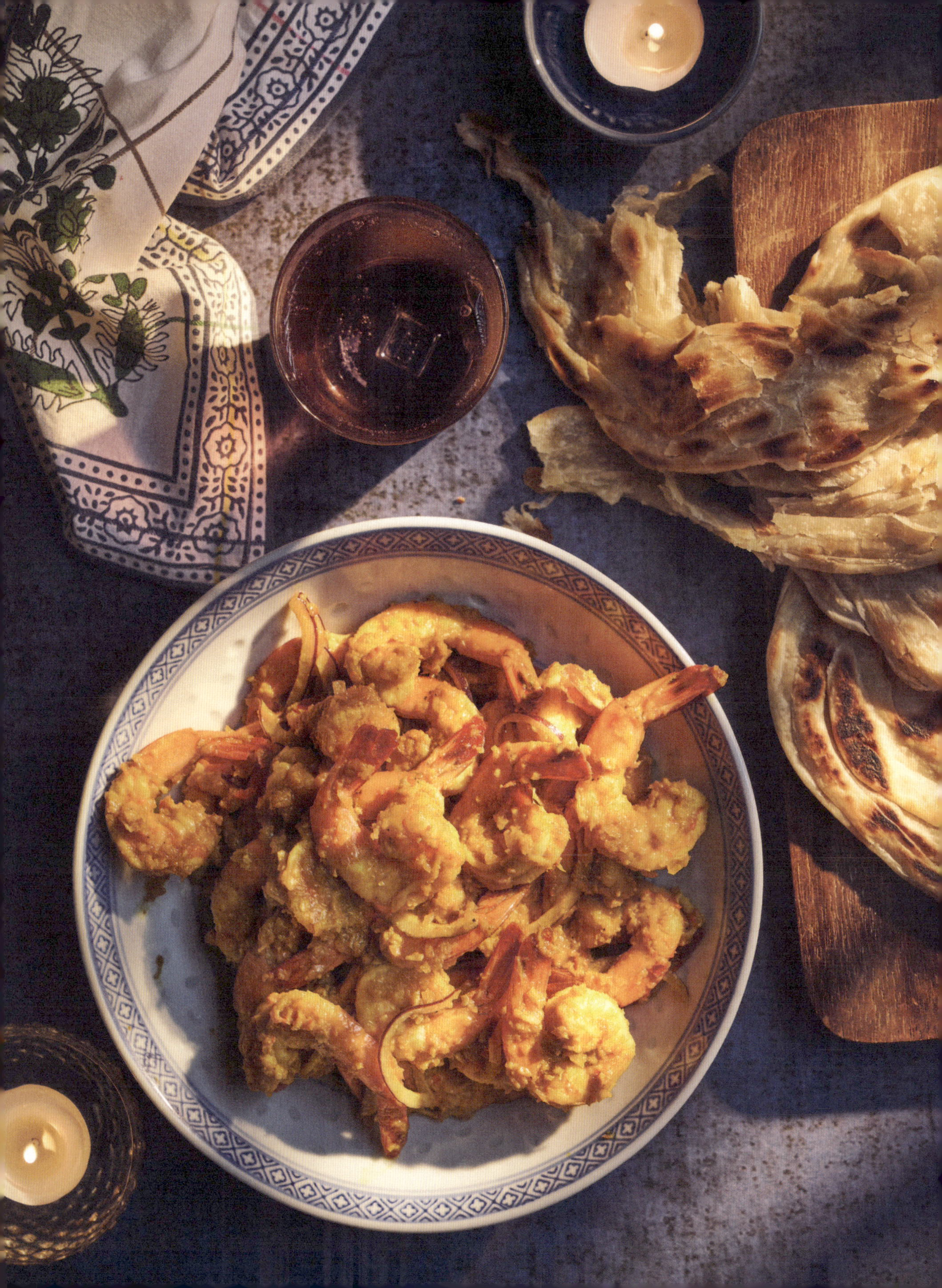

PRAWN SAMBAL
with Roti Canai

Singapore

I love Singaporean food so much. This prawn sambal is aromatic and fragrant and has a depth of flavour unlike anything else. Eaten with the roti canai it is unreal and so worth the wait.

Serves: 6

Start by making the roti canai dough. Put the plain flour in a large bowl with the salt, sugar and oil and use your hands to mix the oil in. Make a well in the centre and pour in the hot water. Use your hands to bring the dough together. Knead for 5 minutes till smooth and shiny.

Divide the dough into six equal balls and place on a plate. Drizzle all over with oil so they are generously coated, cover and leave for 1 hour. You can also do this ahead of time, making the dough the night before and leaving it in the fridge.

While that rests, let's make the paste by putting the onions in a food processor with the garlic, lemongrass, bird's eye chillies, shrimp paste, fish sauce, turmeric, sugar and water. Blend to a smooth paste and set to the side.

Now back to the dough. Take a ball of dough and press out on a greased worktop, rolling till you have a sheet of dough that is see-through and you can see your work surface through it. Make it as large as you can, then fold the edges in and scrunch up the sheet so you have one long strip of layered dough. Lift it up and roll into a spiral that is creating a mound as you lay it down. Press down and pop back on to the plate. Do the same to the other five balls of dough.

Now take each spiral and, using the back of your hand, press down to a circle that is roughly 15cm wide. Do this to all 12.

Pop a non-stick frying pan over a medium heat and cook the roti for 3–4 minutes on each side. Cook all six and then leave to stay warm under a tea towel while we make the prawns.

Put a medium pan on high heat and pour in the oil. As soon as the oil is hot, add the paste and cook for about 10 minutes till it is darker and the paste starts to come away from the sides. If it starts to burn or stick, just add a splash of water.

For the roti canai

600g plain flour, plus extra for dusting
1 tablespoon salt
1 tablespoon sugar
4 tablespoons oil
300ml hot tap water
oil, for drizzling

For the paste

2 onions, roughly chopped
10 cloves of garlic, peeled
1 lemongrass stalk, roughly chopped
10 bird's eye chillies
2 teaspoons shrimp paste
3 tablespoons fish sauce
1 teaspoon ground turmeric
1 teaspoon brown sugar
100ml water
oil, for frying
750g raw prawns with tails on

To serve

1 red onion, thinly sliced

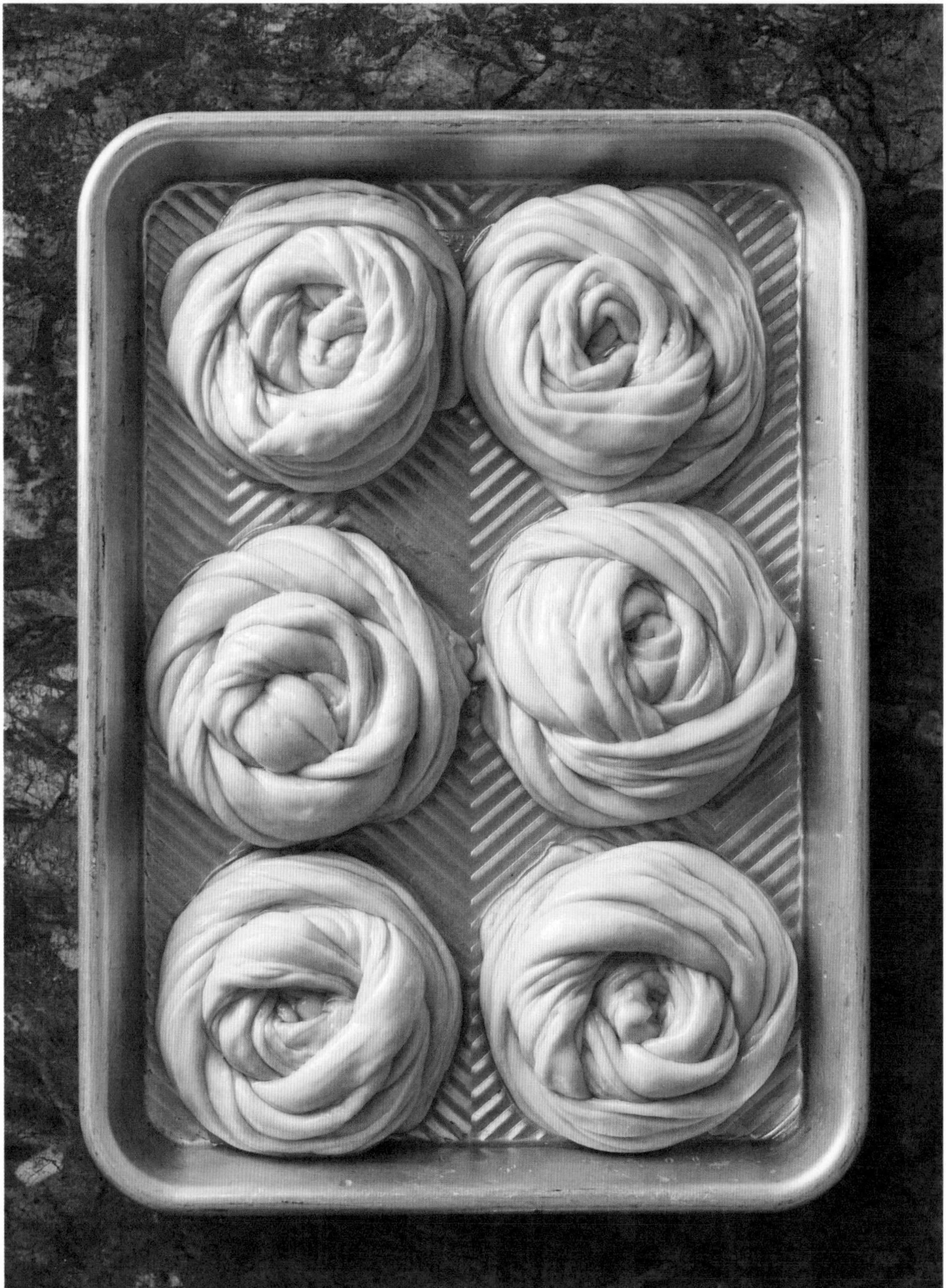

When the mixture is dry, add the prawns and stir through, then cook for 8 minutes till they have turned pink and are covered in that delicious sauce. Take off the heat, stir the sliced red onion through and it is ready to eat with the roti.

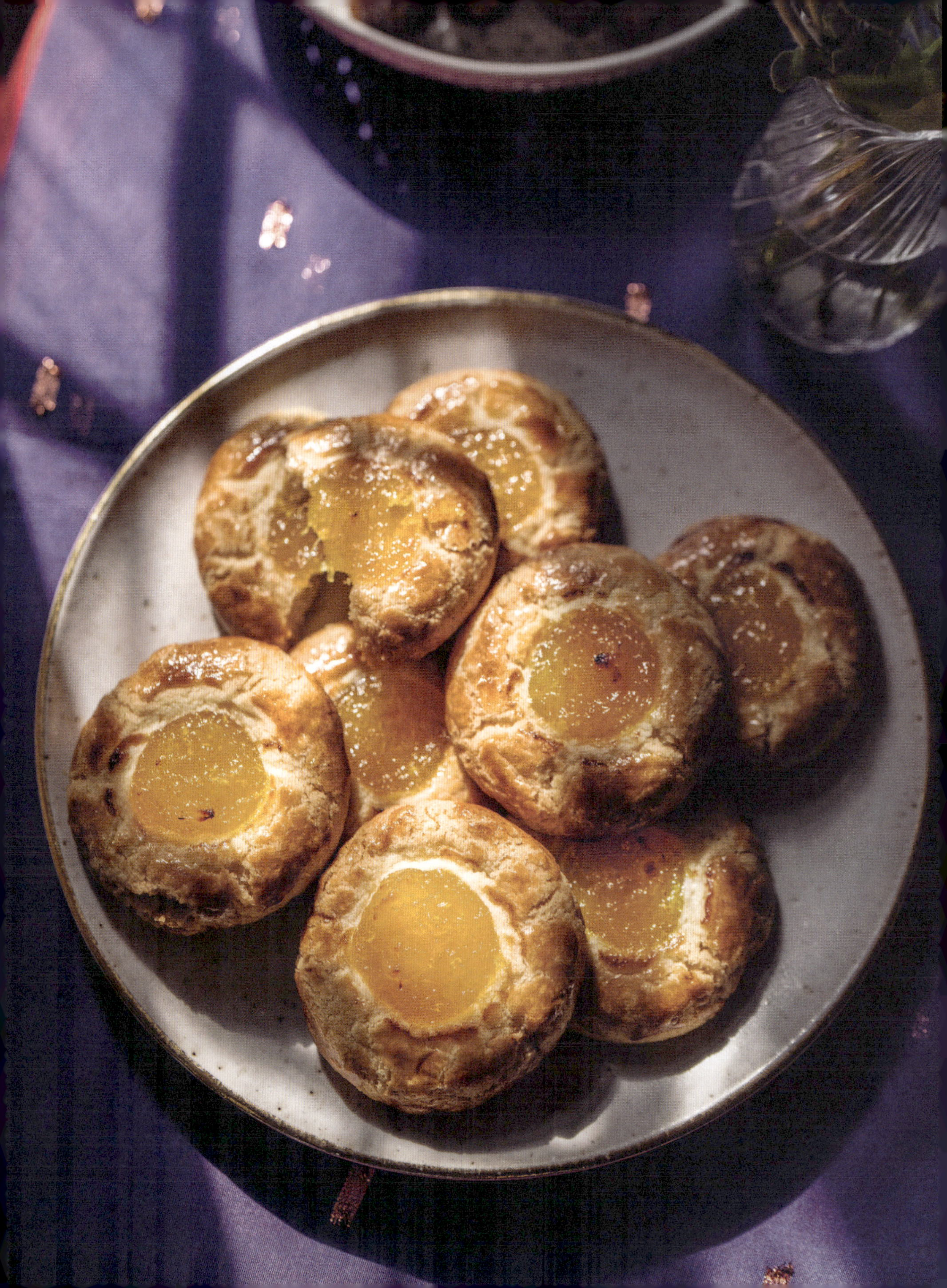

PINEAPPLE TART COOKIES

These cookies may not look like very much, but they are everything. Soft but with a tart pineapple centre and salted egg yolk glaze, which makes them a very special cookie.

Let's start by making the filling for the cookies. Put the drained pineapple chunks into a food processor with the caster sugar, lemon zest and juice and cornflour and blitz to a smooth paste.

Put the mixture in a small pan and cook for about 5 minutes till the mixture has thickened and can coat the back of the spoon. Leave to cool, spoon into a piping bag and pop into the fridge.

Line a large baking tray with some baking paper.

Make the biscuit dough by creaming together the butter and caster sugar – the mixture should be light, fluffy and pale. Add the plain flour in and mix together till you have a dough that comes together. Divide the mixture into 12 equal balls.

Flatten a dough ball and then use your thumb or something rounded to create an indentation for the pineapple filling to go in. Place each one on the tray. Pop the cookies into the fridge for 30 minutes.

Preheat the oven to 170°C.

Make the egg glaze by putting the egg yolks, salt and milk in a small bowl and mixing them up.

Take the tray out of the fridge. Brush the edge of the cookies with the egg yolk mix. Fill each indent with the pineapple filling and bake in the oven for 30 minutes.

Take the cookies out and leave to cool completely before eating.

Singapore

Makes: 12 cookies

For the filling
227g tin of pineapple chunks, drained
50g caster sugar
1 lemon, zest and juice
1 teaspoon cornflour

For the biscuit dough
200g unsalted butter, softened
100g caster sugar
300g plain flour

For the egg glaze
2 egg yolks
½ teaspoon salt
1 tablespoon whole milk

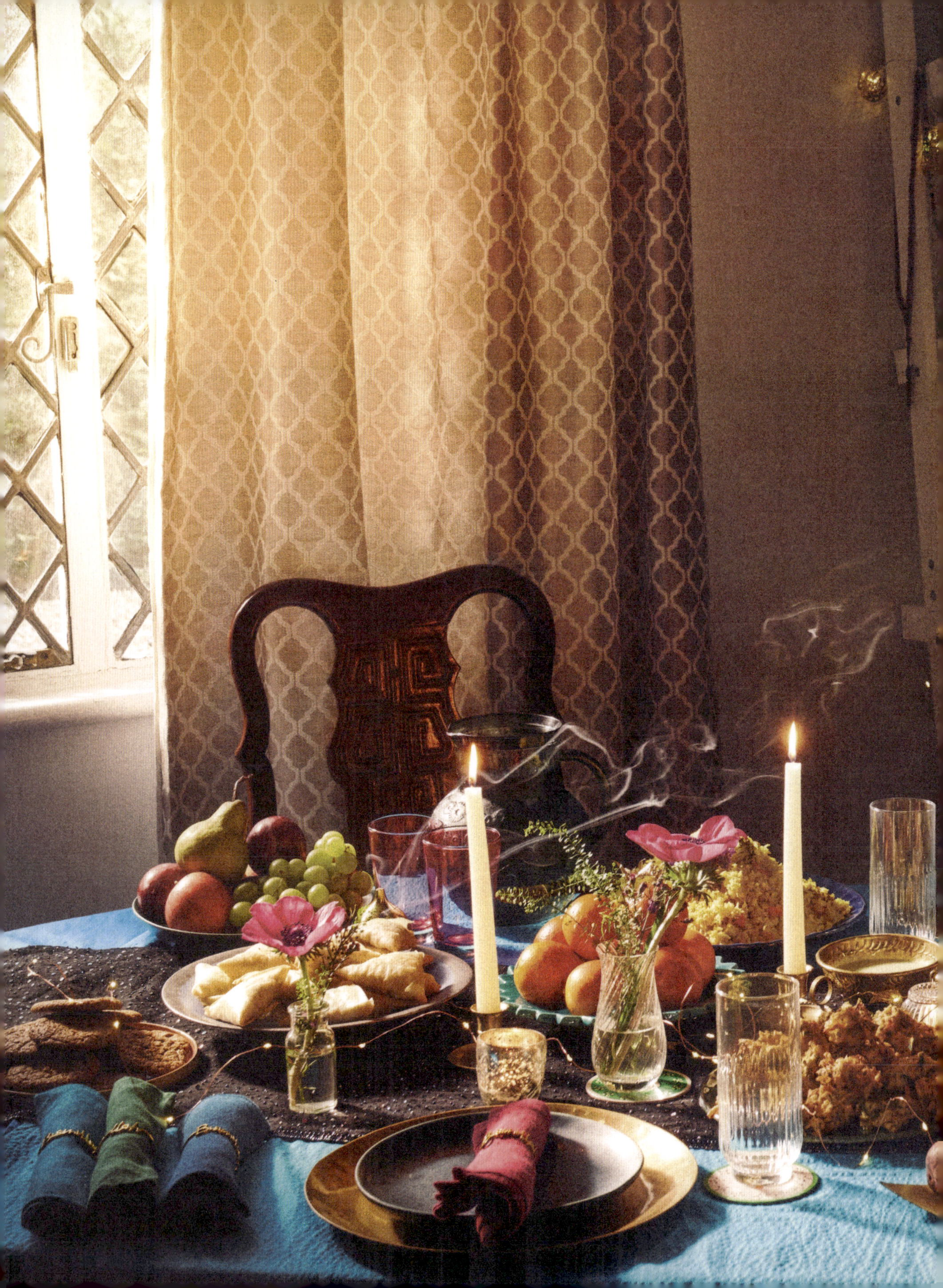

Eid-ul-Fitr

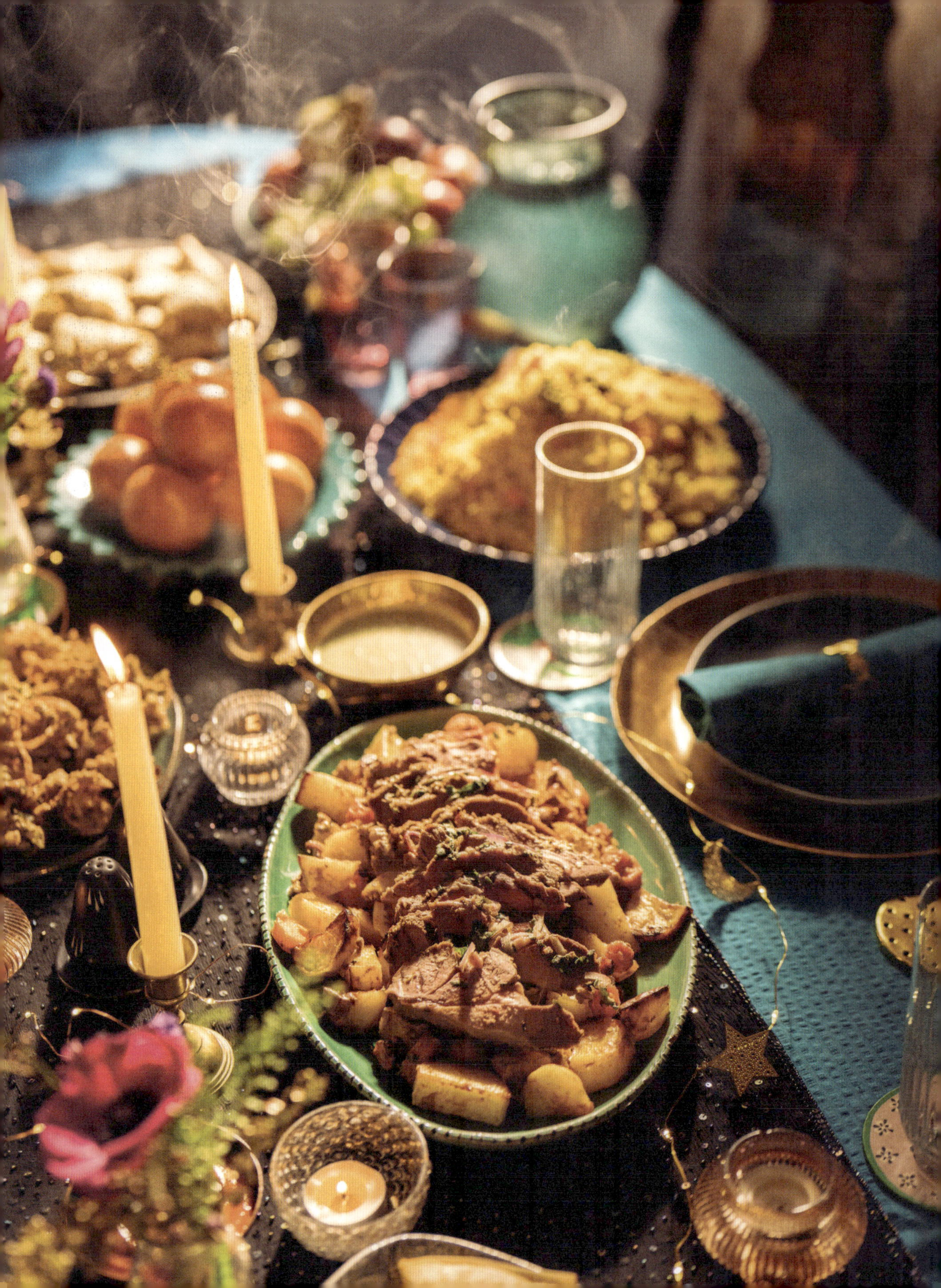

Eid-ul-Fitr

WHOLE STUFFED LEG OF BUTTERFLY LAMB

You can't have an Eid celebration without having a huge centrepiece and this is that centrepiece: marinated lamb stuffed with onions and roasted on a bed of potatoes and carrots. It has to be special for Eid and nothing says special like a whole leg of lamb.

Serves: 10–12

Start by marinating the lamb. Put the plain yoghurt in a bowl with the oil, chickpea flour, blended onion, garlic and ginger pastes, salt, coriander and cumin seeds, chilli flakes and the garam masala and whisk to combine everything.

Pop the lamb leg fillets on a large tray and smother the delicious spiced yoghurt all over with your hands. You could do this the night before if you wanted to prep sooner, which will really help to deepen the flavour.

Make the stuffing by putting the red onion, salt, coriander and green chilli in a bowl, then mix and set to one side.

Preheat the oven to 160°C.

Take the roasting dish that you are going to cook the leg of lamb in and add all the potatoes and carrots. Mix the oil and tamarind in a small bowl along with the salt and turmeric. Drizzle the lamb generously with the oil so everything is coated in it.

Pop the first leg of lamb right on top with the inside of the leg facing upwards (the side the bone has been removed from). Add the onion stuffing on top in an even layer. Place the other leg of lamb on top with the inside of the leg facing down on to the onions.

Bake in the oven for 50 minutes–1 hour.

For the lamb

250g plain yoghurt

50ml oil

75g chickpea flour

2 onions, blended to a purée

4 tablespoons garlic paste

4 tablespoons ginger paste

3 tablespoons salt

2 tablespoons coriander seeds, toasted and crushed

2 tablespoons cumin seeds, toasted and crushed

2 tablespoons chilli flakes

4 tablespoons garam masala

2 x 750g lamb legs, butterflied

For the stuffing

2 red onions, thinly sliced

2 teaspoons salt

large handful of fresh coriander, finely sliced

4 green chillies, finely sliced

For the potatoes and carrots

1kg potatoes, peeled and diced into 2–3cm pieces

500g carrots, peeled and sliced into 1cm coins

100ml oil

120g tamarind paste

2 teaspoons salt

1½ teaspoons ground turmeric

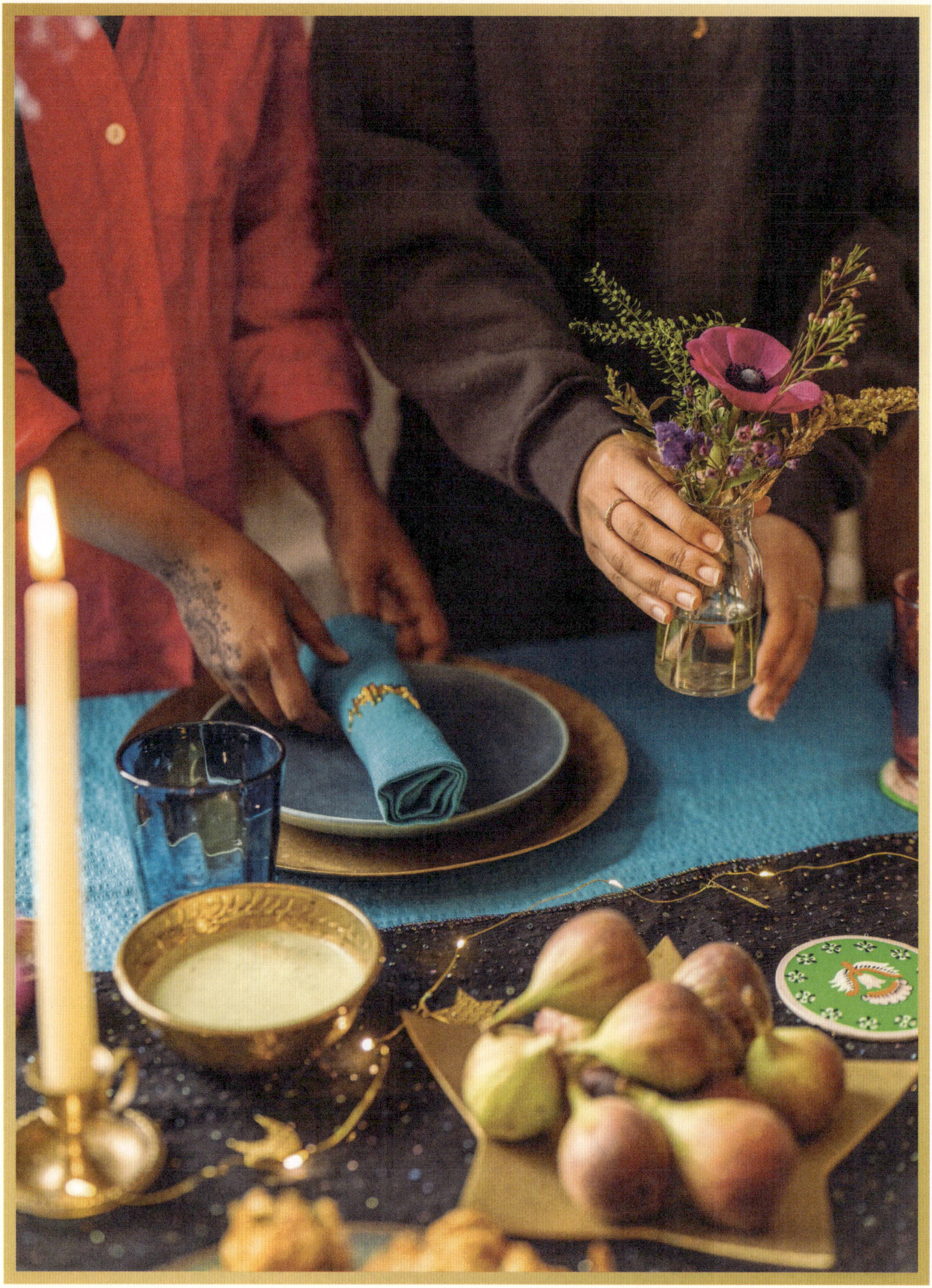

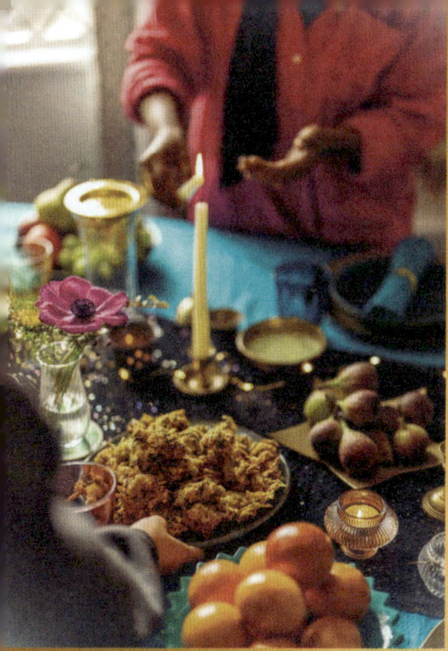
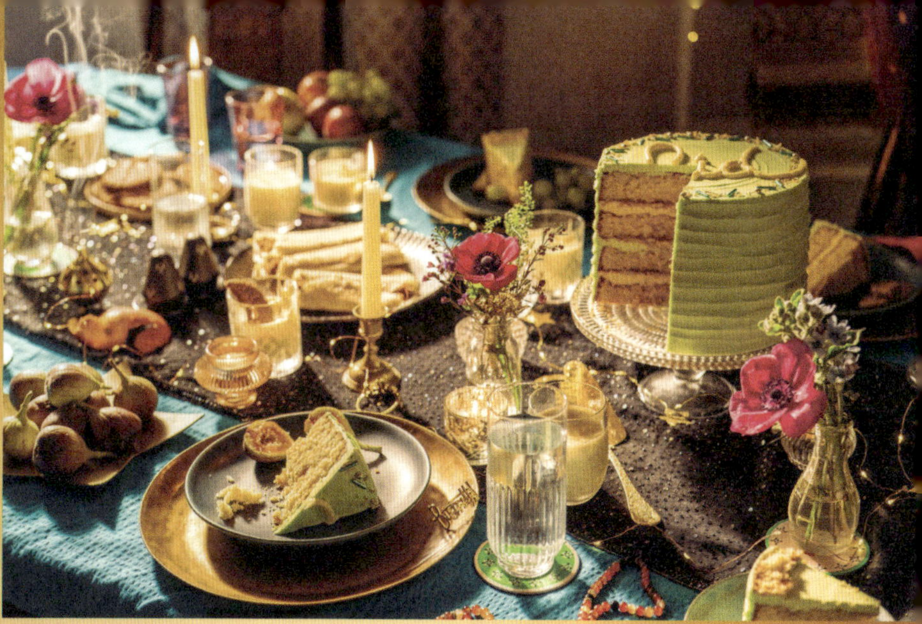
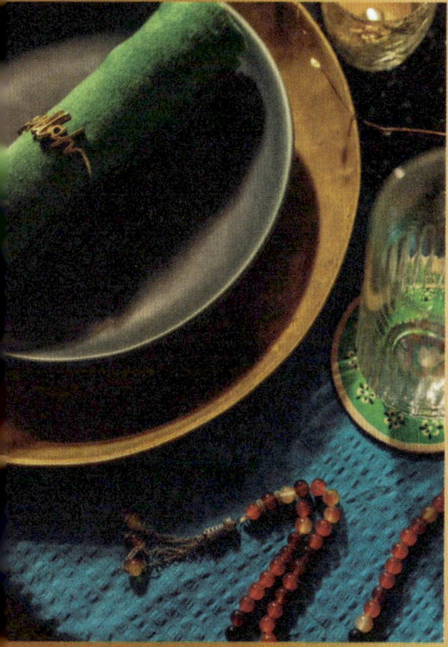
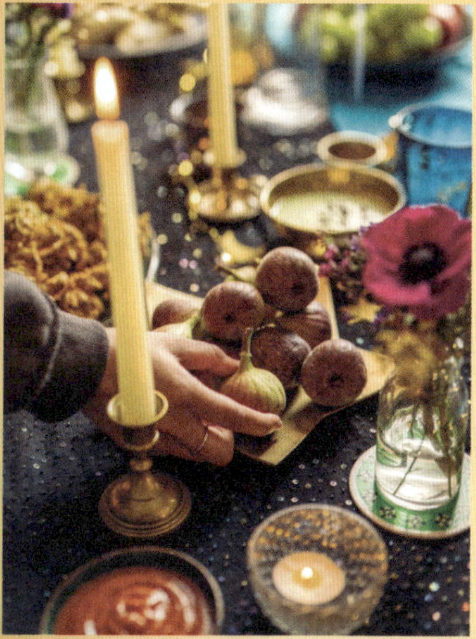
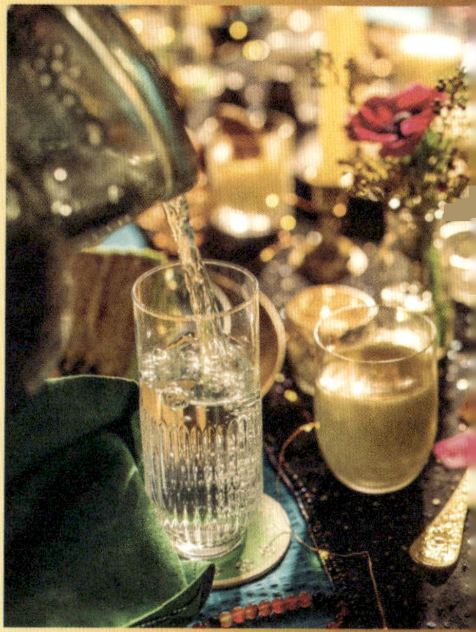
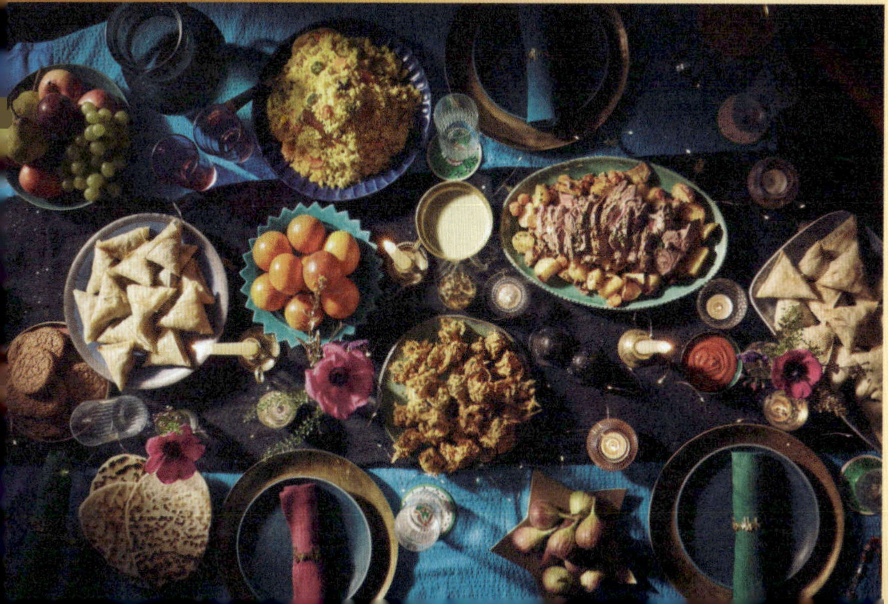
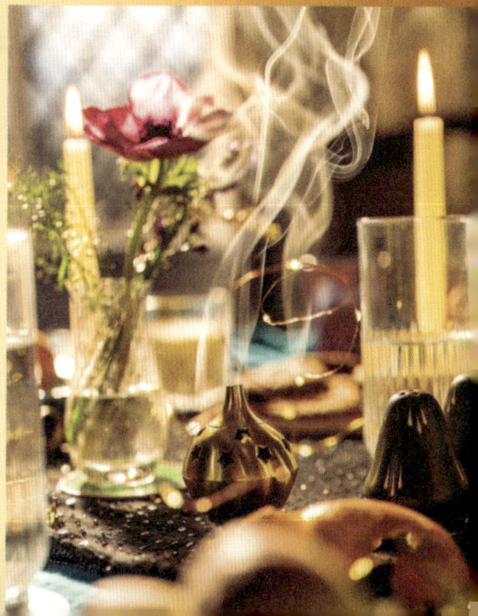

MANGO AND LIME CELEBRATION CAKE

You have to have a layer cake for an Eid celebration. Something that stands tall. This is a cake with four layers of mango and lime and it is perfect for a showstopper dessert worthy of a celebration.

Start by tipping the mangoes into a small pan. Mash them up using the back of a fork, tip in the sugar and the lemon zest and mix through.

Pop on to a medium heat, bring the mix to the boil and as soon as it boils, reduce the heat and keep stirring occasionally but leave to simmer away for about 35 minutes. Once it's a very thick, gooey texture, strain through a sieve, removing any bits, cover and pop into the fridge.

Now let's make the lime curd. Put the lime zest, lime juice, caster sugar, egg and egg yolks in a bowl and whisk together. Set the bowl over a pan of simmering water and keep stirring till the mixture gets thicker. This can take up to 10 minutes. When it coats the back of a spoon, take off the heat, add in the butter and whisk till melted. Pass the mix through the sieve and leave to chill in the fridge.

Make the mango buttercream by putting the butter and salt in a stand mixer bowl and whipping on a high speed for 5 minutes - the texture should be light, smooth and pale. Add half the icing sugar and whisk till really well combined, making sure to scrape down the sides. Add the rest of the icing sugar along with the mango sauce and whip till you have a mixture that holds its shape. Reserve 8 tablespoons of the mango sauce for the cake batter. Cover and leave in the fridge.

Make the lime buttercream by putting the butter and salt in the stand mixer bowl and whipping on a high speed for 5 minutes - the texture should be light, smooth and pale. Add half the icing sugar and whisk till really well combined, making sure to scrape down the sides. Add the rest of the icing sugar along with the lime juice and few drops of green food colouring and whip till you have a mixture that holds its shape. Cover and leave in the fridge.

Eid-ul-Fitr

Serves: 12-18

For the mango sauce
400g tin of mango slices, drained
125g caster sugar
1 lemon, zest only

For the lime curd
2 limes, zest only
65ml lime juice
65g caster sugar
1 egg
3 egg yolks
50g unsalted butter, chilled and cubed

For the mango buttercream
250g unsalted butter, softened
½ teaspoon salt
375g icing sugar, sifted
4 tablespoons mango sauce (see above)

For the lime buttercream
250g unsalted butter, softened
½ teaspoon salt
375g icing sugar, sifted
1½ tablespoons lime juice
few drops of green gel food colouring

For the sponges
500g caster sugar
330g unsalted butter, softened
135ml olive oil

➜

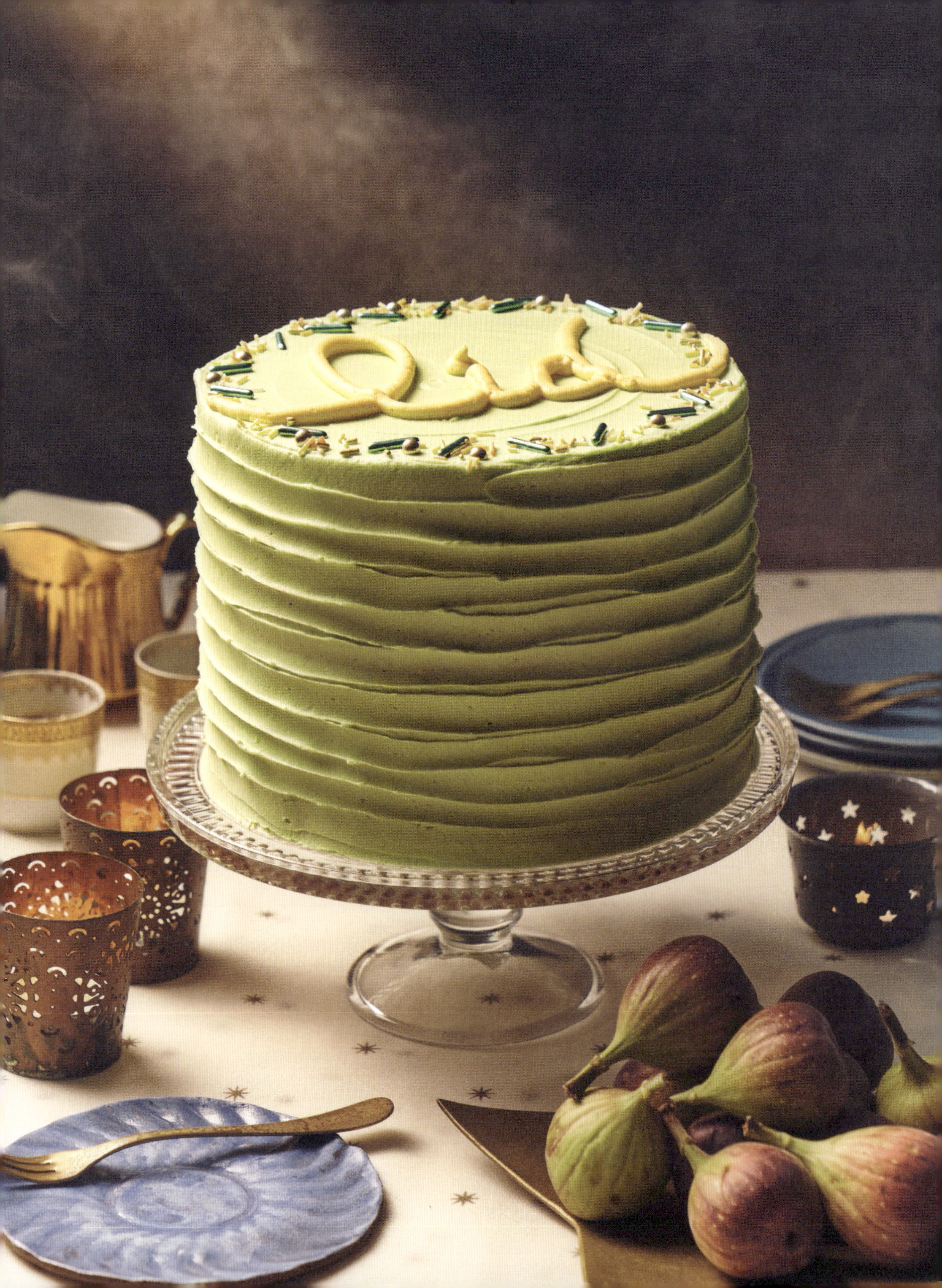

Now on to making the cake. Preheat the oven to 170°C and grease and line the base and sides of four x 20cm round cake tins.

Put the caster sugar, butter and olive oil in the bowl of the stand mixer and whip till the mixture is really light and fluffy and almost white in colour. Crack an egg into the centre, one at a time, making sure to incorporate well between each addition. Add the flour in and, using a spatula, mix the batter. Pour in the whole milk and mix till you have a smooth light batter without any floury bits.

Divide the mixture equally into the four tins. Level off the tops by tapping the tins a few times on the work surface. Drizzle 2 tablespoons of the mango sauce all over the cake batter in each tin and use a skewer to ripple it through.

Bake for 35 minutes till the cakes are golden and just coming away from the sides. Leave to cool in the tins for 20 minutes, then remove and leave to cool on a wire rack.

Take a cake plate or board and add a few smatterings of buttercream to help secure that first layer. Put some mango buttercream on the first cake layer, using your spatula to create a large circular crater with a raised edge, so you can add the mango sauce without it spilling over, then drizzle in the mango sauce.

Add the second layer of cake and this time smother on the same amount of lime buttercream with a drizzle of the lime curd.

Place the third layer on top and add the mango buttercream and lime curd and then pop the fourth and last layer of cake on top.

Make sure the cake is straight and level, smooth off any edges and pop into the fridge for 30 minutes.

Take the cake out, add a crumb coat of buttercream - a thin layer on top of and around the edges of the cake to catch any of the crumbs. Pop back into the fridge for another 30 minutes.

Use the lime buttercream to give the cake another smooth layer on top and on the sides. Use the rest of the buttercream to decorate the cake however you wish, then top with sprinkles or gold leaf.

8 medium eggs
500g self-raising flour
6 tablespoons whole milk
8 tablespoons mango sauce (see above)
sprinkles or gold leaf, to decorate

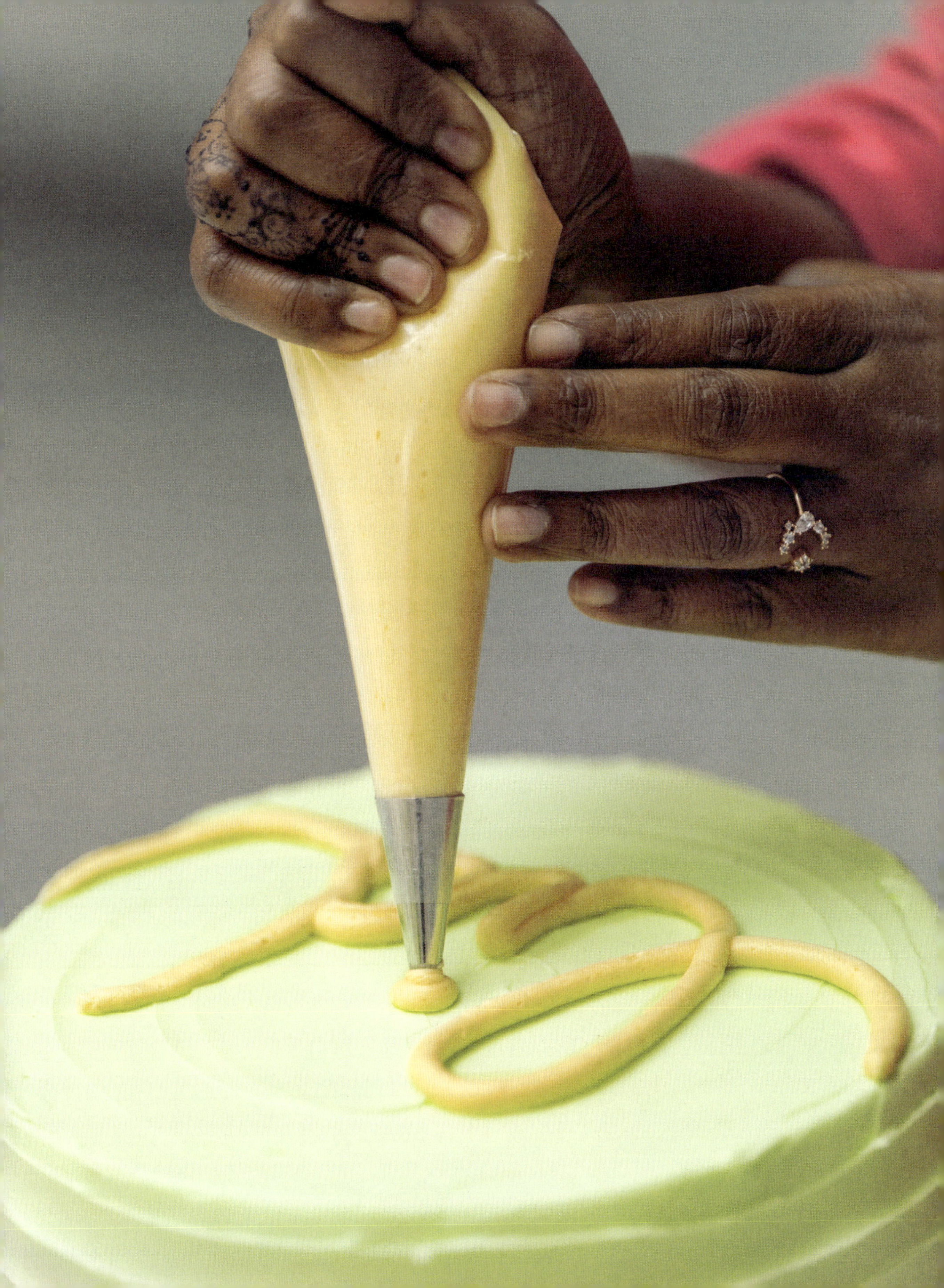

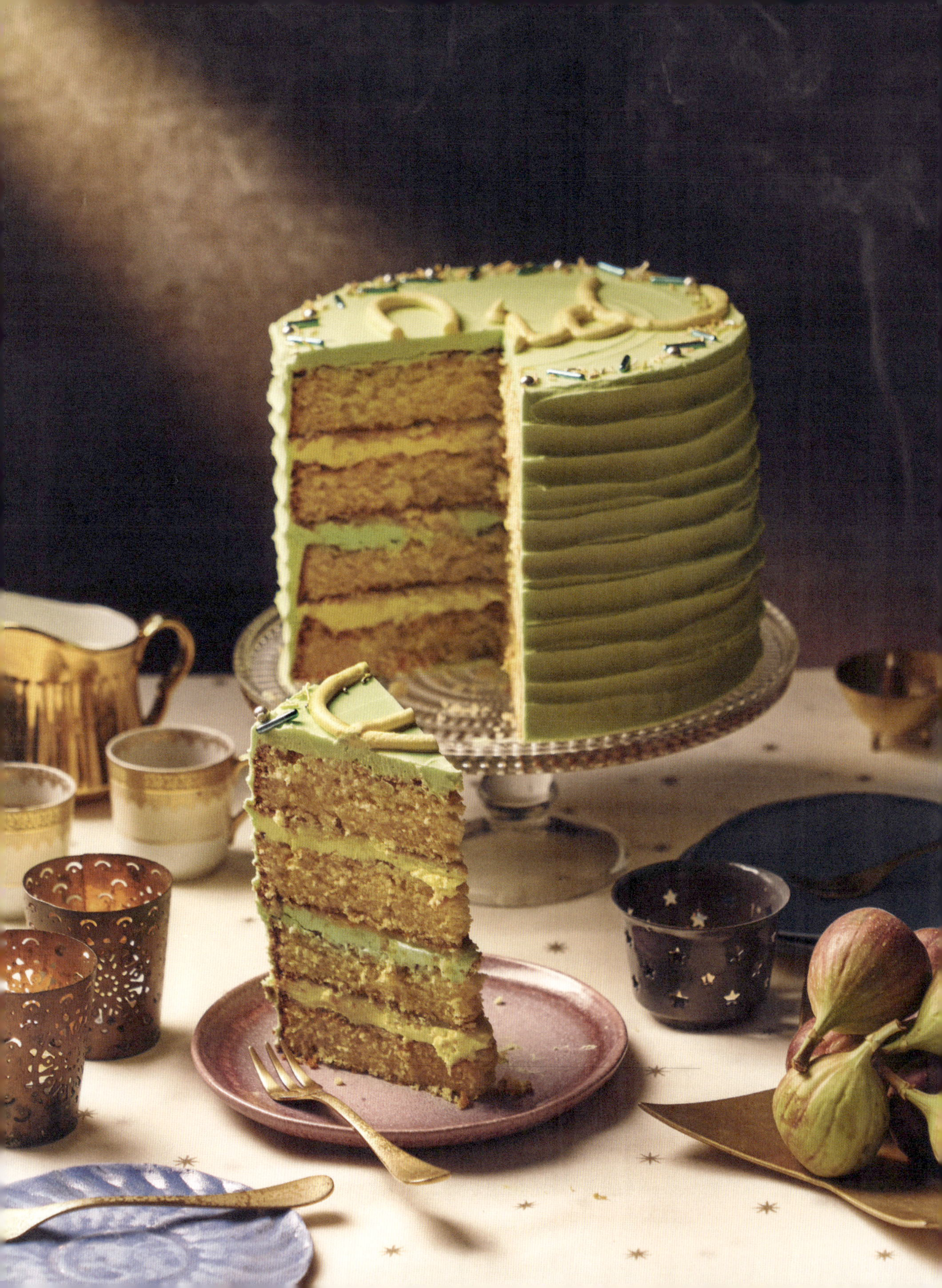

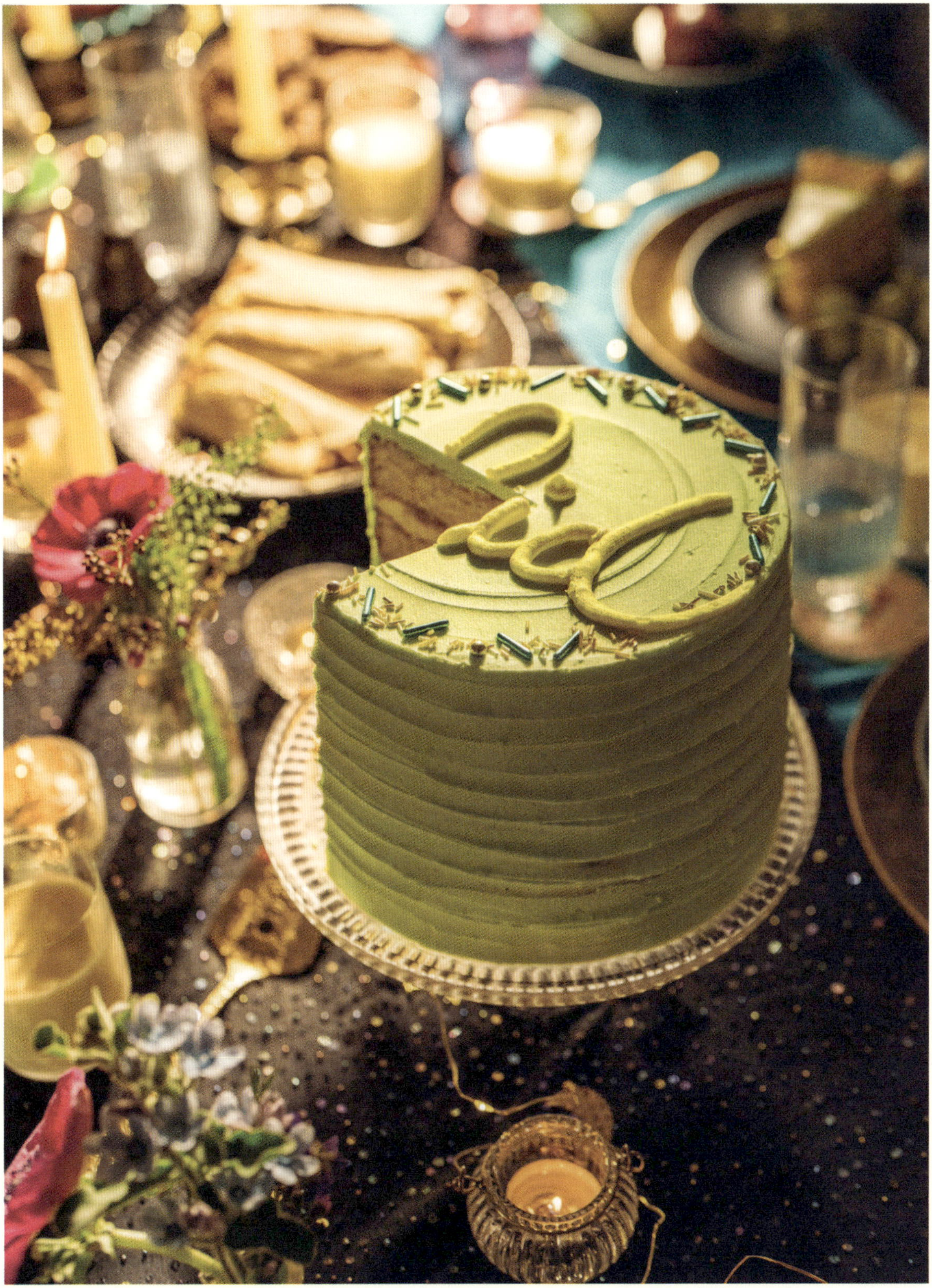

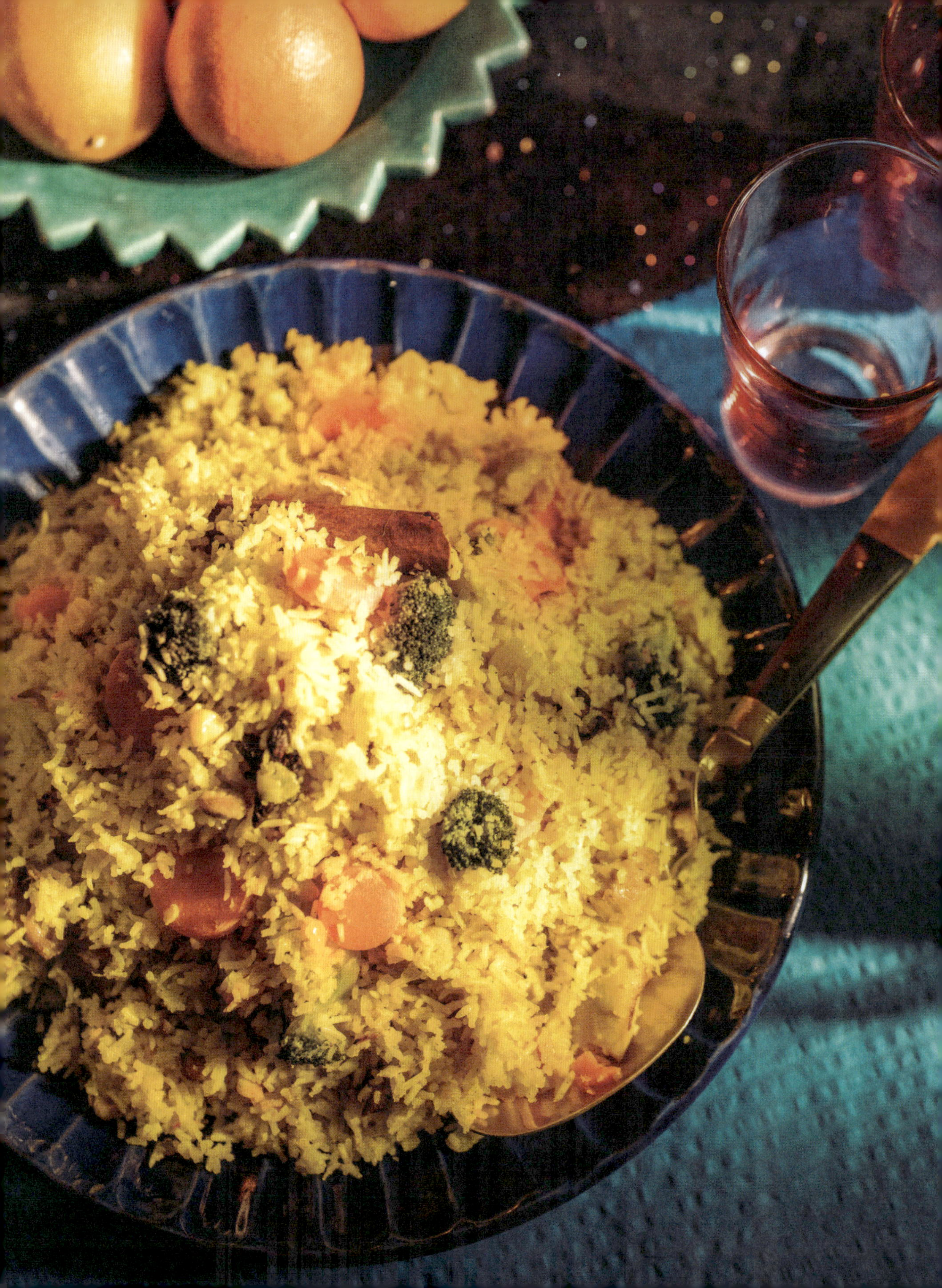

EID CHICKEN PULAO

Rice plays such a huge part in the celebration of Eid, certainly for us as a family. With a history deep-rooted in the growing of rice, it has been, and always will be, a staple in our homes. This huge pot is aromatic, colourful and abundant.

Serves: 10–12

Take a large pan 30cm wide and 30cm high, place it over a high heat and add the ghee. When the ghee has melted, add the cardamom pods, cinnamon sticks, bay leaves and star anise.

Let the whole spices sizzle and then add in your onions and salt and cook the onions until they are really soft but not too dark in colour – low and slow. Add the minced garlic and ginger and cook through with the chicken. The chicken will release some liquid, so we want to keep cooking the chicken till none of that liquid remains. Now get the frozen mixed veg in with the turmeric and again cook till the moisture has been removed.

For the rice, wash the basmati till the water runs completely clear. As soon as the water is clear, drain. Add your rice to the pan with the chicken and stir through for about 5 minutes over a high heat. Pour in your boiling water and cook till the water has evaporated. Lower the heat, cover the pan with a lid and leave to steam for 20 minutes.

Put the saffron in a mortar and pestle with the sugar and grind down with a few spoons of warm water to create a beautiful colour. Take the lid off the rice and drizzle all over. Steam for another 5 minutes.

Before serving, fluff up the pulao and serve on a platter.

300g ghee
6 cardamom pods
3 cinnamon sticks
5 bay leaves
3 star anise
4 onions, diced
4 tablespoons salt
1 bulb of garlic, cloves peeled and minced
13cm piece of peeled ginger, minced
750g boneless chicken thighs, diced
300g frozen mixed veg
2 teaspoons ground turmeric
1kg basmati rice
1.5 litres boiling water

For the colour
1 large pinch of saffron
½ teaspoon sugar
warm water

Eid-ul-Fitr

DALCHINI BISCOOT
Cardamom Biscuits with Elasi Lemon Posset

I like to have lots of different types of puddings so everyone has something they enjoy, especially if they don't like cake. These are perfect little pudding pots. Made with lemon, they are fruity and tart with a hint of fragrance from the cardamom and are best served with a cinnamon biscuit.

Makes: 12

Pour the cream into a pan with the cardamom pods. Add the caster sugar and whisk the sugar in well. Place over a low heat and then bring the mixture to the boil and boil for 3 minutes.

Take off the heat and leave to cool for 10 minutes. Add the lemon zest and juice and whisk till it looks like it's starting to thicken. Strain through a sieve into a bowl. Ladle carefully into 12 small individual pots and leave to set overnight.

Now let's make the biscoot. Preheat the oven to 160°C. Line two baking trays with some baking paper.

Put the unsalted butter in a pan with the golden syrup and heat till everything is evenly combined. Pour the mixture into a bowl and allow to cool to room temperature. Add the egg yolk and mix through.

Put the plain flour, soft brown sugar, ground cinnamon, baking powder and salt in a separate bowl. Whisk to combine, tip into the wet ingredients and mix till you have a smooth dough.

Take 1½ teaspoons of the mixture and shape into rounds. Place on to the baking trays with some space between them and bake for 15 minutes.

Leave to cool on the trays and serve alongside the possets.

For the elasi lemon posset
1.2 litres double cream
8 cardamom pods, crushed
300g caster sugar
4 large lemons, zest and juice

For the dalchini biscoot
50g unsalted butter
125g golden syrup
1 egg yolk
125g plain flour, sifted
50g soft brown sugar
3 teaspoons ground cinnamon
½ teaspoon baking powder
½ teaspoon salt

Eid-ul-Fitr

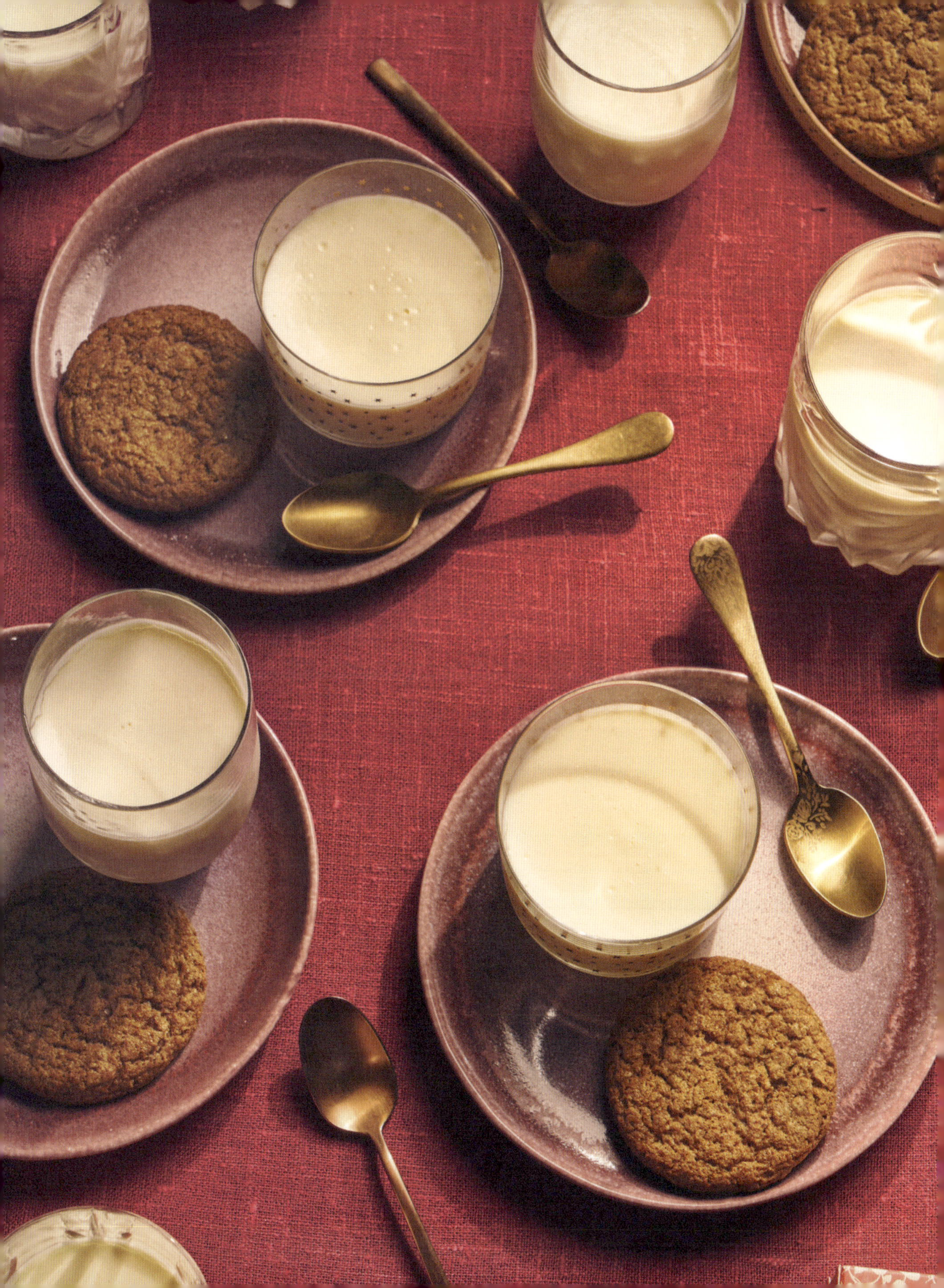

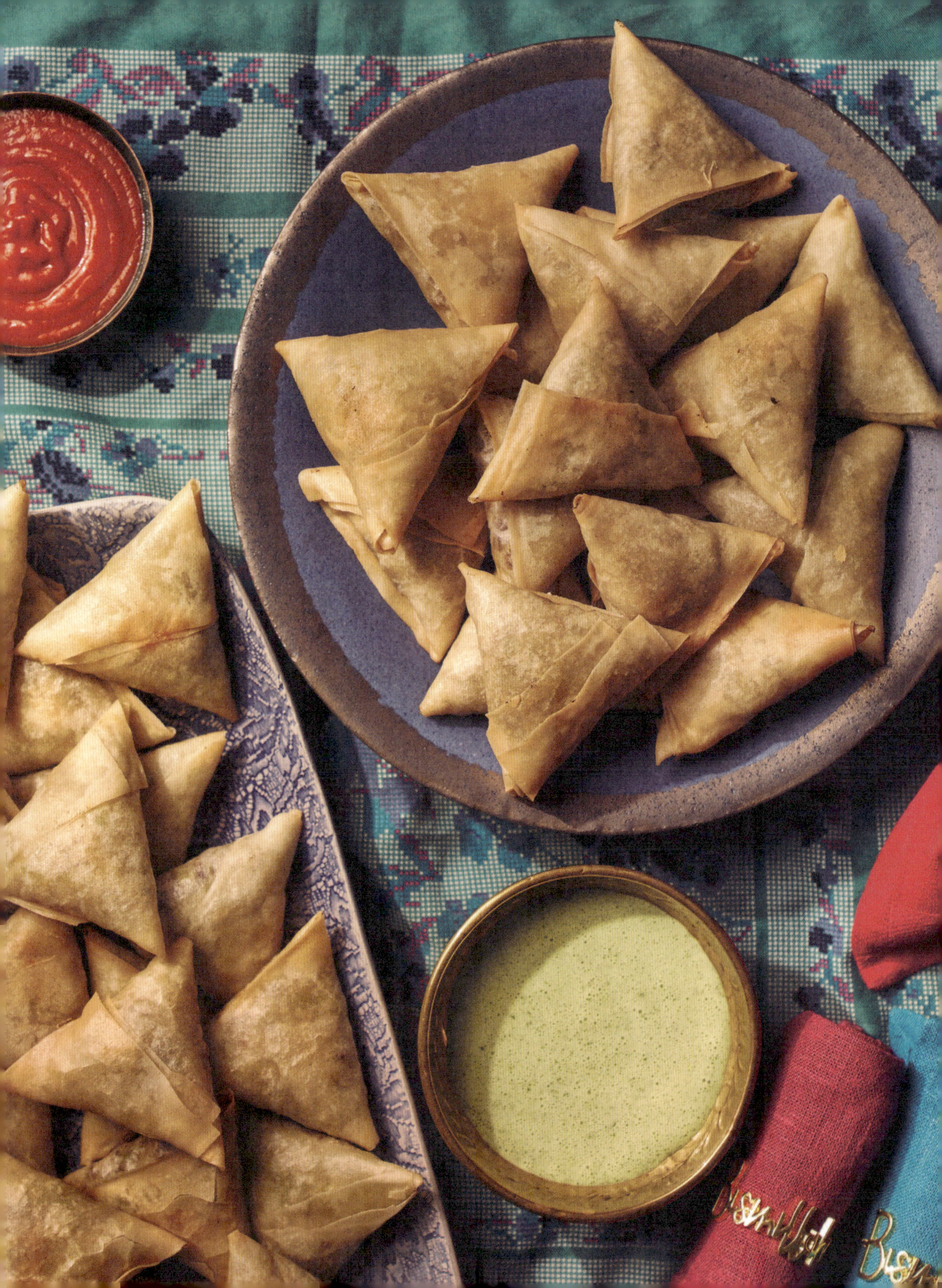

BEEF AND PEA SAMOSAS

It is not Eid if there are no samosas – you have to have samosas. Piles and piles of samosas is the only way to go. So, you will need the recipe for my classic beef and pea.

Makes: 45 samosas

For the filling

50ml oil

3 onions, diced

3 teaspoons salt

2 tablespoons ginger paste

2 tablespoons garlic paste

1kg beef mince

4 tablespoons garam masala

2 tablespoons coriander seeds, toasted and lightly crushed

2 tablespoons cumin seeds, toasted and lightly crushed

2 tablespoons chilli flakes

300g frozen peas

2 red onions, diced

4 green chillies, thinly sliced

large handful of fresh coriander, thinly sliced

For the glue

7 tablespoons plain flour

7 tablespoons cold water

550g pack of spring roll sheets, defrosted (30 sheets)

oil, for frying

For the chutney

260g tamarind sauce

50ml cold water

1 teaspoon chilli powder

1 teaspoon ground cumin

1 small red onion, diced

small handful of fresh coriander, finely sliced

Start by making the mince. Put a pan on the hob on a high heat. As soon as the pan is hot, pour in the oil with the onions and salt and cook the onions till they are golden and tender. Add the ginger and garlic pastes and cook through for a minute or so, then promptly add your beef mince and cook that, stirring and breaking it up as you cook to remove any hard clumps.

When the mince is evenly browned, add the garam masala, coriander seeds, cumin seeds, chilli flakes and frozen peas. Cook till the peas are cooked. Pop everything on to a wide tray and leave to cool completely.

Once cooled, add the raw filling ingredients – the onion, chillies and coriander – and mix through till evenly distributed.

Make up the glue by mixing the flour and the water to a gloopy paste, then set that aside.

Take the spring roll sheets and mark the pastry so you have three equal rectangular strips. When you are happy, place on a board and, using a sharp knife, cut the rectangles. You should have three piles. Place two of the piles back into the packaging and wrap up tightly so they don't dry up.

With the rectangular chunk of pastry that you do have, look at the corner and you will see 30 layers of pastry tightly packed together. We need to peel this pastry, but in twos not single sheets. From the corner take two sheets and peel them together. Do this till you have 15 strips.

Lay a strip so the shortest side is closest to you, hold the bottom left corner and diagonally move the sheet towards your right, creating a triangle. You should see a visible triangle. Flip the triangle over to the flat edge. Carefully glue that edge.

➜

174

175

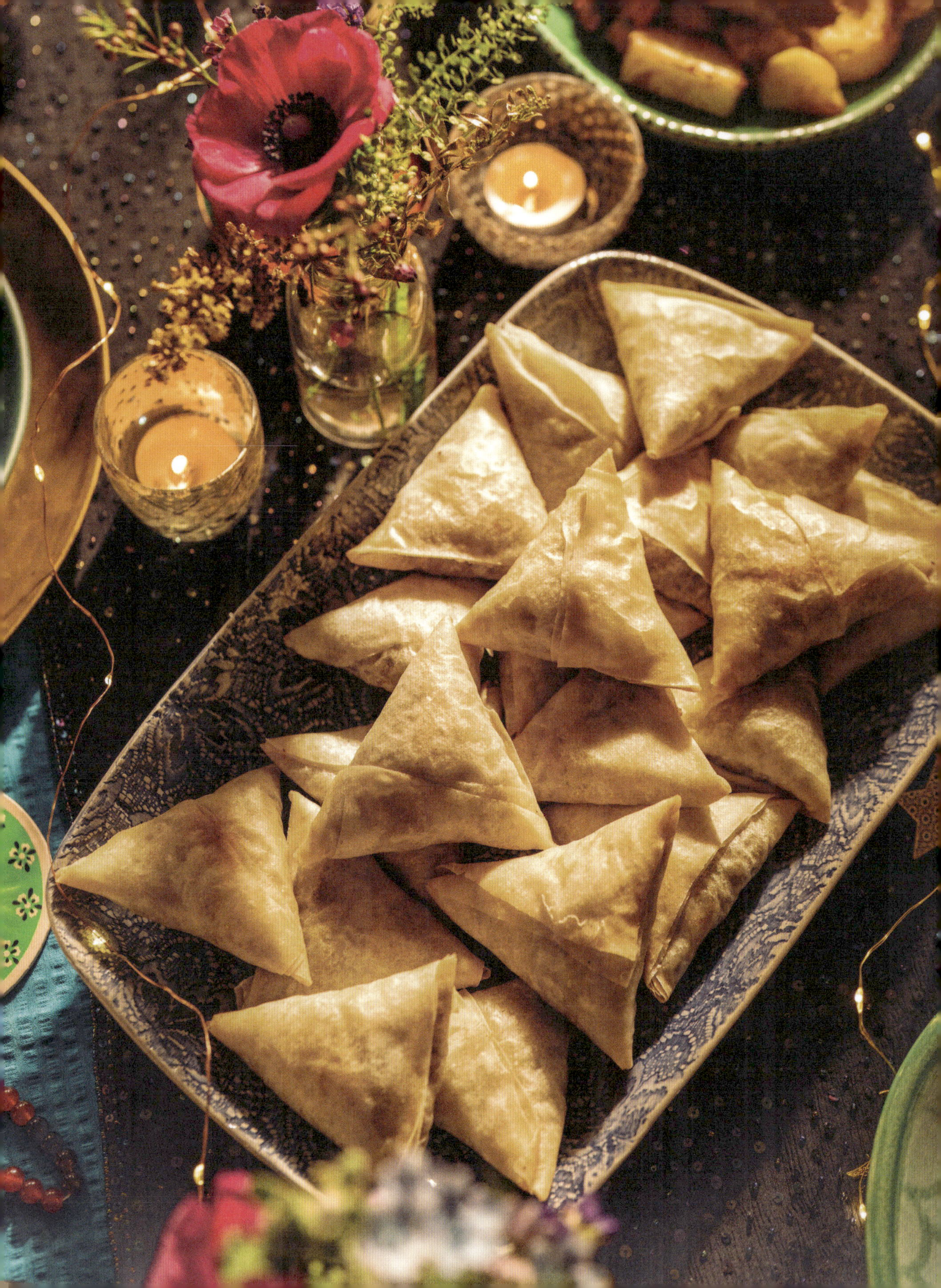

You should now have a pocket. Fill the pocket with mince and glue the flap around the edges. Bring the flap over, sealing tight against the edges and going over till you have a triangle. Then do the same again and again, moving on to the last pile and then the last pile of sheets.

To fry the samosas, place a pan on the heat with oil coming two-thirds of the way up. Heat the oil to 180°C. Fry till golden and drain on a plate lined with kitchen paper.

Make the chutney by putting the tamarind sauce into a serving dish with the water, chilli powder, cumin, red onion and coriander. Mix through and serve with your samosas.

Eid-ul-Fitr

PATHISHAPTHA
Coconut Crepes

This is a classic Bangladeshi sweet treat that only ever comes out on special occasions and Eid is certainly an occasion for its grand entrance. These pancakes are filled with a sweet, smoky, coconut and molasses mixture.

Makes: 16 pathishaptha

Start by making the batter. Put the fine semolina in a bowl with the rice flour, plain flour, caster sugar and pinch of salt and mix through. Make a well in the centre, pour in the milk and water and whisk to a smooth, even batter. Set aside and leave covered for 1 hour.

Meanwhile, make the filling by putting the desiccated coconut in a non-stick saucepan. Add the cinnamon stick, cardamom pods and bay leaves. Toast the coconut with the spices till the coconut is a deep golden colour.

Pour in the water, bring to the boil and leave to simmer till all the water has evaporated and the coconut is plump.

To the same pan add the ghee and date molasses and cook gently till the mixture is rich and thick. Take off the heat, transfer to a plate, remove the whole spices and leave to cool.

Now make the pancakes by taking a small non-stick pancake pan and lightly greasing with oil. Heat the pan and ladle in the batter, swirling to create a simple crepe. Over a low heat, cook till the surface begins to look dry and is no longer shiny.

Add a few tablespoons of the filling down the centre in a log shape and fold the two halves over to cover it. Take off the heat and make the rest.

Before serving, dust with a little icing sugar.

For the batter
75g fine semolina
75g rice flour
150g plain flour
2 tablespoons caster sugar
pinch of salt
400ml whole milk
50ml cold water
oil, for greasing

For the filling
200g desiccated coconut
1 cinnamon stick
7 cardamom pods
2 bay leaves
500ml cold water
1 tablespoon ghee
225g date molasses

To serve
icing sugar

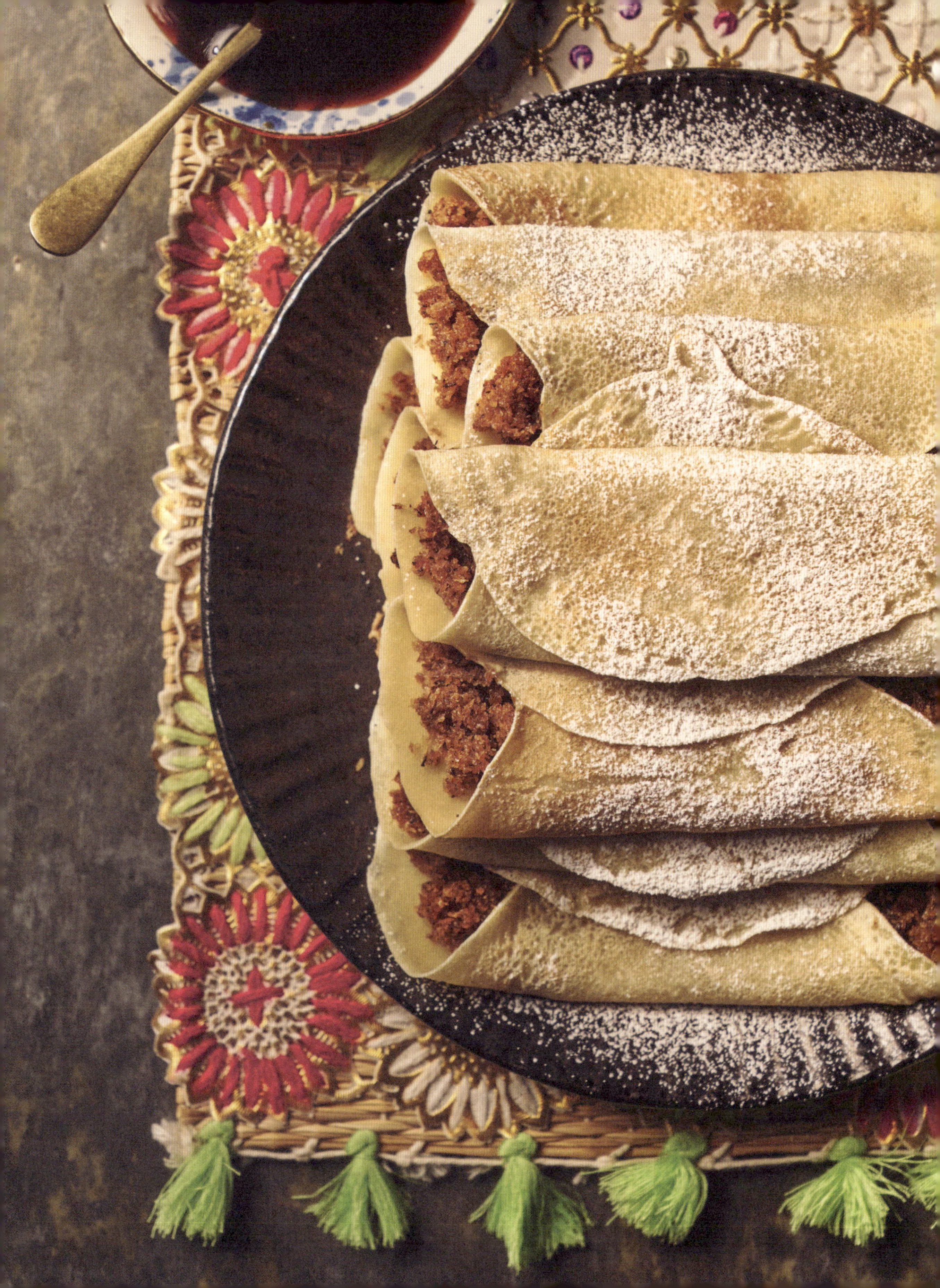

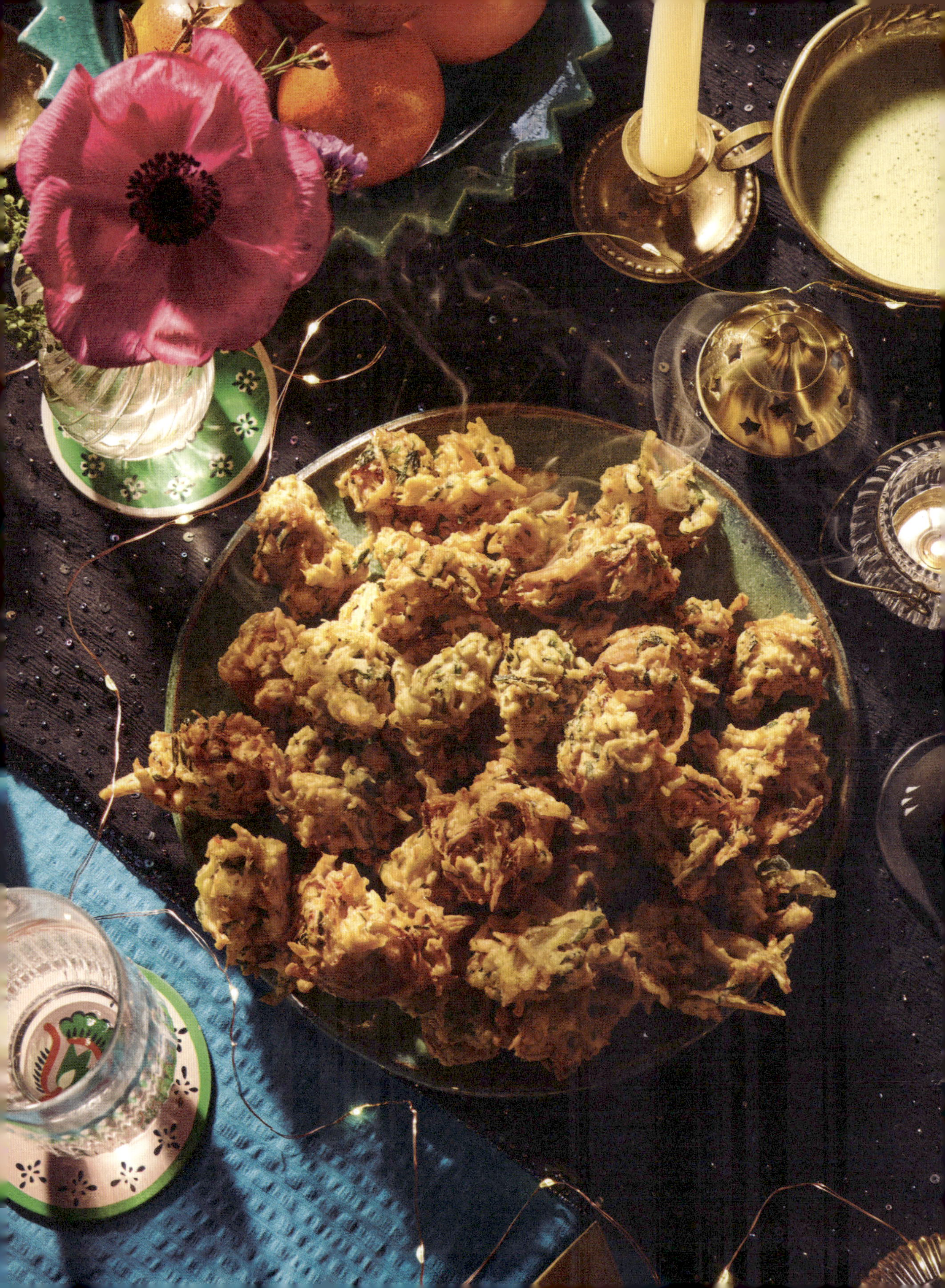

SPINACH AND PARSNIP PAKORAS

As the oil is already out, why not make some pakoras. I love to deep-fry and these are perfect for having some crispy, crunchy pakoras to go with everything else or just a picky snack as you enjoy Eid day.

Makes: 10–12

Start by putting the thinly sliced onions in a large bowl. Add the salt, chilli flakes, coriander and cumin seeds and fresh coriander. Get your hands in and really squeeze all the ingredients together to extract as much moisture as you possibly can. Cover and leave for 20 minutes.

Add the parsnips to the onion mix along with the spinach and mix really well. Add the chickpea flour and use your hands to bring together, adding the water a little at a time till you have a mixture that holds its shape when clumped together. When you get there, stop adding water.

Place a large pan on the hob and pour in oil two-thirds of the way up. Heat the oil to 180°C and start to add clumps of the pakora mix. Fry for 6–8 minutes, till golden and crisp. Drain and leave on a plate lined with kitchen paper while you fry them all up.

For the dip, put the small handful of coriander into a food processor with the garlic and salt and blend till everything is an even texture. Spoon the plain yoghurt into a serving dish with the mayo and mint sauce, add the contents of the processor and mix really well.

Serve this easy yoghurt mint dip with your hot pakoras.

4 onions, thinly sliced
3 tablespoons salt
2 tablespoons chilli flakes
1½ tablespoons coriander seeds, toasted and lightly crushed
1½ tablespoons cumin seeds, toasted and lightly crushed
large handful of fresh coriander, finely sliced
600g parsnips, grated
100g spinach, finely sliced
600g chickpea flour
200ml cold water (you may need less)
oil, for frying

For the dip
small handful of fresh coriander
4 cloves of garlic
pinch of salt
300g plain yoghurt
4 tablespoons full-fat mayonnaise
3 teaspoons mint sauce

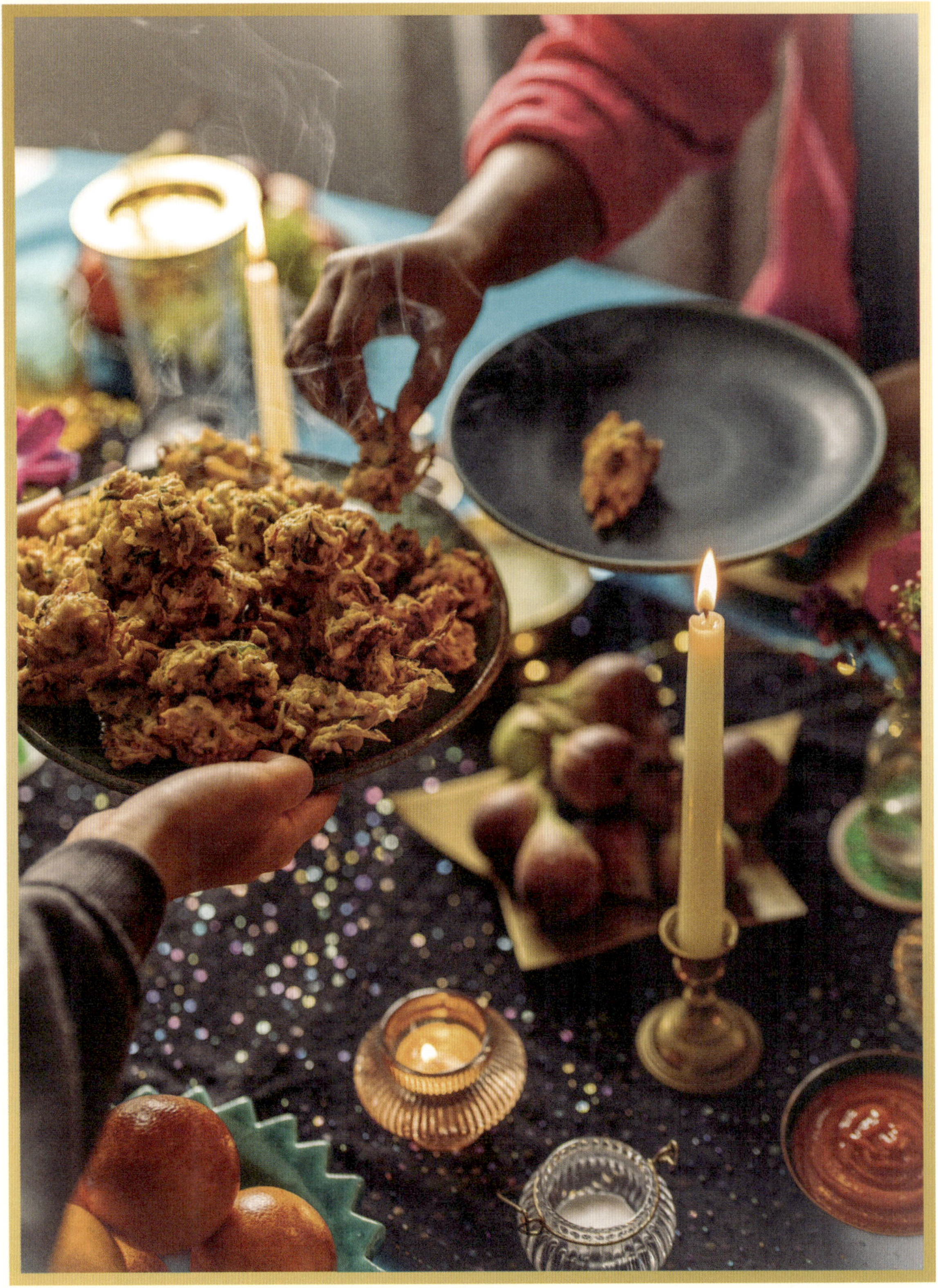

183

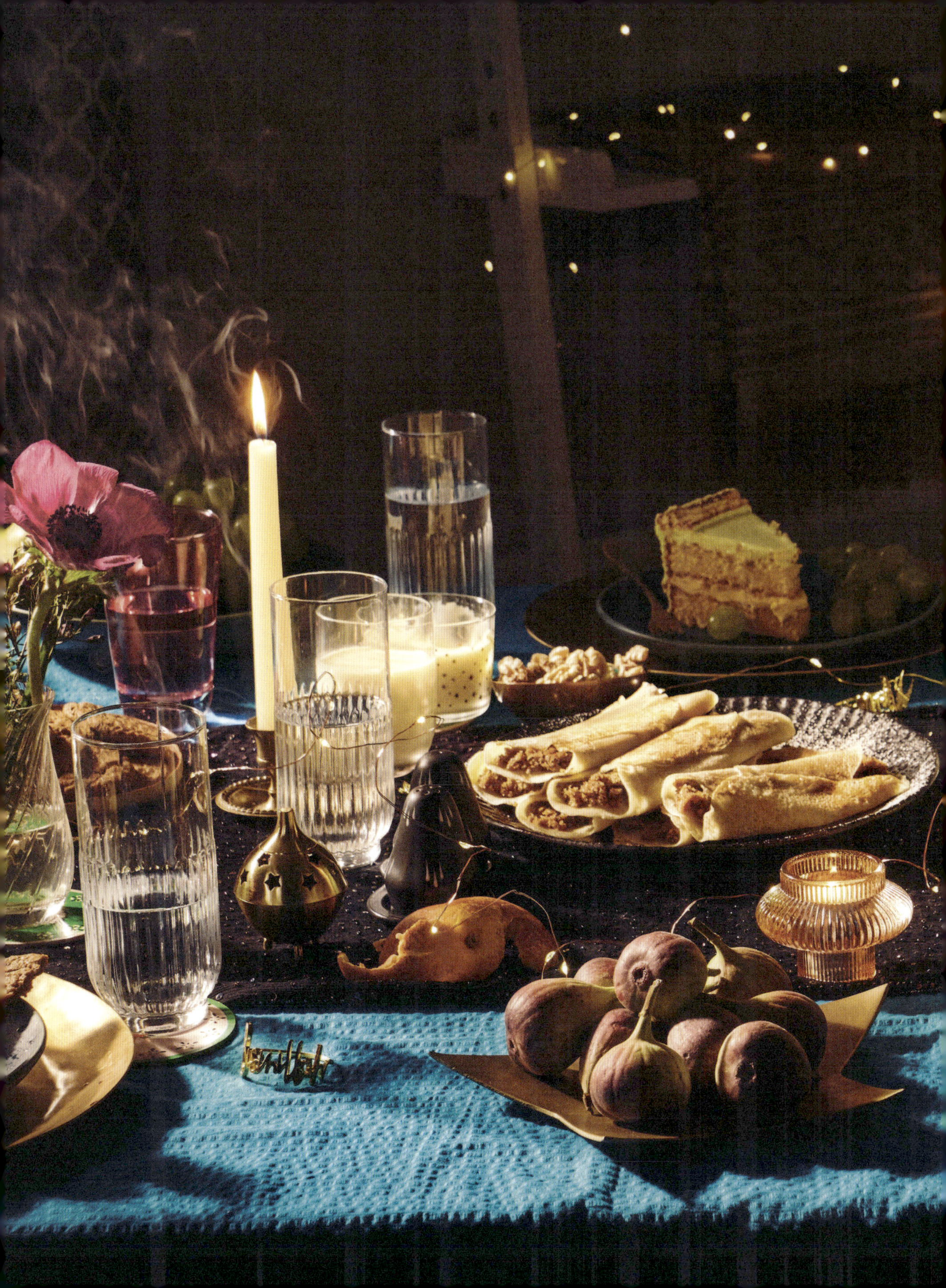

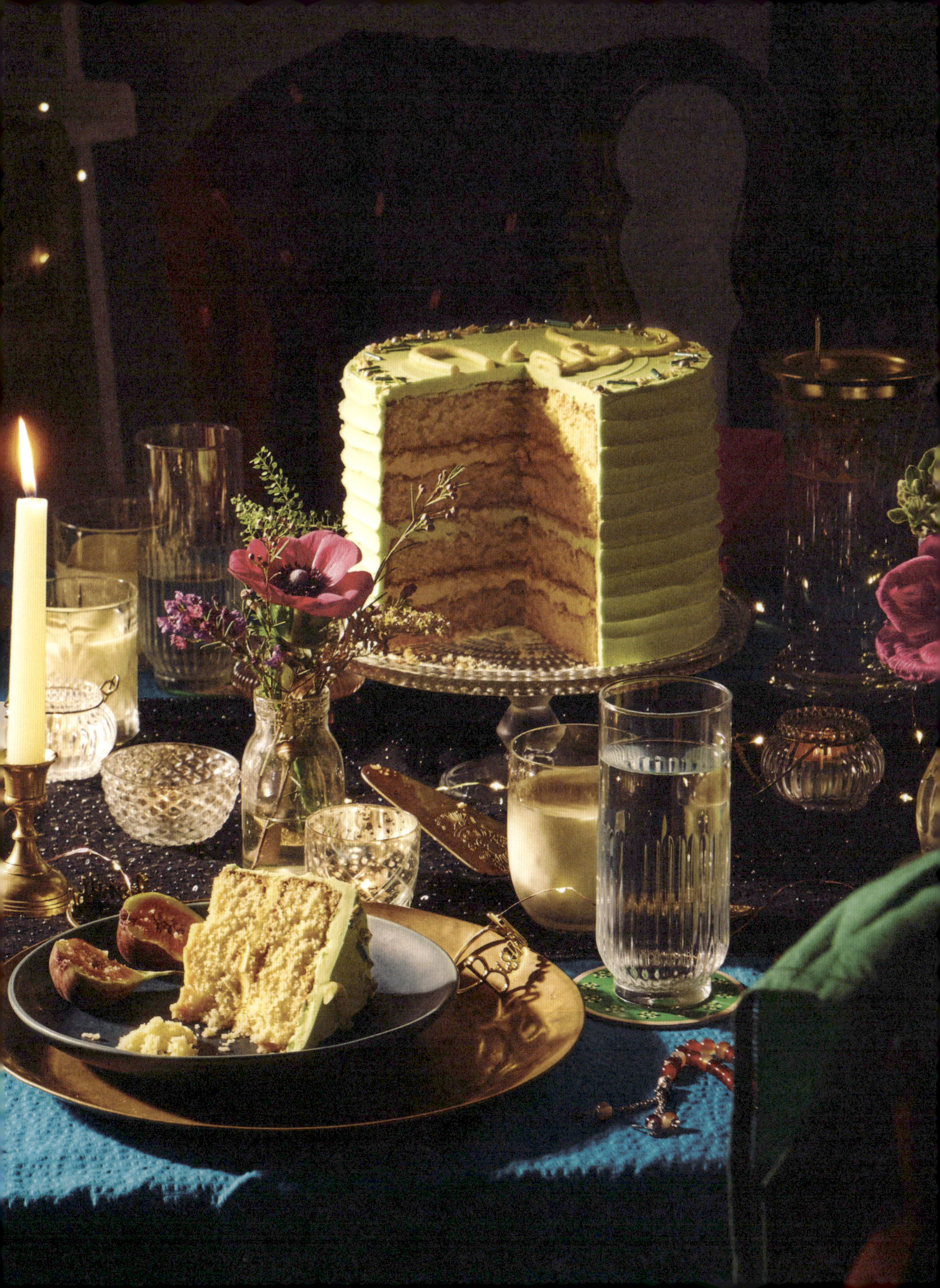

Thanks

Thank you to everyone who worked alongside me to get this book out into the world. This is the book that I never imagined I would ever write, yet here it is.

Abdal, Musa, Dawud and Maryam: Ramadhan would be dull without you guys, you are the added sparkle to our already twinkling month of love and gratitude.

Thank you to Anne, for always believing in my visions, because when I said I wanted to write this book, you believed in me and this book from day dot.

Thank you, Ione, for always talking to me, for listening and for getting it every time.

Thank you, Dan, for being one of my biggest cheerleaders.

Thank you, Georgia and Jess, these recipes cannot go anywhere till they are tested, thank you for cooking, testing and being so complimentary.

Thank you, Roya, for always just getting the vision on point every single time, especially with a book like this that is so close to my heart.

Thank you, Chris, for first and foremost asking questions, listening and trying to understand my vision and for capturing it so perfectly.

Thank you, Aggie, so much, for always being available, from start to finish, I appreciate you.

Thank you, Sarah, for being so diligent and careful to get this book to be exactly what I wanted it to be.

Thank you, Rob and Holly, without you guys there would be no food to photograph; I appreciate you both more than you will ever know.

Thank you to the entire MJ team that work tirelessly to put it all together and send it out into the world. Thank you Bea, Alice, Gaby, Ciara, Hattie and Anjali.

Thank you to everyone who buys this book, whether you observe or not, I hope this book gives you a sense of warmth and understanding for such a beautiful month.

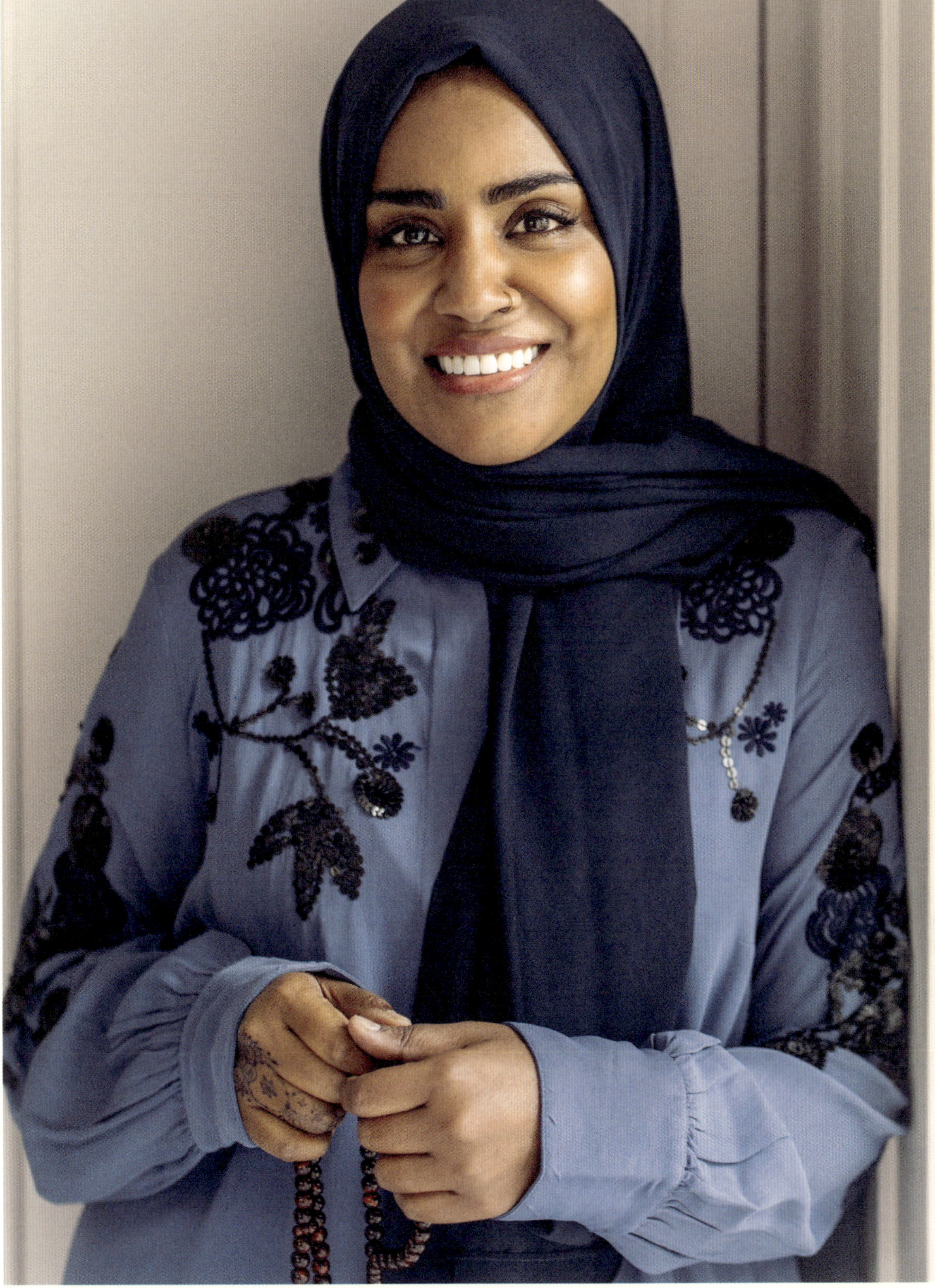

Index

A

Afghanistan 26–31

Aleppo, Syria 36–39

Algeria 44–49

aloo pakora 97

atayef bil ashta 102

aubergine 41, 64, 72–74, 97, 100, 126

B

babousa 94

baghrir 48

baklava 16–17

banana 71, 82

banana spring rolls 82

Bangladesh 68–71

bazin 92

beef 19–23, 54–57, 100, 118, 173–77

beef kibbeh 19–23

beef and pea samosas 173–77

beef rendang 118

Bengal 126–29

bis halva pots 63

brinjal bhaji, ghee pulao and aloo pakora 97

bulgur pot 36

bulgur wheat 19, 26

C

Cambodia 108–13

carrot rice 144

carrots 26–28, 44, 105, 144, 159

cheese, sweet crispy 125

chicken 12–14, 44, 89, 105, 108, 123, 130, 169

chicken shish taouk 12–14

chicken, spinach and crispy rice 89

chickpea flour 159, 181

chickpeas 33, 54–57, 97, 123

chutney 173–77

coconut 41, 43, 58, 61, 79–80, 82, 94, 99, 108–10, 115, 117–18

coconut ice cream 43

curry leaves 61, 115

curry powder 130, 134

D

dalchini biscoot 170

dates 25, 178

diblah 68

djej mashwee 123

dolmas, battata hara and baba ganoush 72

dough, steamed with meat and fish 92

E

egg stew 130

Egypt 54–59

Eid chicken pulao 169

Eid-ul-Fitr 11, 156–83

elasi lemon posset 170

F

fattoush 123

fish 41, 61, 69, 79, 84, 108, 115, 134, 151

fish rougaille 84

flatbread 12

fragrant pudding squares 91

fudge 30, 128

G

ghee pulau 97

Index

gulab jamun **138**

H

hummus **123**

I

Iftar **36**
India **96–99**
Indonesia **118–21**
Iran **88–91**
Iraq **18–25**

J

jollof rice **130–31**

K

Kabuli pulao **26–28**
kandu kukulhu **61**
khaliat nahal **146–47**
khoresh aloo esfenaj **89**
khoshari with buftek **54–57**
kleicha **25**
koeksisters **133**
kue pukis **120**
kufta bin batinial **64**
kulfi ice cream **99**
kunefe **125**
kuni raal **115**

L

lablebi **33**
lamb **19–23, 26, 36, 50–51, 72, 92, 141, 159**
lamb chops **141**
lamb murag **22–23**
lamb suqaar **50–51**
Lebanon **72–77**
lemon posset **170**
lemon wedges **33, 51, 57**
lemongrass **41, 79, 108, 118, 151**
lemongrass and ginger chicken **108**
Libya **64–67**
lime buttercream **162–64**
lime curd **162–64**
lime juice **79, 108, 162**
lime leaves **41, 118**
lime wedges **41, 54, 61, 105**
luchi **126**
lort cha **108**

M

maas biran **69**
Malaysia **40–43**
Maldives **60–63**
mango **63, 71, 162–64**

mango buttercream **162–64**
mango and lime celebration cake **162**
mango sauce **162**
masghati **91**
Mauritius **84–87**
meat stew **92**
Middle East **100–103**
mishti doi **71**
moussaka **100**
mushabbak **38**
mutton mandi **144**

N

naan **141**
nam van **110**
napolitaines **86**
nasi goreng ikan billis **41**
Nepal **104–7**
Noodles **108, 110**
North Africa **92–95**

P

Pakistan **140–43**
pathishaptha **178**
peanuts **43, 79–80, 99**
pineapple **130, 155**
pineapple tart cookies **155**

189

Index

pistachios 16, 30, 38, 76, 91, 99, 102, 125, 143
plantain 1, 126, 130–31
pomegranates 36, 63
prawn sambal 151–53
puff puffs 53

Q

qorma-e-sabzi 26–28
Quran 6

R

radishes
  pickled 14
  red 126
Rooza 1
roti 84
roti canal 151
roti sel 107

S

saffron 91, 138, 146–47, 169
salmon biryani 134–35
samsas 35
sathni 69
sel roti 107
semolina 19, 38, 48, 76, 94, 178

sesame balls 117
shahi tukra 143
sheer pira 30
shish taouk 12
shrimp topping 115
shukto 126
slaw 130
Somalia 50–53
sondesh 128
South Asia 134–39
spinach 26, 61, 79–80, 89, 181
spinach and parsnip pakoras 181
Sri Lanka 114–17
Sri Lanka ambul fish 115
Syria 122–25

T

tagine de poulet 44
tahdig 89
tarka 135
Thailand 78–83
thala guli 117
thukpa 105
Tunisia 32–35
Turkey 12–17

U

Umm Ali 58

V

vegetable peanut curry 79–80
vegetable tofu curry 41

W

West and South Africa 130–33
whole stuffed leg of butterfly lamb 159

Y

Yemen 144–49
yoghurt 12, 71, 115, 159, 181

Z

zhug 144
znoud el sit 76

190

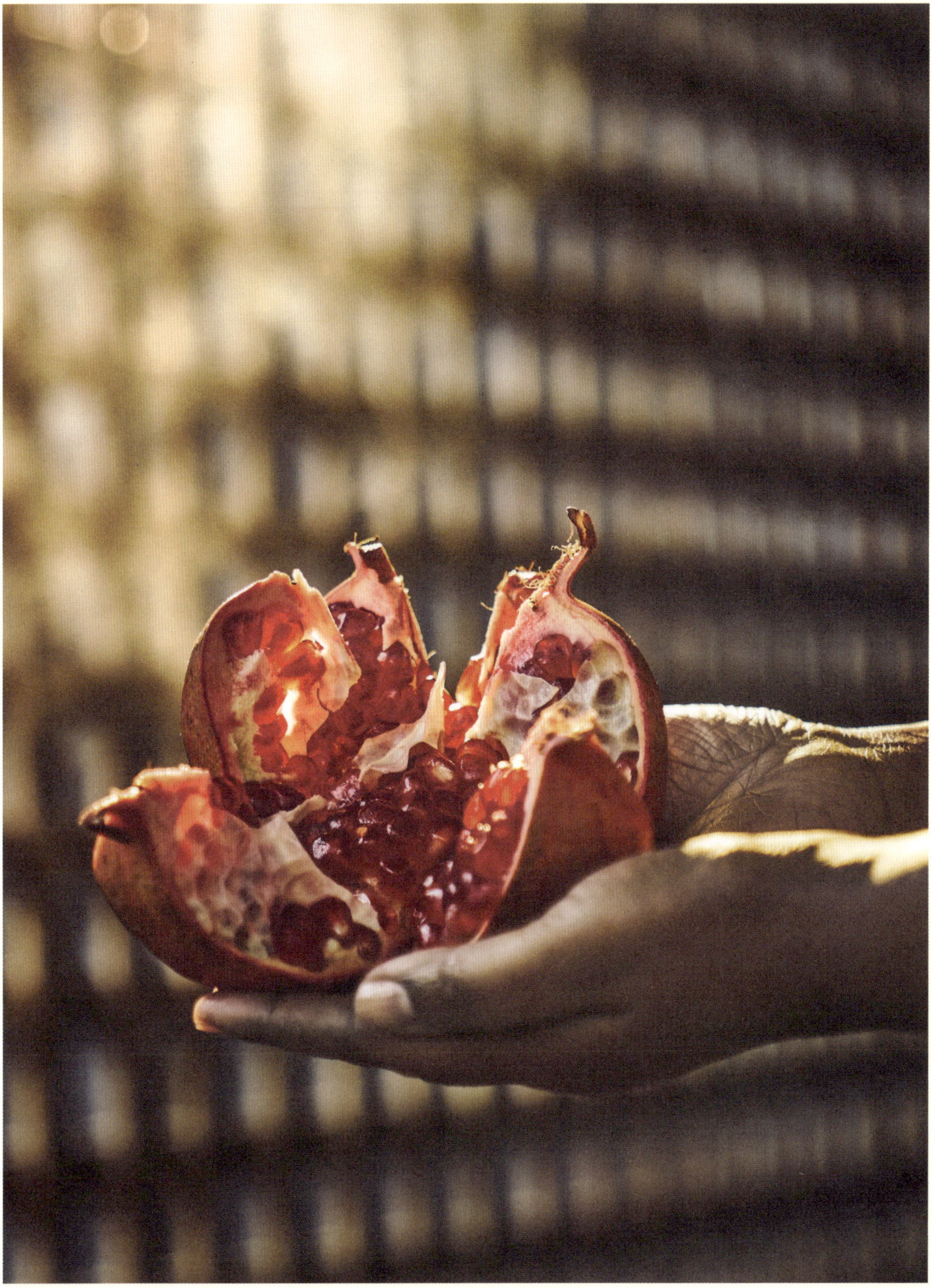

Michael Joseph

UK | USA | Canada | Ireland | Australia
India | New Zealand | South Africa

Penguin Michael Joseph, Penguin Random House UK,
One Embassy Gardens, 8 Viaduct Gardens,
London SW11 7BW

penguin.co.uk

global.penguinrandomhouse.com

Penguin Random House UK

First published 2025
001

Text copyright © Nadiya Hussain, 2025
Photography copyright © Chris Terry, 2025
except page 29 © Shutterstock and page 81 © Getty Images

The moral right of the author has been asserted

Penguin Random House values and supports copyright. Copyright fuels creativity, encourages diverse voices, promotes freedom of expression and supports a vibrant culture.

Thank you for purchasing an authorized edition of this book and for respecting intellectual property laws by not reproducing, scanning or distributing any part of it by any means without permission. You are supporting authors and enabling Penguin Random House to continue to publish books for everyone. No part of this book may be used or reproduced in any manner for the purpose of training artificial intelligence technologies or systems.

In accordance with Article 4(3) of the DSM Directive 2019/790, Penguin Random House expressly reserves this work from the text and data mining exception

Set in Macklin, Moret, Freight Text Pro, Clever and Norden

Colour reproduction by Altaimage Ltd
Printed and bound in China by C&C Offset Printing Co., Ltd.

A CIP catalogue record for this book is available from the British Library

ISBN: 9780241678237

www.greenpenguin.co.uk

FSC MIX Paper | Supporting responsible forestry FSC® C018179

Penguin Random House is committed to a sustainable future for our business, our readers and our planet. This book is made from Forest Stewardship Council® certified paper.